I Was Hitler's Pilot

The Author. Although translated here as Lieutenant-General, Baur's ultimate rank of Generalleutant was in fact the equivalent of Air Vice Marshal in the RAF and Major-General in the USAAF.

I Was Hitler's Pilot
The Memoirs of Hans Baur

by

Lieutenant-General Hans Baur

Introduction by Roger Moorhouse

Frontline Books

I Was Hitler's Pilot

This edition published in 2013 by Frontline Books,
an imprint of Pen & Sword Books Ltd,
47 Church Street, Barnsley, S. Yorkshire, S70 2AS
www.frontline-books.com

ISBN: 978-1-84832-696-5

Publishing History

The first German edition, *Ich flog Mächtige der Erde* ('I Flew with the World's
Powerful'), was published by Pröpster, Auflage in 1956. The first English
edition, *Hitler's Pilot*, was published by Frederick Muller Limited, London in
1958. This edition, published by Frontline Books, London, contains a new
Introduction by Roger Moorhouse.

CIP data records for this title are available from the British Library

For more information on our books, please visit
www.frontline-books.com, email info@frontline-books.com
or write to us at the above address.

Printed and bound by CPI Group (UK) Ltd, Croydon, CR0 4YY
Typeset in 11/14 point Adobe Garamond Pro by JCS Publishing Services Ltd

Contents

Introduction

'BUT FOR THE war,' Hans Baur writes at the opening of this memoir, 'I might have spent the rest of my life in an office.' Born in southern Bavaria in the final years of the nineteenth century, Baur enjoyed an unremarkable youth growing up in Munich, until the outbreak of war in 1914 transformed his life irrevocably. For countless millions of others across Europe, the First World War marked a definite caesura: whether in the wanton slaughter of the battlefields, or the political and economic maelstrom that followed. But for Baur, the war gave him a skill and a career that he would otherwise never have possessed – that of flying.

Serving as a pilot on the Western Front – where, with six victories, he technically qualified as an 'ace' – Baur quickly showed a natural ability and understanding of the pilot's art, not least in the fact that he survived the war, no mean feat in those early days of aerial combat. In the post-war years he rose swiftly, building a reputation for safety and punctuality, and was appointed as one of the first cadre of six pilots of the nascent Luft Hansa in 1926. He also earned a number of honours and accolades: piloting the debut of the Berlin–Munich–Rome route in 1931, for instance, and flying over one million kilometres for the airline.

Thus it was that Hans Baur came into contact with Adolf Hitler. During the election campaigns of 1932, in which the Nazis were expected to make significant gains, Hitler was persuaded that he needed more imaginative methods to reach his audience effectively and Baur was suggested as someone whose flying expertise could help him to campaign by air. Though such a step would be quite normal for any modern politician, it is worth mentioning that it was an extremely radical and innovative idea for the 1930s, when flying was still very much in its infancy and was seen by many as impossibly dangerous and exotic. Whereas his opponents would use radio or give set-piece speeches to the political and media elite, Hitler thus opted to make several grandstand speeches per night, travelling between engagements by air. It was not only a more efficient use of time, it was also a propaganda coup, marking him out with the German electorate as a thoroughly modern, forward-looking politician, ready to embrace new technology.

When the election campaigns of 1932 were successful for the Nazis, Hitler was duly persuaded of the political effectiveness of campaigning by air, not least because he had overcome his own concerns about the safety of air travel. So impressed was Hitler with Baur's proficiency, indeed, that he would never fly with another pilot. With that, Baur quickly became a fixture, and was appointed as Hitler's personal pilot in February 1933. Thus began a personal and professional relationship that would last until Hitler's death twelve years later in 1945. Baur – a bluff, no-nonsense Bavarian – would become one of Hitler's inner circle, one of his intimates, someone to whom the Führer regularly entrusted his life.

Baur, therefore, was in an unusual position within the Third Reich – similar to that of Hitler's photographer Heinrich Hoffmann – in that for all his closeness to Hitler, he was neither politically nor professionally entirely dependent upon him. His thoughts and observations might thus be considered relatively free of the complicating influences of politicking and naked ambition that could colour other accounts. Certainly Baur enjoyed the prestige that his role as Hitler's pilot brought him, and in these pages he clearly relishes the time he spent flying the most prominent men of the Reich and its Allies: Göring, Mussolini and King Boris III of Bulgaria foremost amongst them. It is telling, for instance, that the original German edition of this book was entitled *Ich flog Mächtige der Erde* ('I Flew the World's Powerful').

Baur was also an eye-witness to many of the seminal moments in the history of the Third Reich, including the Night of the Long Knives in June 1934, Ribbentrop's historic flight to Moscow in 1939 to conclude the Nazi–Soviet Pact and the fevered aftermath of Hess's flight to Britain in May 1941. On one level, then, his memoir can be read simply as an engaging chronicle of those tumultuous years, albeit observed by one who was very close to the epicentre of Nazi power. On another level, it is a portrait of the workings of that inner circle: the characters and the petty rivalries that made up the Third Reich as seen from within.

There are a number of highlights. One, certainly, is a passing reference that Baur makes which would have profound consequences and spawn one of the most famous controversies of the twentieth century. On page 177, Baur notes that, whilst Hitler's effects were being evacuated from the Reich Chancellery in April 1945, one of the aircraft used for the purpose failed to arrive at its destination in southern Germany and was presumed crashed. When this loss was reported to Hitler, he was 'very upset', stating that 'extremely valuable documents' were aboard the plane, which would 'show posterity the truth of [his] actions'. That single reference, extrapolated and exploited by a later generation hungry for 'Hitleriana', would provide the factual seed for the 'Hitler Diaries' forgeries of the early 1980s.[1]

Another highlight is Baur's dramatic account of his escape from Hitler's bunker at the end of the war: creeping with Bormann, Stumpfegger and others through the Berlin underground system in a vain attempt to evade the closing Soviet forces. The passage is also notable as it is one of the very few eye-witness accounts

1 Robert Harris, *Selling Hitler*, (London, 1985), p. 72, passim.

(along with those of Artur Axmann and Heinz Linge) that relate to Martin Bormann's fate, which until comparatively recently was still shrouded in mystery.

Like Bormann, Baur also failed to escape the Soviets in Berlin in May 1945. Seriously injured, he was captured close to the Lehrter Station, thereby beginning his long period in captivity. As one of Hitler's former inner circle, Baur was of particular interest to the Soviets, who were keen to investigate the suggestion that he might have flown Hitler out of the beleaguered Berlin, and that he may have had connections to looted art, particularly the fate of the famed 'Amber Room'. Baur would prove a disappointment to his Soviet interrogators, however, not only because of his dogged insistence that Hitler had died in the Berlin bunker, but also because of his apparent ignorance of the broader politics of the Third Reich. In theory, at least, in capturing Hitler's pilot Baur, his valet Heinz Linge and his chauffeur Erich Kempka, the Soviets had secured a unique insight into the workings of the Third Reich and the character of its leader, and they planned to exploit their three captives to compile a 'Hitler Book' for Stalin's pleasure. Baur, however, was swiftly dropped from the project, as his knowledge was not considered to be sufficiently detailed.[2]

As Baur might have put it himself – he was a pilot, not a politician. Yet, he was kept captive for ten years by the Soviets until his release in 1955. It is perhaps a little hard to see what crime – other than guilt by association – might have motivated such punishment, and Baur certainly excels in playing the role of the innocent, political ingénue in this volume. Baur claimed elsewhere not to have known about the Holocaust, for example, until after the war, and, even then, not to have believed it.[3] And, in his defence, one might add that proximity to events is often as likely to result in myopia as in insight.

---

2   Henrik Eberle and Matthias Uhl (eds), *The Hitler Book*, (London, 2005), p. 289.
3   C.G. Sweeting, *Hitler's Personal Pilot*, (Washington, DC, 2000), p. 303.

As ever, of course, there is another side to the story. It is notable, for instance, that Baur joined the SS in 1933, though this might be dismissed as an honorary rank to mark his position as the Führer's pilot. What is more interesting is that Baur was also a comparatively early member of the Nazi Party: joining in 1926, long before it was 'fashionable' and long before his first meeting with Hitler. It is also instructive to note that Baur would later become one of the unofficial 'keepers of the flame', along with Kempka, Linge and Hitler's former secretary Johanna Wolf, who maintained a fierce, uncompromising loyalty to their former employer.[4] As late as the mid-1980s, for example, Baur was still lauding Hitler as 'a truly remarkable man' and 'a kind and considerate man' to anyone who would listen.[5] Again, this might be dismissed simply as an enduring fealty to the man who – more than any other – had shaped Baur's career and his life, and a natural desire not to disavow those heady, formative years just because they had become politically embarrassing. However, it does certainly hint that there was more 'depth' to Baur's politics than he was prepared to admit to his Soviet interrogators. In the absence of any further evidence either way, it is left to the reader to decide for himself the degree of Baur's complicity and the shade of his political conviction.

Aside from such complexities, this is nonetheless a fascinating and illuminating memoir by someone who moved in Hitler's inner circle and who enjoyed his unalloyed trust. Hans Baur is an affable guide through the turbulent, momentous years of the Third Reich. Though he does not engage with the issue at all in this book, his tone suggests that he had few regrets from his time flying for the most powerful men in the world. After all, the alternative might have been to spend his life in an office.

Roger Moorhouse, 2013

---

4   Harris, p. 70.
5   Quoted in Sweeting, p. 303.

PART ONE

The First War in the Air

I WAS BORN in Ampfing near Mühldorf on the River Inn in southern Bavaria in the year 1897; but when I was only two years old my parents moved to Munich. I began my career as a commercial apprentice in Kempten, and but for the war I might have spent the rest of my life in an office.

I was seventeen when the First World War broke out. A wave of patriotic enthusiasm went through the country, sweeping me with it, and I volunteered for service. Too young and not big enough to carry a heavy pack, was the verdict. And this was what first turned my attention to the air – after all, airmen didn't have to carry packs, so I decided to try my luck again, in the air this time. And to make quite certain my application would not get lost anywhere on the way I wrote direct to the Kaiser. I didn't get a reply from the Kaiser, but a letter did come after a while from the air force depot at Schleissheim informing me that for the moment they needed no further recruits; if, however, at any time in the future . . .

That was in September 1915. I waited impatiently for about a month, and then I wrote to the Kaiser again. In due course another letter arrived from Schleissheim, and this time I was told to report on 25 November, which I did with tremendous enthusiasm, quite convinced that within a few weeks I should be in the air.

As a very raw recruit I was given two months' training – but not in the air – and then posted to Bavarian Air Detachment 1B. When I arrived I was welcomed amiably enough, but my extreme youth induced a general 'Germany's last hope' sort of atmosphere, which wasn't very encouraging.

After several months in the office I asked my commanding officer whether I couldn't put in a little time in the evenings with the planes – and with a grin he agreed. After that I was allowed to help the mechanics clean the engines. That wasn't my idea at all, but at least I was actually nearer the planes than before. From time to time notices came in asking for volunteers for flying service, and as I was in the office I saw them first, so one day I approached my commanding officer again and asked him to let me volunteer. After a while he gave way, and sent me off to Verviens, where the volunteers were sifted. There were one hundred and thirty-six of us in all, and most of the others were big, strapping fellows who made me feel very small; many of them were already veterans with decorations. But to everybody's surprise, four weeks later 'Pioneer Hans Baur' (that was my exalted rank) received instructions to report to the Air Training School at Milbersthofen.

I was already keenly interested in technical matters, and I had learned a good bit at Schleissheim, so I found it easy enough to reach the technical standard required. After that came actual flying training at Gersthofen, where we were formed into groups of six, each under an instructor. I was the first of my batch to take my solo test – after I had done only eighteen flights with an instructor; the usual number was between thirty-five and forty. So far we had learned only take-offs and landings, and now I enquired from a more advanced pupil how you spiralled – our instructor hadn't told us anything about that.

When a pupil made his first solo flight no other machine was allowed in the air; everyone concentrated on the test, and it created quite a tense atmosphere. I did mine in an Albatross with a hundred-horsepower engine, a reliable trainer which did about seventy-five miles an hour. I felt calm and confident, and I took off without incident and went up to about two thousand five hundred feet. I had never been up so high before – not more than a thousand feet with the instructor. Then I shut off the engine and did exactly what the advanced pupil had told me. Turning left I spiralled round, and when I thought I was dipping a little too much I easily corrected it. It was all quite simple, and at about six hundred feet I flattened out, flew my obligatory round and then made a perfect landing.

My instructor was far more excited about it than I was, and he didn't know what to do: dress me down or praise me, so he did both alternately. The second and third tests I did without the spiral, and with that I qualified. I was obviously cut out for a pilot. After that I was sent as an observer to an artillery training school (where they used live shells) to take the place of a pilot who had been killed in a crash. I was there six weeks, and after that my application to be posted once again to my old 1B was granted and I was back again on active service – and not in the office this time.

My first nine days in France were spent chasing my old comrades around, because they were constantly being transferred, but I caught up with them at last, and this time my reception by the old hands was enthusiastic. There was a particularly good reason for it, because I had been reported killed in a crash. The victim turned out to have been a comrade of the same name.

It was some days before the weather became fit for flying, but at last I was able to get into the air. It was a DFW, and I put it through its paces very thoroughly, trying out everything I had learned. When I came down to a perfect landing the ground personnel and the observers cheered, though the other pilots, mostly strangers to me, weren't so enthusiastic. After that there was no shortage of observers anxious to go into the air with me, for an observer is completely dependent on his pilot.

A few days after that came the big German offensive, and I flew an armoured infantry-support machine. No less than five thousand guns had been massed, an unprecedented number for those days, and they put up a creeping barrage, which was probably our chief danger, for we naturally had to fly very low. Heavy mist made visibility poor, but from time to time we could see the trenches below. Our men were gathering in their advanced positions, but there was no sign of the French, and their front-line trenches were empty. No doubt the heavy barrage was keeping them in their dugouts.

After about three hours of flying backwards and forwards along the front line we flew over into French territory, and there we saw long columns of men, and horse-drawn carts and lorries. We decided to machine-gun and bomb them, our 'bombs' being hand-grenades in clusters of six. Our attack produced a panic; horses reared, carts overturned, and the column came to a halt in confusion. Of course, we were soon under heavy fire, and our wings were riddled. My engine was hit, too, and we had to get back behind our own lines, which we just succeeded in doing; but in landing I hit a telegraph pole, and the machine turned upside down. Fortunately my observer and I sustained only superficial injuries, but we had to tramp about twelve miles before we could find a telephone to let our squadron know what had happened to us. In addition to our accident, our squadron had lost two other planes and their crews.

After that I spent a few days at base and then returned to duty. This usually consisted of two and sometimes even three flights a day, each of between three and four hours, so we were kept busy. So far our machines had not been suitable for air combat, but now we were equipped with the Hannoveraner, the CL.3a, a small and reliable double-decker powered by a 185-horsepower Argus engine capable of a speed of over a hundred miles an hour, very fast for those days, and armed with two machine-guns, one fired by the pilot, the other by his observer. Up to the end of the war I shot down nine French planes, which was the top ace record for pilots flying artillery observation and infantry-support planes. But one of them gave me the fright of my life. We shot it down in poor visibility, and as it crashed we suddenly thought it was one of our own. Fortunately it turned out to be a French 'Breque', and we discovered that we had mistaken a black and white squadron marking on the plane's rudder, for the familiar black and white German cross.

The war ended on 9 November. As Squadron-Leader I was instructed to take back my squadron from Sedan, where we were at the time, to Fürth in Bavaria. The weather was very poor, and visibility was low, but as far as I was concerned that wasn't the trouble at all. We had machine-gun belts in a case between me and the engine, and the armourer had forgotten to chock them so that the munitions case didn't slip. It did, and I could no longer control the plane properly. When I realised that I was losing height and practically out of control, I did my best to land, but we crashed. My observer was flung clear and came off with a few scratches, and French peasants who had been at work in the fields ran up and released me from the wreckage. We set fire to the plane and did the rest of the journey by car. But when we got to the old imperial city not one of the other planes had arrived. They had all been compelled to make forced landings on account of the weather.

PART TWO

The German Lufthansa

A PERIOD OF uncertainty and impatient waiting followed, for I didn't know quite what to do, but on 15 January 1919, the first military air-mail service was founded, and out of five hundred Bavarian wartime pilots six were chosen – of whom I was one. The Entente Powers allowed us ten old Rumpler C.1s, each powered by a 150-horsepower engine and capable of just over ninety miles an hour – nothing extraordinary, but good enough to start with. Later on we were allowed a couple of Fokker D.7s, the last word in one-seater fighter planes. I was delighted to try them out, and this was the plane with which I first looped the loop.

These were the days of the revolution in Germany, with a Soviet Government in Fürth and another one in Munich, and for a time I served as a pilot with the Free Corps founded by Ritter von Epp; but things gradually settled down again. Soviet Governments – at least in Germany – became a thing of the past, and the great idea now was to earn a living. What other way was there for me but in the air?

By the terms of the Versailles Treaty, Germany was not allowed to manufacture planes, and the authorities had to obtain Entente permits for any they had in use. Such permits were not easy to get, even for civil airlines. For example, the Bavarian Luft-Lloyd was allowed four machines, and the Rumpler Air Line, which had its headquarters in Augsburg, the same number. The Rumpler planes maintained a service Augsburg–Munich–Fürth–Leipzig–Berlin.

I applied for a pilot's job with the Bavarian Luft-Lloyd. On 26 October 1921, I received my civil air-pilot's licence (Number 454) from the Reich Ministry of Transport and on 15 April 1922, I became a pilot for the Bavarian Luft-Lloyd in Munich. There were three of us in all: Kneer, Wimmer and myself, and even in 1922 we had only old wartime machines: three Rumpler C.1s and an Albatross B.2. The Rumplers were powered by Benz 150-horsepower engines, whilst the Albatross had a Mercedes 120-horsepower engine.

Before the official opening of the new line, Wimmer and I made a trial flight to Constance. We had been in the air about an hour when the engine began to knock. I advised Wimmer, who was piloting the plane, to land, but we disagreed about the cause of the trouble and he decided to fly on. We actually got as far as Friedrichshafen, but then there was a big bang and the cabin filled with smoke. My diagnosis had been right, but Wimmer managed to crash-land us. He was uninjured, but I got a nasty bang in the face. Unfortunately the plane, a Rumpler, was a total wreck, and this meant that we now had one machine less for the line, for in those days replacements were almost impossible to obtain.

However, with the three old machines we had left we did manage to run a fairly regular daily service to Constance, a distance of one hundred and twelve miles; a mere nothing nowadays, but with the machines we had, and against constant west winds, it was quite an achievement. Each of us had his turn of duty every third day. If we were unlucky we got the Albatross, an old training plane with a top speed of about seventy-five miles an hour – which meant that when we had to fly against headwinds of fifty or fifty-five miles an hour, which was often the case in the spring and autumn, we were really doing only about twenty or twenty-five miles an hour, so that five hours and more for the short journey was nothing unusual. But we couldn't carry enough petrol with us for such flying times, and this meant that we had to make intermediate landings to tank up, which delayed us still further.

It sounds almost unbelievable now, and present-day airline pilots can have no conception of the difficulties we had to contend with. Our first passengers had to be tough, too, and I often felt sorry for them as they sat there wrapped up like Arctic explorers. There was no room in the plane even for what little luggage they were allowed to take, and it had to be strapped on outside, where it broke the airflow. In summer, though the flying time was shorter, the old engines would often lose oil, and headwinds would spray it back into the passengers' faces. The windscreen was small and right in front, so that when we flew through rain and hail, as, of course, we often had to, the passengers got it full in their faces, and it was as though they were being scourged. Such experiences weren't particularly good publicity, either, and very often a man who had chanced it once decided that he'd go by train next time. But we did our best for our passengers, and in the end . . .

Late in 1922 we obtained the first plane that was ever specifically built as a passenger-carrying machine. It was the Junkers F.13. It had a proper cabin with four passenger seats, and as there was a second seat beside the pilot – in those days we didn't have mechanics with us – it could carry five passengers. In the following year, Junkers Luftverkehr took over our Bavarian Luft-Lloyd. Professor Junkers was aiming at a Trans-European Airline Union, and he succeeded in linking Switzerland, Hungary, Latvia, Estonia, Sweden and Austria with Germany into a really big network of air services.

Progress was fairly rapid now: new services to Vienna, Zürich and Berlin were opened, and, in addition, various special flights – for example, to the Passion Play in Oberammergau – were organised. This latter was very difficult, because although it was easy enough to find a place to land there, the take-off was a very different matter because of the soft, boggy ground. However, we managed it. We would take off from Munich at 07.00 hours and fly back again at 18.00 hours when the performance was over for the day.

It was on one of these flights that I had my first really prominent passenger: Nuntius Pacelli, the present Pope Pius XII. For his benefit I was instructed to make a detour on the way back to fly over the Zugspitze, because he was an enthusiastic mountaineer. It was perfect flying weather that day, and in the evening sunshine as we returned the view over the Alps was simply breath-taking in its beauty. The Nuntius was enthralled, and when we landed in Munich he shook hands with me and thanked me warmly for an unforgettable experience.

The lines from Munich to Vienna and Zürich were opened on 14 May 1923, and with this the first civil air-mail services were in operation. My colleague Kneer inaugurated the Zürich line, and I did the same for Vienna. Our high-ups and representatives of the Bavarian Government were present when we set off, for air transport history was about to be made.

From Munich I flew direct eastward by compass until I came to the Inn. From Linz I reached Traun, and there I picked up the Danube, and flew along it – which was just as well, because the weather had greatly deteriorated and visibility was poor. I made a safe landing on the airfield, thanks in part to an improvised landing cross which had been laid out for me.

A large crowd had assembled to greet us – I had two journalists and a third passenger with me – and we were welcomed by representatives of the Austrian Government and of the Austrian airline company, whilst many reporters and press photographers recorded the epoch-making event for posterity. The distance was two hundred and eighty-four miles, and we flew it in two hours and forty minutes.

I took off again at 13.00 hours for the return journey to Munich, where I landed safely, to be welcomed once again by a large crowd. The next day I flew the Munich–Zürich line, whilst my colleague Kneer took over the Vienna trip, and thenceforth we changed turn and turn about.

After a few weeks of this we began to have trouble with our engines, both with the 160-horsepower Mercedes and the 185-horsepower BMW. Neither of them was made to stand up to such constant use, and the number of engine-trouble emergency landings increased, though fortunately they all went off smoothly. Our directors made no difficulties when we had to break off a scheduled flight in this way, but they didn't much care for it when there was any damage, for our machine park was still very inadequate. To encourage us to avoid damage they began to pay us accident-free bonuses for each trip.

As we had to reckon increasingly with engine-trouble, we spent most of our flying time keeping our eyes open for emergency landing sites; as soon as you had found and passed one you looked out for the next, until you happily landed at your destination – or had to use one of them. This naturally meant a greatly increased strain on us, but with care we managed to avoid trouble. Such forced landings were, of course, a great nuisance for our passengers, who had taken the plane in order to get to their destination quickly, and now perhaps found themselves in some remote village with no idea when they would finally arrive.

We had a good deal of trouble with headwinds, too, and they were very frequent on that line. On one occasion on the return journey it took me four hours to get to Linz, which isn't even half-way to Munich – and I had a big-business man on board who had to get from Munich to Karlsruhe on important business. Instead of going on to Munich, we had to land in Wels to tank up, and by that time the weather was so bad I couldn't take off. I told my passengers truthfully that it would be madness to fly in such weather, because the mountains would be invisible in the rain clouds. At that time, of course, instrument flying was unknown, and it would have meant flying low along the valleys, following the railway lines – and keeping a weather eye open for church steeples. But my passenger declared that unless he got to his destination in time he would be ruined; and he made such a song and dance about it that, against my better judgment, I agreed to make the attempt.

I managed to take off, and the flight to Munich along the railway line through the valleys was successful, and so was the landing. But the whole flight took over seven hours. He could have done it in nine by train. The next day we flew back to Vienna in two hours and ten minutes, a new record.

One day in Zürich my first crowned head came on board: King Boris of Bulgaria. He flew with me to Munich and on to Vienna, and went on from there by train, later I was to fly him to Hitler a good many times.

Our biggest difficulty was still with our engines, because Germany was as yet not allowed to manufacture any, but we finally obtained British Sidley Puma engines, and with these our troubles were over.

On 20 July 1923, we extended our lines down to the Balkans, and the connection from Vienna to Budapest was maintained by a Hungarian company using a Junkers F.13 on floats, a so-called hydroplane. Later on the service was carried on by flying-boats. The following year the line was extended from Zürich on to Geneva, so that we now had a really long air service Geneva–Zürich–Munich–Vienna–Budapest. The outline of the great network of air services which was later to cover Europe was already beginning to take shape, and the regularity of our flights and the absence of any serious accidents were gradually winning the general public over to air travel, which people were at first inclined to regard as foolhardy and dangerous.

But accidents were not always easy to avoid. I well remember what would have been a very bad one, but for the extra care I took because I happened to be flying Dr Schürff, an Austrian Cabinet Minister who was a great supporter of air travel. Although the machine had been overhauled, I decided to make a trial start from the hangar. For some reason the machine swung round to the right. I taxied back to the start and tried again – with the same result. And my efforts to correct the swing made it even more pronounced. Then I tried a third time, telling my mechanic to keep an eye on the vertical rudder. And with that we found the trouble. During the general overhaul the rudder cable had been reversed so that it operated the opposite rudder. If I had gone into the air like that . . .

The Lufthansa was founded on 15 January 1926, by the amalgamation of the two big existing lines: our Trans-Europa Union and the Aero-Lloyd. Germany was now allowed to build aeroplanes again, though, of course, only civil flying machines; so the Government offered subsidies which enabled not only Junkers, but also Rohrbach, Sablatnik and Focke-Wulf, to design and build, and at the same time carry on research work. The new airline organisation had a hundred and thirty pilots and as many planes, and in the following years it was to become internationally famous, with a reputation second to none for safety.

On 18 April 1926, I flew another very important person: Dr Hainisch, the President of the Austrian Republic. This special flight was a great event for Austria, and large numbers of reporters and photographers were present to see the take-off and to welcome us when we returned. It was a perfect flight in perfect visibility, and the sun shone down on the Vienna woods and on Dr Hainisch's own modern estate. I flew three circles over Vienna low enough to see all the famous buildings, including the historic Stefan's Cathedral. At the end of it Dr Hainisch was as deeply impressed as the Nuntius had been, and when he shook hands with me afterwards he assured me that he would remember the experience with deep pleasure to the end of his days.

Sometimes I flew on other routes – for example, Berlin–Frankfort–Essen–Stuttgart–Saarbrücken–Paris – and I often made test flights to try out new material. On one occasion, for example, I tested a four-bladed propeller manufactured experimentally by Schwarz, because experience had shown that the slip-stream of the central propeller affected the side engines to such an extent as to produce distortion. My side engines were now being tested with shorter propellers, and to make up for the loss of power I had these four-bladed propellers.

I was on my way from Berlin to Munich – with passengers – and near Schleiz I was flying low on account of bad weather when there was a sudden loud crack and the propeller of the port engine burst into pieces and the engine itself was almost ripped out of its housing. Fortunately the possibility had been reckoned with, and a special safety catch had been built in. But for this the engine would have been hurled out altogether and we should have gone spinning down. As it was, the whole plane was shuddering so violently that I could hardly hold the controls. I shut off the engines and made a successful landing, for which I received a special letter of congratulation from Milch, who was at that time the chief of the Lufthansa.

Apart from the big passenger planes, I occasionally flew smaller machines: for example, Udet's famous 'Flamingos', the little planes he used in his world-famous 'air-circuses'. Hungary had bought a number of them; as Udet had no pilots available who knew the route, he asked me if I would fly some of the machines to Stamanger, and I agreed. On a test flight with one of these Flamingos I had one of his designers, a certain Herr Stubenrauch, with me. I was anxious to try out the capacities of this wonderful little plane, and I looped the loop at speed. As I came round to normal again Stubenrauch managed to attract my attention. He was as white as a sheet – and not strapped in. Had I done that loop slowly . . .

On one of my normal flights from Zürich to Munich I carried another famous passenger, the Norwegian explorer Fridtjof Nansen, who was understandably enthusiastic at his first sight of the Alps from the air. A little later I received a dedicated copy of his book, *Siberia, the Land of the Future*.

A no less famous passenger was Toscanini, who flew from Milan to Munich, from where he was to go on to Bayreuth to conduct *Tannhäuser* and *Tristan*. I instructed my wireless operator to pay particular attention to Toscanini's comfort, and, in particular, to be ready at a moment's notice with the oxygen apparatus. But Toscanini declared that great heights suited him admirably, and so it seemed they did, for at no time did he use the oxygen apparatus. He had a big pile of music and notes with him and he worked all the time, though occasionally he did allow himself a glance out of the window at the magnificent Alpine panorama below us: and it was particularly wonderful that day because the weather was perfect. When we touched down in Munich he was met by a number of colleagues and friends, and he talked to them enthusiastically about his first flight over the Alps, and told them that he had felt perfectly safe with the German plane and its crew.

Air flight was popular enough now for the film companies to interest themselves in it, and from time to time I flew for them. On one occasion I flew over and around the Grossglockner whilst cameramen in a second plane filmed the scene. The weather was excellent, and many thousands of cinema fans were able to enjoy the magnificent panorama of the snow-covered Alps. Later on I flew a camera party for the all-German small-sports-plane rally which ended with a flight over the Zugspitze, and it was then that I first made the acquaintance of the future Reich Minister Rudolf Hess.

In 1927 we obtained our first Rohrbach machine, the Roland 1, which was a nine-seater. The pilot's seat was high up, and he had an uninterrupted view all around – a very important safety factor. Although its engines were not particularly powerful, they were highly efficient, and they gave us about twelve miles an hour more than we had been getting.

I was flying one of these planes to Vienna when my mechanic reported that the starboard tyre was flat. Now with such big wheels it was obviously dangerous to land with one tyre hard and the other flat, so my mechanic jabbed away at the sound tyre in the hope of puncturing it, but without success. I even thought of putting a bullet in it, but I was afraid that the bullet might bounce back amongst my passengers, who were by this time all aware that something was wrong. In the end I decided to attempt a landing with the one tyre flat and the other hard, so I let Vienna know the situation and when we flew in there was a whole column of vehicles in readiness, including ambulances and fire-engines.

I came in to land, and kept the plane on the one good tyre as long as the rapidly reducing speed would allow me. As soon as it dropped, I applied the counter-brake and turned a hundred and twenty degrees – to come to a halt safely.

Once on a flight to Berlin I had to fly low on account of bad weather, and whilst we were in the Main valley I felt a number of hard jolts and saw panic-stricken flights of swallows speeding away on either side. Soon afterwards the cabin filled with a terrible stench. When we landed in Leipzig we found a swallow which had slowly been burnt to a cinder. Several birds had been killed by the propellers, and others had hurtled against the wing edges, doing a certain amount of damage.

To fall in with flights of swallows was quite common; usually they just dived steeply away below us – unlike hawks and buzzards, which would stay where they were no matter how close we came to them.

On 22 June 1926, I completed my 300,000th kilometre in the air for the Lufthansa, or a total of about 185,000 miles, and on that day my pilot's seat was festively garlanded. In Zürich I was honoured with a sheaf of roses by the Swiss Air Corporation 'Ad Astra'; in Munich I was presented with a special mug of the Bavarian national drink, Munich beer; and in Vienna they gave me a laurel wreath of honour and stood me a celebration dinner. At the same time the newspapers in Germany and Austria published appreciations of my career and my airmanship, whilst the various airlines used my performance – '300,000 kilometres without an accident!'– to advertise their services: 'Speed and Safety! Save time and money by flying there!' and so on. It was, of course, primarily this question of safety which prevented a good many people from going by air in those days, but gradually the splendid safety records of the civil airlines were removing those fears. In September 1927 I reached my 400,000th kilometre, and this was similarly celebrated. The Lufthansa introduced its golden pin of honour for flying personnel completing this distance, and I was one of the first to receive it.

By July 1927 the political situation in Austria had become very tense. A General Strike was declared; there was rioting on the streets, and the Law Courts – or the Palace of Justice, as the buildings were called – went up in flames. Both the postal and railway services were temporarily discontinued, and our air services represented the only connection between Vienna and Munich, so we made several flights daily carrying post and freight in and out of Vienna.

One day our flight manager asked me whether I could fly four important passengers to Salzburg. I knew that the airfield there was not suitable for landing big planes like ours, but I promised to do my best. When I got there I circled round and examined the ground beneath us. The outlook was not inviting. The airfield was an old exercise ground with rolling terrain, no doubt excellent for infantrymen looking for cover, but literally shocking for landing a big plane. However, I came down on the flat behind a line of rising ground and made a safe landing.

Quite a crowd of people quickly gathered, for no one there had seen a big plane close at hand before. Our machine had no wheel brakes, so it wasn't possible to turn by using one brake; to do it by operating one motor meant too wide a turn, so when we wanted to turn a machine round into the start direction a few strong men just lifted up the plane's tail and carried it round. I now asked the airfield chief to lend me half a dozen men for this purpose, and volunteers from amongst the spectators came forward. Once we were facing right for the take-off I made a sign to the ground personnel and I received the flag-off.

The machine seemed a bit over-heavy in the tail, but we got into the air all right. However, in flight the tail-heaviness remained. The trim indicator was correct for the load I was carrying, and I couldn't understand what was wrong, but I managed to get the plane in trim. I was a thousand feet up now and flying towards the Burg. As I was going back to Munich, I turned and flew over the airfield again, and when we looked down it was like a disturbed ant-heap, with people running wildly and waving handkerchiefs and what were probably towels. And then signal rockets started to come up in all possible colours: white, green, blue, red – with stars and without. There were, of course, agreed light signals for emergencies, but we couldn't make anything of these, though something was obviously wrong.

We were about thirteen hundred feet up now, and I circled round the airfield again; in the meantime discussing the strange situation with my mechanic and wireless operator, neither of whom could think of a thing to explain it. With a larger airfield we could have enquired by wireless, but in those days Salzburg had no wireless equipment. I thought of getting in touch with Vienna and waiting until they had telephoned to Salzburg and found out what was wrong, but finally I decided – much against my will – to land again on that wretched exercise ground. I landed safely once again in the same place, and then the mystery was cleared up. A man had been hanging to my tail!

It turned out that he was an unemployed small-part film actor. By causing a sensation he hoped to draw attention to himself and get a job – at least, that's what we found out in the end, for at the moment he was as white as a sheet and not in a position to utter a word. He had thought we were flying to Vienna, which wasn't far; a landing there hanging to the tail of a plane would have been a sensation – but he would never have lasted as far as Munich! We had been only about seven minutes in the air, and that had been almost too long for him.

* * *

In 1928 it was decided to open a new airline Munich–Trent–
Milan, which meant flying over the Alps. I was sent to Trent
– Trento, as the Italians call it – to study landing conditions
there, which were said to be difficult. They were. The chief
difficulty was the *ora*, a wind caused by the wide difference of
temperature between the Lago di Garda and the heated rock face
of the Brenner massif. This wind would rise at about 10.00 hours
and blow until about 17.00 hours, at times reaching a force of
fifty feet per second. A plane coming in to land from the north
could suddenly find that instead of a headwind it had a tailwind,
because a change within a matter of seconds was on the cards.
As the Trent airfield was considerably less than a thousand yards
long, a big plane with a strong tailwind would find it impossible
to come to a halt on the landing space, and would crash on into
the vineyard slopes beyond.

I told the airfield chief that the Lufthansa would certainly
not be prepared to take such risks. He suggested placing wind
indicators at all four corners of the field so that a pilot coming
in to land could see the situation immediately, but this did not
meet the objection that the wind was liable to change suddenly.
In an emergency, and certainly in war, you have to take risks,
but never deliberately in civil flying. How right I was became
very evident when on one occasion the indicators at one end of
the field gave the wind as north, whilst those at the other gave
it as south!

I reported back that if it were impossible to avoid the
intermediate landing in Trent, then the planes should start from
Munich early enough to reach Trent before the *ora* rose. For
three months test flights were carried out with post and freight
but no passengers, and then in the following April the new line
was officially opened. I was chosen to pilot the first passenger
plane; and, as usual with such starts, there were celebrations at
both ends, important delegations from governments, and so on,
speeches and champagne.

I took off in beautiful weather, but when I got to Trent I could see from the behaviour of the wind indicators that the *ora* had, in fact, already risen. I therefore instructed my wireless operator to explain the situation to Trent and tell them that a landing was out of the question, and that we would go on. We landed safely in Milan, to the accompaniment of the usual official reception, etc. Everything went swimmingly until about half an hour later, when I was summoned to the office of the airfield commandant and informed that according to a message from Trent I had flown over at a height of ten thousand feet without making any attempt to land. Fortunately it was possible to rebut that charge at once, and I invited the Italian to inspect the barograph in my machine – which he did, and assured himself that over Trent I had come down from ten thousand feet to about fifteen hundred. On the next flight out we started still earlier; we reached Trent before the *ora* had risen, and were able to make a safe landing. The new line was now well and truly in operation, and on an average we covered the two hundred and eighty miles in two and a half hours. But we had a good deal of chicanery to put up with, for the Italians appeared mortally afraid that we would spy on them on the way. For example, our exact route was laid down and we were not allowed to depart from it by more than about half a mile or so in either direction; five minutes before we arrived over the Brenner Pass we had to warn a specially established wireless station; a control point was set up from which the Italians could note the exact time of our passing, and our exact course – and there were a lot more regulations of the same sort, which we did our best to comply with.

On 20 July 1928, the Lufthansa promoted me to flight captain as from 1 July. A flight captain had to have flown at least 500,000 kilometres, or over 300,000 miles, of which 200,000 must have been during the hours of darkness. In addition he must have had at least eight years' flying experience, of which five must have been with a civil airline. The ranks for pilots with the Lufthansa were: pilot, leading pilot and flight captain. Although I have known a number of promotions in my life, there was none that gave me greater satisfaction than this one, and a good deal was made of it in the German press and in the publicity of the Lufthansa.

By this time, of course, civil flying had developed tremendously. All the dismal prophecies had come to nothing, and even those who had fought tooth and nail against it were now being forced to come round. It was, of course, not only passengers we carried, but post and freight, and under the latter heading we had flown some very strange things. In the autumn of that year we were to fly perhaps our strangest to date.

The winter of 1928 set in with a very severe and very unusual cold snap, and it caught the birds napping, with the result that many of them were unable to fly across the Alps to the warm south. It looked as though many thousands of normally migratory birds, particularly the swallows, would freeze to death in our bitter northern winter; but then a society for the protection of birds and animals got into touch with us to charter a plane to take the birds south. The people of Bavaria were then urged by press and wireless to collect the cold and miserable birds from stalls, hedgerows and so on everywhere and forward them to a collecting station.

When we took the first cargo of swallows on board in Munich it was about forty-five degrees Fahrenheit. This was much too cold for them, and they were very quiet, but half an hour later, when the temperature in the cabin rose, they began to twitter and show more signs of life. When we rose above the thirteen-thousand-foot mark they behaved as human beings do: they looked tired and they relapsed into silence. On their own flights they rarely go higher than perhaps half that height, and, of course, in those days there were no pressurised cabins. Over the Lago di Garda they came to life again, and the cabin was full of their twitterings –we were lower now and it was warmer. When we landed on the Taliedo airfield in Milan the sun was shining and it was beautifully warm. We carefully lifted out the cases in which the birds had made the journey, and released them. In a moment all our passengers were out and flying in the air under their own steam. They circled around for a while; then they joined the swallows already there, and made off.

About three thousand swallows were gathered throughout Havana and carried over the Alps to warmth and safety by the Lufthansa.

The Lufthansa made a good deal of publicity for the flight over the Alps, and many people took the trip for the pleasure of enjoying the tremendous Alpine panorama. There was one trouble, though: it was in the days before pressurised cabins and artificial oxygen, and when we flew at thirteen and fourteen thousand feet passengers with weak hearts were apt to go blue and lose consciousness. As soon as we came lower, they recovered – in fact, some of them didn't even know that they had temporarily passed out – but all the same it wasn't a satisfactory situation, and the first thing to be done was to introduce oxygen apparatus for passengers. (Aircraft personnel were supposed to be used to doing without it.)

The journey took sixteen hours by train, and we did it in an average of two and a half hours. Now, with the introduction of oxygen apparatus, we could take children and even babies. My wireless operator had the job of keeping his eye on the children. As soon as he noticed blue lips he would go into action with specially constructed oxygen apparatus, and carry on until the lips were normal again. Each adult passenger had his own apparatus fixed by his seat, to be used at need.

In those days the flights over the Alps ended in October, but even earlier than that things were not always pleasant. In good weather the flight across the Alps is the loveliest I have ever flown. I was to fly it many hundreds of times, and each time – providing the weather was good – it was a renewed experience of elevating grandeur. At those heights the visibility is unbelievable, and you can see between two and three hundred miles all around – an incredible spectacle.

But in bad weather the situation is very different, and storms over the Alps are an intimidating experience. One of our chief sources of trouble was the *föhn*, a destructive southerly gale. In those days we hadn't enough ceiling to rise above it, because between fourteen and fifteen thousand feet or so, depending on the load, was about our limit, whereas *föhn* winds reach a height of perhaps seventeen thousand feet. Above that the atmosphere is quite still – and the ultimate solution of the problem was to rise above the *föhn*, but before that became possible I have known my machine to be swept three thousand feet higher into the air without engine power, and to be forced down even further despite my engines. And when flying blind over mountains between eleven and twelve thousand feet high you can imagine what a feeling the pilot gets in the pit of his stomach when he sees that his altimeter is registering even less.

In 1930 technical development made a big leap forward. Up to this time any extended flying in mist or cloud was a big risk, and the instruments indicating the plane's position, height and so on, were very primitive, being still more or less at wartime level. The margin of error could be very great, and many a pilot depending on his instruments crashed his plane and killed himself and his passengers. But now we received what we soon began to call an artificial horizon: an apparatus which took a very great deal of the risk out of blind flying, a so-called gyro-rectifier, which allowed us to determine the position of our plane within reasonably narrow limits. It was very reliable in operation, and was independent of any jolting of the plane or other outside interference.

I was one of the first to test this new apparatus, and my experience with it over the Alps was very encouraging. At first many of my colleagues were incredulous when I told them that with this new device I had flown blind through clouds and mist for sixty miles and more with visibility down to zero. And when, as now happened quite frequently, I landed in Milan in very bad weather, the Italians were flabbergasted, because their own machines had all been grounded.

'Herr Baur,' I remember one of them saying to me indignantly, 'it is absolutely impossible that you should just have flown in from Munich!'

'Impossible or not, that's what I've done.'

'But there's no visibility at all over the Alps.'

'You're telling me! But with my new apparatus it doesn't matter.'

It was some time before they were convinced. At first the new apparatus indicated only altitude changes and not lateral course deviations, so that it was always possible to fly off course when blind flying, but this was rectified after a while by an improved instrument which showed deviations both vertically and horizontally. After that it was possible to fly blind over long distances with very little risk.

But as a consequence of our ability to fly blind through mist and clouds, a new danger now arose – or rather it was an intensification of an old danger which previously hadn't worried us very much: icing. Before we were able to fly blind we had always avoided flying through clouds for any length of time, but now we plunged into vast accumulations of water particles and stayed there for long periods. According to temperature, this could mean icing-up.

It is a mistake to suppose that the colder the weather the greater the danger. When the cold is intense, water droplets freeze before they have a chance of coming to rest on a plane's wings and freezing there. The temperatures just around freezing-point are the most dangerous, because then the droplets collect on the plane, and the freezing process, being more gradual, takes place on the plane itself, causing ice formation. In consequence, when there was a danger of icing around freezing-point we used to fly high in order to get into much colder zones, where the danger of icing was much reduced.

The most dangerous time for icing was not in winter, but in early spring and late autumn, when sudden showers could swiftly turn to ice. I have known ice to form on my wings a couple of inches thick within a matter of minutes – and not only on my wings. Ice also forms on the propellers, and then there is an added danger. The swift revolutions throw off hard lumps with the speed and force of bullets, with the result that the fuselage is subjected to a fierce bombardment which makes the passengers wonder anxiously whether the thin metal skin will stand it. And for the pilot there is a particular danger in this – the ice is sometimes hurled off centrifugally from one side only, and then the propeller no longer spins true.

Of course the scientists were at work all the time in our laboratories to discover ways and means of remedying these things, and many counter-measures were devised and introduced, until today the problem has been reduced to reasonable proportions.

The newspapers made a splash of my hundredth civil flight over the central Alpine area, plugging the general theme that flying over high mountains had meant many new difficulties previously unknown and that now all these difficulties had been tackled and surmounted, which was very largely true.

When I returned from this flight to Munich I was formally presented with a bronze statuette of an eagle with out-stretched wings, and round the base was an inscription: 'Presented to Flight-Captain Baur on the occasion of his hundredth flight over the Alps and in grateful recognition of his outstanding services, from the South German Lufthansa.'

In March 1932 I was to receive another honour which profoundly moved me. Three captains of the German Lufthansa were chosen to receive the Lewald Prize, which was awarded for the most outstanding services to German civil aviation, and I was one of them. By this time I had flown not far short of a million kilometres, or something like 600,000 miles; I had crossed the Alps a hundred and fifty times, and it was for my special services on this route that my medal was awarded. But the particular achievement of all three of us, and of our colleagues and the organisation behind us, was that we had brought civil aviation to a very high pitch of safety, regularity and reliability; in consequence, the name of the German Lufthansa was internationally synonymous with the greatest possible degree of safety in the air.

But now a far-reaching change, as yet unsuspected by me, was to take place in my life.

PART THREE

With Hitler Over Germany

ONE DAY IN March 1932 on returning to Munich after a schedule flight I was told by our flight manager that 'a certain Herr Hitler' had rung up and wanted to speak to me. Would I come to see him at the 'Braun Haus', which was the Nazi headquarters in Munich? It appeared that he wanted to charter a plane to fly him round Germany on a speaking tour during the coming general elections, and I had been recommended to him as a reliable pilot.

I had never been in the place before, but I drove there now in my car and was received in a very friendly fashion by Hitler himself, who occupied a modest room on the first floor. He explained what he wanted, and pointed out that it would be a very onerous job, because he wanted to make a lightning tour, perhaps visiting as many as five towns a day. Chancellor Bruening could broadcast to millions of people at once; if he, Hitler, had to rely on the railway and on cars, he could address a couple of meetings in perhaps two different towns in one evening, but hardly more. Therefore he had to use an aeroplane to get him around, though, frankly, he hadn't much confidence in air travel. However, I had been recommended to him by several people as a first-class pilot.

When I had agreed to pilot his plane and after I had explained the technical possibilities to him, he told me why he was so suspicious of the aeroplane as a means of transport. At the time of the Kapp putsch in 1920, Ritter von Greim, who later became a General, had flown him from Munich to Berlin on critical business in a wartime plane. Visibility had been bad, and they had been so shaken up that he had been sick. In addition, von Greim had been compelled to make a forced landing in Jüterbog, which was in the hands of the 'Reds'. As Hitler explained, fortunately he had papers for the 'Whites' and for the 'Reds', so as soon as he saw soldiers with red armlets he presented his 'Red' papers and asked for petrol to get him to Berlin on urgent business. But by the time they finally got to Berlin the Kapp putsch was over. Hitler said that he would have done better to stay at home!

I pointed out that civil flying today with our modern three-engined planes was very different from flying wartime machines in 1920, and that, in any case, he didn't look to me like a type who would easily get air-sick. As a matter of fact I have a very keen eye for that sort of thing; I have often astonished my crews by taking a quick look at our passengers and telling them just who was likely to be sick, and I was usually right. But, just in case, I suggested that Hitler should sit next to me in the mechanic's seat, because there was so much to be seen and so much to take the interest there, that there was little opportunity for air-sickness, which is largely psychological. I had often done this with doubtful cases before, and I had never known it fail.

Hitler allowed himself to be encouraged, but not altogether convinced. For him air travel was a necessary evil if he were to get his message to the masses during the election campaign. As most of the meetings were to take place in the evenings, we should often have to fly after dark; the towns in which the mass meetings were to take place were chosen fairly far apart so that we could cover the widest possible area in the shortest possible time; and Hitler would spend not much more than a quarter of an hour, or twenty minutes, at each meeting.

The election tour was to last a fortnight, with a pause of one day, or at the utmost two, at the end of the first week in order to give Hitler time to recover from the strain of speaking several times in the course of an evening for a week on end.

Hitler then handed me over to his adjutant, Brückner, to discuss the details, and the plan of the speaking tour was laid before me. Some of the towns had to be struck out because of the lack of a convenient airfield to land on, but finally we agreed on between sixty and sixty-five towns, and settled the dates and times of the meetings.

This first election flight began on 3 April 1932, and ended three weeks later on 24 April. We set off from Munich and flew to Dresden. The weather was excellent; Hitler stood the flight well, and was in good form when he addressed his mass meeting in Dresden. Half an hour later we flew to Leipzig, where he spoke in the famous Exhibition Hall. Three-quarters of an hour after that we were on our way to Chemnitz, and from there to Plauen, where we landed in the dark. At the end of the first day Hitler picked out the biggest of all the numerous bunches of flowers with which he had been presented during the day and handed it to me with the words:

'Baur, you've done your job well. I'm enthusiastic about air travel from now on.'

The next morning at nine o'clock we flew to Berlin. Despite the exertions of the previous day Hitler was fit and well, and obviously very delighted at the success of his meetings. On the journey he read the various reports from a pile of newspapers. In Berlin he was welcomed by a great crowd, and that evening he spoke in the vast Berlin Sport Palace.

Another German Lufthansa plane was now chartered, an F.13 flown by Flight-Captain Steidel, and in this Sepp Dietrich and one or two journalists flew ahead of us. Wherever we landed, Dietrich was there to report on the situation and then fly on to the next town.

On 6 April we flew from Berlin to Würzburg, and on to Fürth, finishing at Nuremberg. But the following day the weather had deteriorated to such an extent that all air services were suspended. The weather forecast threatened storms, snow and hail from the west – and it kept its promise; so much so that on Fürth airfield we had to fasten our machine to the ground to prevent its being blown away.

Hitler was worried about his speaking tour and wanted to fly, and I told him that it was possible but that it wouldn't be pleasant. I thought I could get over the Spessart, but mountains were a real problem in such weather. Hitler no doubt remembered his flight with Ritter von Greim, but he told me to carry on. I took off without difficulty, but over Neustadt we ran into the first hail showers. I flew fairly low, but even then we were flying practically blind as far as Würzburg, where for a while the weather improved. But as we came nearer the Spessart the hail grew worse. However, we got over the Spessart safely and landed in Frankfort. Despite the rough passage Hitler was not air-sick. He told me that he had been deeply impressed by the sight of the Spessart below us, lashed by rain and hail against a dark background of threatening clouds. It had reminded him forcibly of the 'Walküre', he said.

At the end of our air tour on 24 April Hitler thanked me warmly, and told me that the flight had justified his highest expectations. A couple of days later I was back on my ordinary job, flying the Munich–Berlin route. From 4 May on I began to fly the Munich–Rome route, which now went over Venice and not over Milan as previously. The airfield at Venice was on the Lido, and consisted of a narrow strip of land less than three hundred yards wide and less than nine hundred yards long. It therefore wasn't long enough to land our regular Rohrbach planes, because they still had no brakes and needed a long run-in; we therefore had to fall back on the old Junkers G.24s, which did not need such a long run-in and were less susceptible to the lateral winds which were a real problem in Venice.

* * *

At the end of June I was again approached by Hitler's adjutant to arrange the details of the second election flight, which was to take place from 15 June to 30 June. The first flight took us from the Isar valley to Tilsit. After this seven-hour flight, which was chiefly above the clouds and out of sight of the ground, we flew on in the night to Königsberg; from there Hitler drove around to various smaller places by car. On the 17th we flew to Marienburg, and from there he made the same sort of tour by car. On the 19th we went on to Schneidemühl and Kottbus. From Kottbus we wanted to fly on to Warnemünde, but the weather forecast was very unfavourable: cloud-cover below a hundred and fifty feet, storms and heavy rain. I didn't know the place, and I should have had to land in the dark at 22.00 hours – and there was no wireless there to help me.

I had to refuse the risk, and Hitler then agreed that we should fly on to Rechlin and land there so that he could speak in Stralsund. But the cars with his staff were already on the way to Warnemünde. From Kottbus, Berlin was informed, and the local Nazi groups en route were able to get into touch with the cars and divert them to Rechlin.

The little machine that went ahead of us landed on Rechlin airfield in pitch darkness at 21.00 hours. We were to have landed at 22.00 hours, but about thirty miles to the north of Berlin we received a wireless message forbidding us to land. I had to turn back to Berlin, where a furious Hitler immediately rang up Göring, who was already President of the Reichstag. Göring succeeded in obtaining permission for us to land at Rechlin – but only on condition that I was to take off again at once, in order, for reasons of military secrecy, to avoid drawing any undesirable attention to what was going on at this small airfield. We took off at 23.00 hours, but in the meantime the weather had grown worse in Rechlin too. The airfield there had no ground lighting and no boundary lights, and the only assistance I would have were rocket signals. It was a very difficult landing. The first time I touched down I hadn't reached the airfield at all, and was digging up potatoes in an adjoining field. To make matters worse, there was a high wind and it was raining in torrents, but I touched down safely in the end. The first thing I was told by the officer in charge was that I must take off again at once; which I did, and from the air I called up Stettin. It was some time before I could get any reply – it was now 00.30 hours, but in the end someone woke up and I was given permission to land.

The following day I flew to Warnemünde, a combined airfield and seaplane base. Captain Christiansen was there with his famous flying-boat, Do. X, waiting for Hitler's arrival before taking off. When Hitler came he told me that he had been particularly pleased with his meeting the previous evening. He had been very late, but a great mass of people had waited patiently in the cold until two o'clock in the morning – just to hear him speak for twenty minutes. Whilst he was in Warnemünde he inspected the Do. X, but he told me afterwards that he much preferred our smaller land planes.

Later we flew to Kiel, Hamburg and Alt-Harburg. Here the Communists were strong, and there was a bit of trouble, but Hitler managed to speak and hold his meeting to the end. 'Give me ten minutes, and they're quiet,' he said. 'By that time they want to hear what I've got to say – suspiciously at first, but afterwards with enthusiasm.'

Bremen, Hanover, Brunswick, then Kassel, Breslau, Neisse on the 22nd; Gleiwitz, Görlitz, Dresden, Leipzig, Dessau on the 23rd; Düsseldorf, Essen, Osnabrück and Erfurt on the 24th. And then to Weimar for a rest. The next day I accompanied Hitler on a visit to the Belvedere, and he questioned me keenly about my flying experiences during the First World War.

Whilst we were out Hitler turned round to Sauckel, who was walking behind us with a group of other party leaders.

'See that we have some female companionship at table tonight, Sauckel. All day long I'm surrounded by men, and I'd like to hear women's voices for a change.'

At 17.00 hours we were sitting together on the Schloss terrace, and Sauckel had produced about fifteen girls between eighteen and twenty-three years old. In the meantime the news of Hitler's presence in Weimar had got around, and crowds were beginning to gather to see him, whilst cars were being driven slowly past. A little while before when I was sitting alone on the terrace with Hitler an attractive woman drove by in a car. Hitler spotted her at once.

'Look, Baur: there's a lovely little woman for you! As pretty as a picture!'

I didn't know much about Hitler's private life in those days, or what his attitude to women was, but the eagerness in his voice made me reply:

'I feel quite sorry for you.'

'Why, what do you mean, Baur?'

'I mean that it sounds as though women were something only at a distance for you.'

'As a matter of fact you're right,' he said reflectively. 'And I have to keep it that way. I'm in the spotlight of publicity, and anything of that sort could be very damaging. Now if *you* were to have a passing affair, no one would bother his head about it, but if I did there'd be the devil to pay. And women can never keep their mouths shut.'

Afterwards I saw Hitler surrounded by a group of attractive girls. At first they had been a little shy, but then they began to chatter away merrily. I tried to start a conversation with one of them, but she had no time for me – only for Hitler. And the same thing happened to everyone else. None of the girls had eyes for anyone but him: they were all around him in a circle now. But when Hitler noticed that he was the centre of attention he became less and less talkative, and finally declared the coffee interlude at an end – though he invited them all to come on afterwards to the Künstler Café as his guests, an invitation they all joyfully accepted. Once again he was surrounded by women, but after a while he asked Dr

Hanfstaengel, who was an excellent pianist, to play something; Hitler then left the company of the women and stood by the piano. Soon after that he said good-bye to the party and went away.

I wondered what women really thought about him, and from time to time I questioned some of them. Without exception they were enthusiastic about him, some of them fanatically so, even to the point of hysteria. On that particular evening I talked to the girl who was sitting beside me. She was twenty-two, and very attractive, but she told me that she was afraid she would never get married, because when she compared all the men she had ever met with Hitler they were so far inferior to him that none could possibly satisfy her.

I was malicious enough to tell her what Hitler had said about women: that none of them could hold her tongue. She stared at me almost in horror.

'He said that! Oh, how mistaken he is! Please, please tell him that I could. I'd sooner have my tongue cut out than whisper a word.'

I had to laugh at her, but she was very serious. When I told Hitler about it the next day, he laughed too.

I mention this in itself unimportant incident, because it is typical of Hitler's relationship to the many women we met – he meticulously avoided anything which might have damaged his reputation.

From Weimar we flew back to Berlin, on to Eberswalde, and then to the west again: Aix-la-Chapelle, Cologne, Frankfort on Main, Wiesbaden, Stuttgart, Neustadt and Freiburg in Breisgau, where thousands of people had come to the airfield to meet Hitler. The way to the place where the meeting was to be held was lined with people, and the car could go forward only slowly. Suddenly a shower of stones was aimed from behind the front ranks at Hitler's car, and a stone struck him on the head and injured him slightly. In a moment he was out of the car swinging his raw-hide whip, but his attackers had fled.

The same evening he was to speak in Radolfzell, and I had to land at Friedrichshafen. Their wireless post had closed down, so I had to fly by dead-reckoning. It was quite dark when I decided that we must be over Lake Constance, and I went down far enough to see the surface of the water glimmering. I flew around for about ten minutes, but I couldn't identify the landing-ground. After a while, however, my flare signals were answered from the ground, and then two big green lights were switched on for me to land between them. I switched on my own wing lights and swept in over the trees to land, but before I could do so the green marker lights went out. I had my searchlight on, but it didn't help me a great deal. I knew that right in the middle of the field was the great girder mast used for anchoring the Zeppelin, and there was a real danger that I would collide with it. But I was going down rapidly now and there was nothing I could do but hope for the best. The airfield was pitch dark, and not even obstacles and hindrances were lit up. I landed only a few yards from that anchor mast . . .

My second election flight for Hitler ended with Fürth, Nuremberg and Munich.

After a couple of months' flying on the Munich–Venice–Rome and the Munich–Berlin and Munich–Zürich–Vienna routes I was once again called on to fly Hitler on an election tour. It lasted from 13 October to 15 November. This time I flew the Junkers 52, which had been taken into service by the Lufthansa in 1932. It had won first prize at an international air-meeting in Zürich; it was nearly twenty miles an hour faster than the Rohrbach, could carry sixteen passengers, and had a higher ceiling. The Lufthansa wanted it for the trans-Alpine flights, and at first our directors were very unwilling to let Hitler have the use of one of these machines for a whole month. However, Göring used his influence as President of the Reichstag, and it was in the Ju.52 that we started. On our previous tours we had first Sefton Delmer, and then Ward Price with us. This time it was James Kingston of Reuters.

During the course of this tour we visited about sixty towns throughout Germany. Autumn flying conditions were poor as usual, and I had a good many difficulties to contend with, but I overcame them all, and not a single one of the many meetings had to be cancelled on account of any failure of our flight programme. But on 18 October a different sort of trouble faced me in Königsberg. The airfield mechanics there refused to service our plane, which was, as usual, guarded by a squad of SA men. After a certain amount of negotiation, during which I insisted that my machine was a Lufthansa plane on charter and should be treated in accordance with the standing agreement, the men in charge agreed with me and promised that they would do their best to get their mechanics to do the work, but when I arrived at eleven o'clock the next morning – which was in any case a rest day – I was informed that unless the SA guard were withdrawn not a mechanic would touch the plane. I then secured the withdrawal of the SA men and the mechanics started work.

In Ulm we landed in an ordinary meadow, and we were to take off again that evening after dark. As that would have been dangerous without marker lights, I went into the town and bought ten hurricane lamps, and with their aid we got safely away.

When the election tour was over, Hitler thanked me warmly once again. He told me that he was thinking of buying a Ju.52, and asked me to get in touch with Junkers on his behalf. This I did at once, and they quoted a price of 275,000 marks. Hitler called me to the Brown House.

'It's too dear,' he said. 'I shall wait. Before long I shall be master of the Third Reich, and then I'll establish a Government Flight, and put you in charge of it.'

After that I went back to my normal flying duties with the Lufthansa, but on 30 January, by which time Hitler had become master of the Third Reich, I was seconded to him as his personal pilot. It was a job that lasted until his death in 1945.

Once he was head of the German Government Hitler flew far more than before, and I also flew a good many of his ministers. By this time he trusted me absolutely, almost blindly one might say; and he always insisted that I should fly him and any of his special friends. Later on I brought in other pilots from the Lufthansa to fly ministers and other VIPs. The man I liked best as a passenger was Rudolf Hess, who was himself an enthusiastic pilot. I taught him instrument flying on board my plane. Hitler had given him strict orders to fly only with a first-class pilot.

I flew Göring on his first visit to Air-Marshal Balbo in Rome. It was April 1933, shortly after Hitler had come to power: I was an air captain, or wing-commander, now, and off we flew to Rome in our brand-new uniforms. Göring sat next to me in front and flew the plane. We hadn't been more than about ten minutes in the air when his valet arrived with ham laid on bread and butter, and I took over whilst he ate. After that there was coffee with cakes, a Steinhäger liqueur, and then oranges. That would have seen me through to Rome, but Göring's valet obviously had very different instructions, because every now and again he appeared with sandwiches, coffee, cakes and so on, and Göring steadily ate his way to Munich.

He was anxious to circle over Schloss Grafenwöhr, where his mother was living, so we went down to below two hundred feet whilst Göring waved his handkerchief, and various people below waved up at us. It was a wonderful day, and Göring then had his first flight over the Alps. In Berlin I had negotiated with the Italian Ambassador, Cerutti, about the air escort which the Italians proposed should meet us as soon as we flew into their air space. I wasn't very enthusiastic about the whole thing. I had already had a rather disagreeable experience with an Italian air escort when flying Minister Guerard, so I strongly opposed the first suggestion that the Italian air escort should meet us over the Brenner; in the event of bad weather the danger of collision in the narrow valley of the Adige was considerable, so in the end it was agreed that we should be met over Ravenna.

When we were ten minutes' flight distance away from there, I wirelessed our imminent arrival and suggested that the escort should take off. When we flew over Ravenna the eighteen escort machines were still lined up on the ground, so I cruised around until they were all in the air and in position and then I flew on. Before long I could see nothing of our escort, so I sent my observer to the back of the plane to report. He returned with the information that the Italian planes were almost out of sight. We were doing about a hundred and thirty miles an hour, and as the Italians had informed me that their planes could do a hundred and sixty, I had thought my speed would be appropriate, but their claim was obviously inaccurate.

I asked Göring what I should do – by this time the Italians were out of sight. He decided that we should fly back, and this I did and picked up the Italians again. When I turned on course again I throttled back to a hundred and seventeen miles an hour – but it was still too fast.

Then a storm loomed up ahead. I suggested that we should fly through it, which meant instrument flying, and Göring agreed, but he immediately vacated his seat next to me, because he knew nothing about blind-flying and didn't want to betray his ignorance. The only other place he could sit was on the broad bench at the rear, because the ordinary passenger seats weren't big enough to take his huge rump comfortably. We flew through the storm and we were shaken up a bit, but by the time we got to Perugia the sky was fairly clear again – quite clear of our escort anyway. The weather on the rest of the way was favourable, but by the time we sighted Rome we were still alone.

We made a perfect landing on the military airfield of Cento Cello, and rolled accurately to a stop, where we were greeted by German and Italian flags, a company of honour, a band playing the German and Italian national anthems, and, of course, Air-Marshal Balbo himself with his retinue. The first thing he did was to congratulate Göring on the expert way he had landed the plane – Göring had taken his seat up in front with me again, and he now winked at me, but no one said a word. Then Balbo wanted to know what had happened to the Italian air escort, and I had to explain; which I did as mercifully as I could, but the story obviously upset him.

When the reception ceremony was over we were led to a nearby military barracks where a huge table was loaded with every possible delicacy. Göring's eyes sparkled, and he set to with a will – the colossal quantity of food that man could put away was astonishing! After the traditional glass of vermouth we went out on the airfield again – just in time to see the Italian escort coming in to land. Air-Marshal Balbo looked annoyed, and I subsequently heard that my unfortunate Italian colleague who had led the flight had received a tremendous rocket – not that it was his fault, poor man; his planes just weren't fast enough.

That evening Balbo took us around Rome's night-spots, from restaurant to restaurant, and so on. Everywhere we were welcomed enthusiastically. There was no doubt that Balbo was very popular with the Italians. But at midnight the German Embassy informed me that I was to fly back to Berlin first thing in the morning – Hitler wanted me.

Göring was to return by another plane. When I got back to Berlin I discovered that Hitler wanted to be flown to Munich and refused to be flown by anyone else. That was all. During the thirteen years I flew for Hitler he used the services of another pilot only once, and that was when I was in Moscow with Ribbentrop; Moscow was rather too far to recall me just like that. Because of the importance of Ribbentrop's mission Hitler wanted to be in Berlin when we returned, so he actually flew with another pilot from Berchtesgaden to Berlin.

On his return from Rome Göring flew to Obersalzberg to report to Hitler, and I was instructed to fly him from there back to Berlin. When I met him in the morning he nearly fell on my neck.

'Baur,' he exclaimed, 'I thought I was going to die on that return flight without you.'

It appeared that on the way back over the Alps he had used up oxygen with the same prodigality with which he polished off food, with the result that before long it was all gone.

The machine was flying high between the Adamello group when Milch hurriedly came forward to the pilot and ordered him to fly lower because Göring was going blue in the face and gasping for breath. But the pilot couldn't. The weather was bad, visibility was poor; it was raining and snowing – and just below him were 11,500-foot peaks. Milch therefore ordered him to turn back to Venice.

In the Po valley the pilot was able to go down three or four thousand feet, whereupon Göring recovered at once and hardly knew what had happened. He thought they were flying into Munich. When he heard it was Venice he got furious and ordered the pilot to fly to Munich. Milch then explained what had happened, but Göring insisted on being flown to Munich – he was afraid that if they landed at Venice the whole story about the oxygen would come out and Balbo would hear of it – which would be as embarrassing for Göring, as German Air Minister, as the business with the escorting planes had been for Balbo as Italian Air Minister.

But flying back over the Brenner at height the same thing happened. Göring turned blue again and looked as though he were dying, whereupon Milch once again ordered the pilot to go lower. Fortunately by this time they were near the Karwendelstein, and my colleague managed to scrape over the top and go down beyond it towards Munich. And, of course, as soon as they flew lower Göring recovered. Instead of two hours the flight to Munich had taken four.

Hitler told me the whole story a few days later when we were at dinner, and asked me what I would have done in the circumstances.

'If you're trying to save a drowning man and he struggles and threatens to drown not only himself but you, you just KO him,' I said bluntly. 'And that's what I would have done to Göring

– by flying still higher. He would then have lost consciousness altogether, but no harm would have come to him, and as soon as we were able to fly lower he would have been all right. I've had that experience time and time again.'

Hitler laughed: 'You're a brutal fellow, Baur,' he said.

Hitler's complete confidence in me had led by this time to a more intimate and friendly relationship. After all, again and again his life depended on my skill, and he realised that I always did my level best for him, so one day he told me that henceforth I was to consider myself as his personal friend and permanent guest as well as his pilot. From now on I was to be allowed to go in and out of his house and of the Reich Chancellory whenever I liked without special pass or permission. After that I almost always had lunch and dinner with him, and I found it very interesting to get to know the way he lived, and in particular how he relaxed.

In the garden of the Reich Chancellory there were a number of very tame squirrels, and whenever he went out into the garden they would come running up to jump on his shoulders. They wanted nuts, of course, and when Hitler went into the garden he always took some with him. Once when the supply was exhausted I offered to go back to the Reich Chancellory and get some more, but Hitler refused:

'No, Baur. Your job is flying me, not waiting on me.'

And with that he shouted and a servant came running up.

Whilst the former residence of Hindenburg was being prepared for him, Hitler lived in the Hotel 'Kaiserhof', the place he had always stayed at when he was in Berlin before he came to power. I was quartered there too. One evening I was sitting in his private room chatting with him when Dr Hanfstaengl came in and told him that he had now finished a march 'The German Föhn' which he had been composing, and was ready to play it for him. With Hitler's agreement, therefore, Hanfstaengl sat down at the grand piano and played us his march.

It sounded a bit outlandish to me. Hitler, who had listened very carefully, asked Hanfstaengl to play it again. Then Hitler whistled the whole thing through from beginning to end, pointing out this and that to Hanfstaengl, telling him where he would like it altered, and so on. I am not unmusical myself; in fact, I love music and I have listened to a great deal of it, but I couldn't have whistled a single passage after those two performances.

The first official meeting between Hitler and Mussolini as heads of the German and Italian states was arranged to take place on 14 June 1933. The weather was clear when we flew over the Alps, and it was now Hitler's turn to be impressed. We were due to land on the airfield at Venice at 12.00 sharp, but we were five minutes early, and although we could see that Mussolini was already waiting down below, Hitler ordered me to fly around over the town for five minutes.

'We're due to land at midday,' he said. 'Do it on the dot.'

I therefore flew around over Venice for five minutes, whilst Hitler admired the famous town from the air. Then we turned back to the airfield and landed – 'on the dot'. As far as I could judge, the greeting between the two statesmen was sincerely warm and friendly. Afterwards Mussolini came up to our Ju.52, about which he said he had heard such a lot that he wanted to inspect it. I showed him everything; and, of course, as a pilot himself he was not only very interested, but knowledgeable. I was to fly him often, and, like Hess, he was an enthusiastic flyer.

The formal discussions between the two leaders took place in a nearby palace, and apart from them only the Italian Foreign Minister, an interpreter, and the German Foreign Minister, von Neurath, were present. The rest of us were standing too far away to hear anything of what was being said. But one thing we could see: little seemed left of the friendly warmth with which the two leaders had greeted each other. They were both obviously excited, and the discussion soon became a clash of personalities. First one then the other would stamp nervously, and both of them were gesticulating vigorously. The main subject of discussion was Austria. Hitler wanted Mussolini to agree to let the Austrian National Socialists have a free hand, but Mussolini wouldn't; on the contrary, he still supported the Austrian Government. The prospects of agreement looked remote.

A few hours later we flew back to Germany, and the whole time Hitler sat silently by my side looking out at the glorious Alpine scenery beneath us. He never said a word about his discussion with Mussolini, and none of us ever learned just exactly what the two did say to each other.

There was no suitable airfield for our Ju.52 in the neighbourhood of Obersalzberg, and one day when Hitler was in Munich again he called me to the Brown House and informed me that as the Salzburg airfield, which was, of course, on Austrian territory, was not likely to be at our disposal for a while, I had better look for a suitable spot on our side of the frontier, and he would have an airfield built there.

Major Hailer and I therefore prospected the neighbourhood from the air and marked various spots we thought might be suitable, and then we went by car to examine them on the ground. A number of otherwise suitable meadows couldn't stand up to a closer examination because – as so often in mountainous districts – they tended to be marshy. In the end we chose a spot just on our side of the frontier opposite Salzburg, and reported back to Hitler, who immediately gave orders for the building of an airfield there. The field was quickly laid out, and hangars for three Ju.52s and various auxiliary buildings were erected; we used it until 1938, when the airfield at Salzburg on the Austrian side of the frontier became available to us at last.

Tremendous preparations were naturally made for the 1933 Reich Congress of the National Socialist Party, the first since the coming to power. It had to be a tremendous success – something to impress the whole world. Every evening before the Congress Hitler would fly from Nuremberg to Bayreuth, and go from there by car to Berneck, so that he could rest completely to be fit again the next day. One evening whilst we were in Berneck I told Hitler that I had read a report in the paper that Hofer, the National Socialist Gauleiter of the Tyrol, had escaped from Innsbruck prison and managed to make his way over the Italian frontier. He had been wounded, and was now in hospital in Brixen. Wouldn't it be a good idea if we could fetch him from Brixen to Nuremberg by air for the Congress?

Hitler was enthusiastic at the idea. He immediately sent for his adjutant, Brückner, and gave him instructions that his Austrian representative, Habicht, was to fly with me to Brixen and fetch Hofer to Nuremberg. We lost no time, and we touched down in Bolzano at 11.00 hours the next day. Habicht immediately made arrangements to get Hofer from hospital, and at midday he arrived by ambulance from Brixen with his parents and his daughter. We got the stretcher safely into our plane, and at 12.30 hours I was ready to take off, for I wanted to be back in Nuremberg by 15.00 hours.

The Italians gave me back my log, but the airfield commandant informed me that I couldn't start as they had no information about weather conditions over the Brenner. I immediately suspected that something was wrong, but for the moment there was nothing to do but wait. I let an hour pass, and then I enquired again. All I got was a shrug of the shoulders: the commandant was at lunch. In the meantime Habicht was trying to negotiate with the Italian authorities, because the weather-report business was obviously a mere blind. The Austrians, as we knew, had demanded Hofer's extradition, but so far the Italians had refused it, and they obviously weren't keen on letting him leave the country. I now rang up the German Embassy in Rome, and asked them to intervene so that I could get permission to start.

In the meantime we were informed that there were customs difficulties. We were not a regular flight, and therefore . . . And after that it was that our passengers had no passports. Then the official in question got the bright idea of examining our passports too. Zintl, my mechanic, had gone off to lunch, and my passport was locked away. Then an officer appeared and informed me that he was the military commandant and that I should have applied to him . . . In short, the chicanery went on with one excuse after the other. I pointed out that a wounded man was in the plane, and that the sun was turning the cabin into an oven. More shoulder-shrugging.

At last at about 18.00 hours the German Embassy rang up and informed me that the Italian Government had now agreed to let me start with Hofer, and ten minutes after that the airfield commandant came running up to tell me that I could now take off. All the Italians were suddenly as sweet as honey and pretending not to know what all the disagreeable Germans were so angry about. Then came the suggestion that it would be better if I delayed my start until daylight . . . 'To hell with that!' I thought, and aloud I declared that I knew the route perfectly well and was quite accustomed to night flying.

With that I took off and flew to Munich, for I hadn't enough petrol to take me right through to Nuremberg. It was pitch dark before we reached the Brenner, but we flew over the Alps safely; however, when we arrived over Munich airfield I discovered that my wing flares wouldn't switch on, so I had to land without them and rely on the hurricane lamps they put out on the airfield for me. Even at that time there was no flood-lighting to facilitate night take-offs and landings.

We landed safely, tanked up, put in the contacts of our wing flares, and took off again at once for Nuremberg. As we had telephoned from Munich, there were no difficulties when we arrived. In fact, the airfield was as light as day with jupiter lamps, for the film people were anxious to record the arrival of Hofer for their newsreel, and we had a tremendous reception.

In the autumn a village called Öschelbrunn, near Karlsruhe, was burnt to the ground for some reason or other; at the same time there was a collision between lorries near Gosen which cost twelve

SA men their lives, and seriously injured twenty-three others. Hitler wanted to visit Öschelbrunn to express his sympathy to the inhabitants and assure them of government assistance, and directly after that to attend the funeral of the dead SA men. The flight was to be kept secret, in order to avoid any unnecessary delays, and Hitler told me that he was very anxious to be in time for the mass funeral.

I got my machine ready early in the morning on 14 September in order to make the usual test flight before taking off with Hitler, but before I could do so Colonel Kadaniko, the commandant of Berlin airport, came hurrying up to enquire where I was going. As Hitler himself had given me strict orders not to tell anyone, I was unable to inform him. But Kadaniko was supposed to report to the Reich's Air Minister concerning the destination of every flight taken by Hitler so that the necessary precautions could be taken; he therefore did his best to persuade me to tell him, but I still refused. In the end I told him to wait until Hitler arrived. But when he approached Hitler, Hitler only laughed.

'That's our business,' he said. 'If Baur tells me he can get along without special precautions, then we won't bother with them.'

As the weather conditions weren't too bad I was in a position to give him the necessary assurance, and so we took off without poor Colonel Kadaniko's being any the wiser. Actually we were flying to Karlsruhe, but to leave him – and others – completely in the dark we set off northwards, and only when we were out of sight did we describe a great arc and set our course south-west. Throughout the flight we maintained wireless silence in order to give Berlin no chance of getting a bearing on us, and only just before we got to Karlsruhe airfield did I give my wireless operator permission to get in touch and ask for wind strengths at ground-level, and so on.

However, when we got over the airfield it was obvious that Hitler was expected. The field was lined with people, including hundreds of uniformed SA men. Hitler was furious, and he shouted and stormed.

'What damned fool gave our arrangements away?' he demanded angrily but none of us could tell him.

In the end it turned out that the Gestapo had informed the Karlsruhe Gauleiter, Dr Wagner, that Hitler was coming 'secretly' – and Wagner simply had to organise what he considered an appropriate reception. So whether Hitler liked it or not, he had to inspect the SA guard of honour and say a few words.

I remained behind on the airfield to fly him on to Essen for the funeral, whilst he went off in a car through cheering crowds and festively decorated streets – Wagner had been very busy, and it took some time before Hitler's chauffeur could get out onto the road to Öschelbrunn at all. In fact Hitler didn't get back to Karlsruhe, but went on by car to Stuttgart, and a telephone call came for me to pick him up there and fly him to Essen for the funeral. But when I arrived in Stuttgart there had been so many delays, and the weather had worsened so much in the meantime that we needed at least two hours for the flight to Essen, which would have meant that Hitler would arrive after the funeral ceremony had started. This he was determined to avoid at all costs, so he decided not to be present at the funeral but to visit the injured in hospital afterwards.

That same evening we flew to Bonn, and in twenty minutes after that we were in Bad Godesberg by car. Whenever Hitler was in the west he would always stay in the Hotel Dreesen there, and a room was constantly kept ready for him. We were also given excellent accommodation. The Hotel Dreesen is situated in a wonderful position with a splendid view out over the Rhine and to the Drachenfels on the far side. The next day we drove back to Bonn and flew back from there to Berlin.

We had a similar experience when Hitler flew to Nuremberg for the burial of an old comrade. Once again the flight was supposed to be secret, but the Gestapo saw to it that the authorities in Nuremberg knew all about it, with the result that when we arrived the airfield was lined with waiting crowds. This time Hitler was so furious that he refused to land at all, and ordered me to fly on to the military airfield at Fürth, from where he went on by car.

There is no doubt that the precautions Hitler took – or tried to take – to keep his movements secret came from a fear of assassination. Although he had originally disliked and distrusted air flight, he had now realised that he was much safer in the air with me than, for example, in a railway train, where it was much more difficult to take effective precautionary measures, which had, in any case, to be on a much wider scale. For example, if he wanted to go by special train from, say, Berlin to Munich, hundreds of people had to know about the train's movements in advance, so that an attack, perhaps by placing explosives on the line to cause a derailment, was much easier than dealing with a plane, which it was quite simple to guard. The result was that Hitler much preferred to appear suddenly and unannounced, and this he regarded as the best protection for his person. I used to go to the airfield to get my plane in order and make a trial take-off about half an hour before we actually left, but as I often flew other important people, ministers and so on, my presence at an airfield was no definite indication that Hitler was about to follow.

As I had to study the weather charts before each flight, this might have given away our destination, but to prevent it I always asked for the lot – and no one knew in which ones I was really interested. After a long battle with the Air Minister I also obtained permission to keep the old number of my plane, D-2600, although by this time the international numbering codes had been introduced. This meant that wherever we went my plane was known as Hitler's, and we were therefore given every possible facility. We were always served first when we asked for a weather forecast or a wireless bearing, and if other planes happened to be in the air ahead of us when we had to be talked down in bad visibility, then they had to cruise around whilst we were taken first – which could easily save us three-quarters of an hour and greatly enhanced our safety.

In September 1933 I completed my millionth kilometre in the air – about 620,000 miles – and once again I was loaded with honours; but the one which pleased me most was a signed photograph of the famous First World War Ace, Immelmann, which my mother sent to me telling me to keep it in my plane – which, although it was D-2600 to everyone else, was 'Immelmann' to me. Thereafter it was fixed in a silver frame in front of Hitler's seat.

Not all my flights with Hitler went smoothly. On one occasion he wanted to fly to Elbing. I happened to know that if the airfield there happened to be soggy, as it often was, it would be very difficult to land, and still more difficult to take off; so I first made enquiries and received the information that a plane had flown from Königsberg to Elbing specially to examine ground conditions, and had reported that everything was in order. I then made arrangements for lighting in the event of a landing after dark, and with that I thought I had done everything I could to ensure a good landing and a good take-off – and so I had, but the best-laid plans of mice and men . . .

We set off for Elbing on 5 November, a damp and humid time of the year, and as soon as I touched down I could feel my wheels beginning to sink into the boggy airfield, so that the machine was stopped long before it had rolled out. Despite my three engines it was impossible to get it any further, and Hitler had to get out and tramp through the bog. After that, a hundred and fifty men with ropes had to be mobilised to drag my machine out of the mud. They succeeded, but a normal start on that quagmire was out of the question. The only thing I could do was to have lines of wooden boles laid and to lighten the machine as far as possible by jettisoning everything, including the petrol in its tanks except just enough to get me to Danzig, to which Hitler could go afterwards by car when his business in Elbing was completed. From there I could fly him back to Berlin.

Starting on wooden boles is a tricky business. Only too often one of them will up-end and damage the propellers; but I had had enough bad luck for one day, and now my luck was in again and I got off safely. There was no one else on board, and I had just enough petrol to get me to Danzig. In Danzig I tanked up again, and when Hitler arrived I was able to get him to Berlin without further difficulties.

The day after that we flew from Berlin to Marienburg to visit the old Reich's President, Marshal von Hindenburg, who lived on the Neudeck estate near there. From Marienburg Hitler wanted to fly on to Kiel for a meeting, but the weather forecasts were so unfavourable that we had to start earlier than intended because I feared that otherwise headwinds would seriously delay us and cause Hitler to be late. We took off at 11.45 hours, and shortly after passing Danzig we had to fly blind over the Polish corridor against a sixty-mile-an-hour headwind. From Rügenwald I flew low, not more than a couple of hundred feet above the sea, following the coastline, and in this way we got safely to Swinemünde. From there I had to fly blind to Kiel using wireless bearings.

There was no shortage of them, and at first they seemed to be all right. Further bearings provided near Warnemünde and again near Oldenburg confirmed that I was dead in line for Kiel, so now I went down from about three thousand to a thousand feet above the sea in order to do the rest of the journey by direct visibility. But about a quarter of an hour later I was given a bearing which indicated a position about eight miles south of Lübeck, which would have meant that I had flown due south. But I hadn't changed course, so the bearing was obviously wrong. I instructed my wireless operator to ask for another bearing, and this one gave twelve miles to the north-east of Hamburg. In the end the confusion was so great that I got fed up and decided to find my own way to Kiel.

I went down to about six hundred feet and got a sight of the ground again, but to get a horizon sighting I had to go down to about one hundred and sixty feet. As far as I could see now there was water, water everywhere, so I changed course again: to the south-west this time in the hope of sighting land, which we had been able to see a quarter of an hour before. After about ten minutes there was still nothing but water, so I changed course due south.

Hitler now came forward and wanted to know where we were, and I explained to him that the wireless bearings had confused us so much that I couldn't say, but I thought we couldn't be far from Kiel. As we had been flying for over four hours, however, Hitler half feared we must have flown beyond our destination and now be over the North Sea. But then we did come in sight of land, a broad bay with a large town in the background. I couldn't tell Hitler which town it was, so I adopted the old airman's trick in such circumstances: I flew along the railway line to the nearest station and tried to read the name off the board. But when we arrived a train unsighted us, and as it was letting off great clouds of steam we were none the wiser.

Hitler was looking out from the front of the plane with me now, and suddenly he said: 'I know that place. I've spoken there. Look, in that hall! It's Wismar.'

And he was right, though the bearings which were still coming in said anything but. But I wasn't taking any notice of them now: I had my own bearings and I decided to fly by sight. We kept within a hundred and a hundred and fifty feet from the ground, and in this way we reached the River Trave. The weather reports from Kiel were very bad, and I flew up and down the Trave trying to identify Travemünde airport, which I knew quite well, in order to land there; but without success. I had very little petrol left now – enough perhaps for a quarter of an hour, so I warned Hitler that we might have to make an emergency landing in the best place we could find. With my landing flaps down and with my engines throttled back to save petrol I made a last attempt, flying northwards at about sixty feet over the sea. I came to the bay, but I still couldn't find the airfield; so I told Hitler to go back to his seat and strap himself in, because in landing on soft ground, as this would certainly be after so much rain, the braking effect is often so strong that a plane just turns upside down. I turned landwards and found a stretch of grass which looked fairly suitable for a landing; but just as I was circling to come down I spotted something to my right, so switching on my engines again I flew towards it. It was the tower of Travemünde airfield . . .

From Travemünde Hitler went by car to Kiel, returning the following morning for me to fly him to Hamburg. As soon as I had time in Hamburg I went to the wireless station to examine the recorded bearings and find out if possible what had gone wrong. It turned out that Kiel, Copenhagen, Stettin, Berlin, Leipzig and Hannover had all been involved in the confusion. Out of ten bearings taken, seven had been wrong. Weather phenomena connected with the dusk had deflected the beams. Since then, greatly improved methods have made such distortions impossible.

I had already heard a good deal of Eva Braun before I met her. For many people her relationship to Hitler was a surprise, and to some a disappointment, but for me it represented perhaps the most human thing I knew about Hitler.

Eva Braun played no role whatever in the politics of the Third Reich, and she obviously had no desire to do so; her only interest was in Hitler the man. I found her a simple and charming woman, and I liked and respected her.

I had been interested in photography for a long time, and I always took my Leica about with me. One day I showed my snaps – of Hitler and so on – to Hoffmann, the official photographer, and he offered to buy the publication rights of some of them. I told him I didn't need money, but if in future he cared to develop and print my films, enlarging them where necessary, he could have any of them he fancied, and this he agreed to do. In consequence I was often in Hoffmann's studio. One day I went there with my wife, to be greeted by a very good-looking young woman I had not seen before. She didn't know me either, of course, and she asked me my business, but as soon as I mentioned my name she smiled and said she had heard a lot about me and was very glad to meet me. Then she went to fetch the pictures I had come for. When we left the studio my wife remarked how attractive she was, saying that she had seldom seen such a pretty girl.

Shortly before Christmas 1933 my wife came with my daughter Inge – who was nine years old at the time – to meet me at the airfield. Hitler shook hands with them both, and then he said to me: 'Baur, women send me far more boxes of chocolates than I can possibly cope with – some of them are a couple of feet across. Bring your daughter round to see me and I'll see what I can find for her.'

It was in the afternoon on Christmas Eve that I actually took my daughter to Hitler's Munich flat. His housekeeper, Frau Winter, opened the door to my ring, but told me as I went into the hall that Hitler had a visitor.

'Still,' she said, 'I don't think he'll mind. After all, you aren't a stranger.'

She knocked on the door, and Hitler's voice called out 'Come in'. She opened the door and I went in, to find that his visitor was the very pretty girl we had seen at Hoffmann's studio. She flushed, and Hitler looked a little embarrassed. He was about to introduce me, but the girl said at once that it wasn't necessary as we had already met. Hitler now turned his attention to my daughter, talked to her for a while and then gave her the promised box of chocolates. After that there were mutual Christmas good wishes and we left.

After the holidays I flew Hitler back to Berlin, and before I went in to lunch I happened to meet Sepp Dietrich, the captain of Hitler's bodyguard, and I told him about my meetings with Eva Braun. 'What do you think of her?' he demanded, and when I said I had been favourably impressed, he went on: 'Yes, he's not got bad taste, has he?'

I now knew that there was, after all, a woman who had a share in Hitler's life – probably the only woman of whom he was ever really fond. Officially, of course, no one knew anything about the matter, but you can't keep such things secret, and there were soon rumours abroad – truth and falsehood mixed; and in 1935 my wife told me that people were talking about a girl called Eva Braun with whom Hitler was said to be having an affair. Did I know anything about it? Such questions were becoming more and more common; the circles around Hitler which might have been expected to know, and in fact did know, either gave a point-blank denial or pretended not to know anything.

Naturally, as I was so often with Hitler I came into Eva Braun's company a good deal. She was often in my plane, with others flying from Munich to Berlin and back, for example – always, of course, with Hitler's direct permission. In the upshot I got to know her very well, and I liked her more than ever. More than once she begged me earnestly never to take any unnecessary risks whilst Hitler was on board, which I always promised; though, of course, I would not in any case have taken risks.

She had a film camera which she used a good deal at Obersalzberg, and, of course, her peculiar position meant that she had to be very careful, with the result that she was very often alone and left to her own resources. When there were official visits to the Berghof she always kept out of sight, and only when Hitler was with a circle of intimates was she present. After the end of each meal he would rise, kiss her hand and take her into the adjoining drawing-room for coffee. Incidentally, Hitler was always a very attentive host to all the women who ever sat at the same table with him.

I was soon friendly enough with Eva to talk to her of her relationship with Hitler. She was well aware that in the ordinary way she could never hope to be his wife, and that she would have to be content to be his lover; and she certainly did love him. I am sure that occasionally she was depressed at the fact that she could never be publicly acknowledged, but she rarely showed any such feelings, and whenever Hitler came back to her again she was always cheerful and happy. In the end, of course, Hitler did marry her, and although she knew that her marriage would last for a few days only, I believe it gave her deep satisfaction. At least, when her relationship to him was at last officially made known to the world, it was as his wife.

Eva Braun's role has been misunderstood and exaggerated. She was a woman brought to the side of a powerful man by love and not ambition. And when the time came and he was no longer powerful, she freely chose to die at his side.

In February 1934 Hitler informed me that I should once again be flying him to Italy for a meeting with Mussolini. Actually it was 26 March before we set off. It was an official visit to Venice, and a whole retinue of diplomats and officials was to accompany us, so, in all, three Ju.52s were in the flight. Once again we landed absolutely punctually, and once again the greetings of the two statesmen were very warm and friendly – in fact, in the meantime they had really become friends. A military band played the German and Italian national anthems, whilst Hitler, Mussolini and their retinues went along the files inspecting the guard of honour. Subsequently Hitler's hotel was practically besieged by an army of reporters and press photographers.

The following morning the German Ambassador, von Hassel, arranged a trip round Venice in a motor-boat to show Hitler all the famous sights, but Hitler was primarily interested in the Italian naval units – most of them small – which were drawn up with their crews lined up on deck for his inspection.

In the afternoon a vast assembly of about seventy thousand people gathered on the famous Saint Mark's Square, where Mussolini delivered one of his usual dramatic speeches from a window of the palace whilst Hitler and his staff observed the scene from another window. Mussolini was obviously referring to Italy's treaty of alliance with Germany, and from time to time he mentioned Hitler. Then suddenly the crowd realised that

Hitler was standing at the other window, and immediately a tremendous roar went up, 'Hitler–Duce–Hitler–Duce', and in their excitement the crowds flung thousands of hats up into the air, hardly one of which could ever have been recovered by its rightful owner. But they didn't seem to mind that, or anything else except Mussolini. I don't think I ever saw crowds so hypnotised by anyone, not even Hitler. When he had finished his speech Mussolini invited Hitler to come to his window so that the two statesmen could stand there together in full view of the crowd, and when Hitler accepted the invitation the enthusiasm knew no bounds. For at least half an hour the masses cheered, shrieked and flung things into the air – any old hats no doubt this time. Hitler was greatly impressed by this tumultuous welcome.

That evening the two statesmen attended a concert in the palace of the Doges, where the leading talent of Italy sang for them; and where singing is concerned, that is no small thing. In addition to the brilliant assembly actually in the hall, there were many thousands of listeners outside. At the end of the performance there was again tremendous enthusiasm from the crowds, and insistent demands that the two leaders should show themselves, which they did. Hitler, who was a great lover of music, and in particular of operatic music, declared on his return to Berlin that the concert given in his honour in Venice had been truly superb.

The following morning there was a march-past of all the Italian Fascist organisations in the great square, including the youth organisation Balilla. Hitler and Mussolini stood together on a specially constructed platform and took the salute. The Italians march quickly, and what with the playing of music which seemed designed to make them march faster than ever, the march-past became a trot past, and then almost a helter-skelter race past.

In the afternoon Mussolini and his staff saw us off at the airfield and we flew back to Munich. On the way Hitler stayed with me up in front, once again looking at the magnificent scenery, but this time he was not silent. Instead he asked me what I had thought of this and that. I could honestly reply that I had been very much impressed by the enthusiastic gathering in Saint Mark's Square and by the concert in the Doge's Palace. But as for the military march-past of the Fascist organisations, frankly I thought that had been very poor. Hitler laughed: 'I think that about hits the nail on the head,' he said.

Soon after our visit to Italy Hitler told me to prepare for an extended trip to the west. Once again three machines started, first of all to Essen. Later we were to go on to Bonn. Dr Goebbels was with us this time. On the way I was not pleased with the way my port engine was behaving, so when we arrived in Essen I asked Hitler for permission to fly back to Berlin, have a new engine put in during the night, and be in Essen again the following morning. But Hitler declared that he needed me urgently.

'Let someone else fly it back to Berlin,' he said. 'I want you to fly me, so take one of the other machines.'

The first thing Hitler did in Essen was to visit Krupp, which he invariably did, to discuss this or that improvement in Germany's armaments. This took several hours, and we took off for Bonn late in the afternoon; from there Hitler went on by car to Godesberg, where he stayed in the Hotel Dreesen as usual. I had already noticed that Dr Goebbels was not himself. Usually he was witty and cheerful and kept the party, including Hitler, highly amused; but now he was silent, almost morose. Hitler himself didn't seem to be too cheerful either, and I began to wonder what was the matter.

Dinner was served at 20.00 hours in Hitler's special dining-room, and a number of high party officials were present. Once again, Hitler was not very talkative, with the result that no one else was either, and the meal proceeded almost in silence. At about 20.15 hours Dr Goebbels was called to the phone, and when he returned he informed Hitler that Sepp Dietrich had arrived in Augsburg with several companies of the bodyguard.

'Good,' said Hitler, but there was no other comment. I was wondering why it was particularly good that Sepp Dietrich should have arrived in Augsburg with his men, but I couldn't guess.

When the meal was over, we all sat around in the adjoining room or on the balcony, and the general depression was still very obvious. At about 21.00 hours a Labour Service man arrived and declared that the band of the Labour Service and the choir of the League of German Girls wanted to sing in Hitler's honour. It was quite clear that Hitler was in no mood for it, but he agreed.

At about half past nine we were all on the balcony. A crowd had gathered down below with the band of the Labour Service and the choir of the girls, many of whom were carrying lighted torches. The concert began, and the singing was very good. But before long I noticed to my astonishment that Hitler was in tears. I knew that he was more easily moved than most men, but I couldn't imagine why he should want to cry now.

When the concert was over I decided to get away from the depressing atmosphere and go and find something more amusing to do, but when I went up to Hitler to ask his permission to leave he refused.

'I'm afraid I can't let you go, Baur. I may need you tonight.'

It looked as though Hitler might decide to fly off somewhere unexpectedly, as he sometimes did at the last moment, so I got into touch with my crew and told them to have everything ready for an immediate take-off. When we had packed our things again and were ready to leave I went upstairs to Hitler and the others. There had been no change in the atmosphere in the meantime, so I found myself an arm-chair in a corner and dozed. At 23.00 hours Hitler called over to me:

'Baur, find out the weather situation in Munich.'

'Aha!' I thought. 'So we're going to Munich,' and I rang up the weather bureau in Cologne. There were storms all the way, it appeared, but there was a likelihood that the weather would improve during the course of the night. Flying was inadvisable at the moment. I reported back to Hitler, who thanked me and said nothing more. Half an hour later he asked me about the weather again. Once more I rang up Cologne and reported back to him that the storms were dying down as indicated. Twice after that with about half an hour in between I had to make further enquiries. The last report was no more rain, steadily improving weather, no further objection to flying.

At 01.00 hours Hitler asked me when was the earliest we could start, and I told him two o'clock, because although everything was ready it would take us twenty minutes to get to the airfield, and some time to get the tarpaulins off the planes and release the guy-ropes which held them down. And then, of course, the engines would have to warm up. In fact, we had to bestir ourselves to take off by two o'clock, but we managed it.

The second plane was made ready for Goebbels, who was to fly with it back to Berlin the next morning. With Hitler were his two personal adjutants, four police officers, his servant and his chauffeur. We landed in Munich at four o'clock in the morning in perfect flying weather. Gaulieter Wagner was waiting there in a car to take Hitler into the town. When Hitler met Wagner the two of them walked up and down together deep in conversation for about five minutes. Hitler was obviously very excited about something; he kept flourishing the raw-hide whip he always carried with him, and occasionally he slapped his top-boot violently with it. When he finally got into the car with Wagner, he slammed the door, exclaiming: 'I'll settle that swine's hash!'

The rest of us stood behind on the airfield with our mouths open. What on earth could have happened? And who was the swine Hitler meant?

At that moment the Munich Air Controller, Hailer, came running up.

'What's happened, Baur?' he demanded excitedly. 'I've never seen Hitler in such a state. But where's your D-2600? How could I know Hitler was in this plane?'

'What does it matter?' I asked.

'Röhm rang me up yesterday evening,' he explained, 'and instructed me to let him know at once if Hitler landed, telling me he would hold me personally responsible for ringing up SA Headquarters at once.'

I knew that Hailer had a very healthy respect for the powerful Chief of Staff, and now he didn't know what to do – whether to ring up or not. I told him that there was little point in it, because by this time Hitler must be there, and in the end Hailer decided not to telephone.

It was not until later that we learned just how important the whole affair really was. If we had flown in with my D-2600 Hailer would have known at once, or guessed, that Hitler was on board and he would have telephoned Röhm immediately, and Röhm would then have had time to take whatever measures he thought fit. As it was, Röhm did not know of Hitler's arrival, and it was he who was taken by surprise.

I went home from the airfield, and it was not until the afternoon that I learned from the wireless announcements what had actually happened. At about the same time the telephone rang, and I was told that Hitler wanted to leave Munich at 16.00 hours. I had everything ready to take off at that time, and Hitler arrived punctually. When we reached Berlin a big reception had been arranged for him. Göring had his air-troops on the airfield waiting for us, and Dr Goebbels was also there.

During dinner Hitler told me his version of what had happened. It appeared that he had been informed through the Italian Ambassador in Paris that his Chief of Staff, Röhm, was preparing a putsch against him. Röhm was reported to have got in touch with the French, and secured an undertaking that in the event of a change of government in Germany they would take no action. Röhm had already drawn up his cabinet list, and his chief aim was now to get his SA incorporated in the army and to secure the dismissal of the old Hohenzollern generals, whom he regarded as unreliable.

Hitler acted at once on receipt of this information, and nipped the putsch in the bud.

On our arrival in Munich Hitler had driven in Wagner's car straight to Police Headquarters, where the Chief of Police was the SA leader Schneidhuber. Hitler accused him point-blank of being in the conspiracy with Röhm, ripped off his rank insignia and his gold party badge and put him under arrest. After that Hitler drove out to Wiessee, where Röhm was staying at the Hotel Hanselbauer. Röhm had set up guards, but most of them were drunk. Hitler arrived at six o'clock in the morning, just at the time for the changing of the guard, and the night sentries had gone into the guardroom to wake up the men who were to relieve them.

In consequence Hitler marched into the hotel vestibule unchallenged, and wrenched open the door of the guardroom. The men were naturally flabbergasted when they saw Hitler before them. Brigadier Schreck then dealt with the guard, disarming and arresting them all. As Hitler went back into the vestibule, Standartenführer Uhl, who had just come down to see what all the noise was about, spotted him and tried to draw his pistol, but he was seized and disarmed at once by a detective named Högl, who was with Hitler. Hitler asked where Röhm was, but Uhl refused to reply. The proprietor was then called, and from him Hitler discovered which room Röhm was occupying. He went straight up to it and knocked on the door. Röhm's voice called out: 'What is it?'

'News from Munich,' Hitler replied, whereupon Röhm called out again: 'Come in, then.'

Hitler wrenched the door open, and there – according to his account – lay Röhm naked on the bed with a young fellow, also naked. Hitler declared that he had never seen such a revolting sight in his life. He shouted at Röhm: 'Get dressed at once. You are under arrest. And I don't need to tell you why.'

On recovering a little from his astonishment at Hitler's unexpected appearance, Röhm began to play the innocent and pretend that he hadn't the faintest idea what Hitler meant, but Hitler cut him short, and turning to the detective with him he ordered curtly:

'Högl, see to it that Röhm gets dressed, and then bring him downstairs.'

Hitler then went from room to room and hauled everyone out of bed, except Röhm's doctor, whom he left in peace. All the arrested men were brought down and locked in the cellar until the arrival of transport to take them away. It was only then that Röhm's men realised how very few men Hitler had with him: eight men had carried out the whole action against them. A bus arrived and the prisoners were bundled into it, guarded by two policemen with submachine-guns, whilst Hitler drove ahead in his car. He knew that Röhm had already ordered his officers to meet him that morning, which meant that they were probably already on their way, so he personally stopped every car they met, offering his apologies to such people as were obviously not concerned in the affair and allowing them to drive on. But when a car came along with SA officers in it – and there were quite a number of them – he arrested them and put them into the bus with the rest of his prisoners. Only the drivers were left to take the cars back.

They also met a lorry with thirty armed SA men. Hitler stopped this lorry too, and told the men they were to go back, as their orders had been cancelled. But the Obersturmführer in charge temporised. He had his orders, and he wanted to obey them. Whereupon Hitler's adjutant Brückner shouted at him: 'You heard what the Führer said. Obey at once, or I'll shoot you out of hand.' The man then got down at pistol-point, and was loaded in with the others, whilst his men were disarmed and ordered to drive back behind the bus under surveillance. The column moved along the Tegernsee Road towards Munich, and as this passes Stadelheim prison Hitler unloaded them all there.

Röhm had had no intention of killing Hitler, of course; all he had wanted was to push him into the background, but the massacre which crushed the putsch cost seventy-two men their lives.

When Hitler had finished his story, he was still unaware that I had an important detail to contribute: namely, the misunderstanding caused by the fact that we had flown into Munich in a different plane, and not, as usual in the D-2600. He listened with interest to what I had to say, and then remarked: 'You see, Baur, the hand of fate was at work there.'

I had already noticed that Hitler always saw the hand of fate in anything that turned out in his own favour.

One night Hitler came back late to the Reich Chancellory from a gala performance at the opera. It was half past eleven. He came into the smoking-room – in which, incidentally, no one was allowed to smoke – spotted me, and informed me that he wanted to fly to Munich straight away. I immediately rang up the weather bureau and asked for the weather report. The whole route was quiet and cloudless, but there was a thick ground mist in Munich which would make landing dangerous. But when I passed this on to Hitler he declared that it was impossible. It was a beautiful starry night – which was quite true. That mist was just a 'Göring mist', he declared, meaning that Göring didn't like his flying at night and was always inventing reasons to prevent it. I told him that the report had come direct from the weather bureau in Munich. 'I'll soon see about that,' he said. He called Group-Leader Schaub and ordered him to ring up the Café Heck and the Osteria Restaurant in Munich and get the girls who always waited on him to the telephone. This was done, and then Hitler personally asked them to go out into the street and come back and tell him whether it was misty. Each of the girls did as she was told, and came back to say that there was a heavy mist on the streets.

'All right, Baur,' he said. 'You're right this time, but I know I have to be careful with you flyers. You're all under Göring's influence, and he wants to stop me flying at night.'

I didn't care to leave it at that, and I told him the simple principle I had always followed from my Lufthansa days: 'If the weather seems good enough I fly; if it doesn't I don't.'

A little later Hitler gave me instructions to found a Government Flight – as he had told me even before he came to power that he would. I therefore ordered six Ju.52s, established a special hanger at Tempelhof airfield, and began to look around in the Lufthansa for suitable pilots, mechanics and ground personnel to staff the new flight. I was to hold a government appointment, of course, but as yet there was no Luftwaffe and they didn't quite know what to do with me. At first I was going to be under a higher civil servant, but Hitler didn't think this was quite the thing for an old wartime flyer. He decided I should be attached to the police, and so I was made a major of the Schutzpolizei. Formally I remained a policeman to the end, but actually I had nothing whatsoever to do with police matters, and I never attended to anything except my own affairs as captain of the Government Flight.

We started with six Ju.52s, but towards the end we had forty machines. During the war I had sometimes as many as thirteen four-engined Condors, a large number of Ju.52s, and many small planes such as the Siebel and the Fieseler Storch. These small planes were particularly useful because they needed less petrol, but nevertheless had a cruising speed of about a hundred and eighty-five miles an hour, and could carry three passengers. Three Ju.52s were kept at Hitler's disposal, whilst Göring and Hess each had his special machine. Later Goebbels, Himmler, Keitel and Raeder each had his own plane.

I was responsible for the whole running of the flight, of course, and as I was often flying here and there with Hitler and so on, this meant a very great deal of work for me. For one thing, all our machines had to be very closely watched to prevent any kind of sabotage. Hitler's machines each had two guards, one from the SS and the other from the Gestapo. The other planes had only one guard, sometimes from the SS and sometimes from the

Gestapo. When a machine landed after a flight, it was the flight mechanic's job to have it checked, overhauled and made ready to start again. Ground personnel were allowed to work on the planes only under his supervision, or that of some other member of the crew. If for any reason this supervisor had to leave – even for a minute (perhaps to attend to a call of nature) – work was suspended, and the ground mechanics left the plane until he returned or someone else came to take his place. Whilst he was away, the guard, who was always present, took charge. When the work was done the machine would be put away and no one was allowed to go near it. These precautions were introduced and very strictly maintained, because our intelligence service had reported from Prague that attempts would be made to attach devices to our planes, governed by altimeters so that they would explode at a certain height, causing the plane to crash and probably killing everyone in it. We didn't give our enemies much chance, because in addition to these strict precautions, each machine always had a ten-minute trial flight before taking off, and any such device would have exploded by that time.

At the end of April 1934 Hitler decided to go away for a week's holiday to Wiesbaden. We were to fly from Munich to Stuttgart, from where Hitler would go on by car. The whole affair was supposed to be a dead secret, but once again there was a leak, and when we got to Stuttgart the streets were lined with people all wanting to cheer Hitler. They gathered in large numbers before his hotel, and they were told that he was going to take off from Böblingen airfield, where our machine was known to be standing. Hitler's car actually drove part of the way out to the airfield, but then turned off and made at speed for Wiesbaden.

In the meantime I had strict orders to stay on the airfield at Böblingen, and not to land in Wiesbaden before 16.00 hours. I carried out these instructions to the letter, and then I waited for Hitler in the Hotel Kock; but he didn't arrive until 11.00, and he was dead tired when he did. It appeared that along the whole route he had been held up by cheering people, and his car had often had to crawl. The thing had been made worse by the fact that the people hadn't been content just to see him pass, but had run after the car and in front, often for miles. Police had had to be called out – not to clear the way for Hitler but to prevent enthusiastic children from falling under the wheels of his car. Peasants even dragged carts across the road to stop Hitler's car so that they could have a good look at him.

During his stay in Wiesbaden Hitler regularly went for long walks in the park, which was closed to the public as soon as he entered it, though the people already there were not turned out, but merely warned not to interfere in the slightest way with Hitler by staring at him, crowding round him or following him. He also went for walks in the surrounding hills.

In May 1935 I was instructed to fly Reich Minister Rudolf Hess to Stockholm. We took off in the early morning, made an intermediate landing in Malmö, and then flew on to the military airfield to Wäserös near Stockholm. From there we flew on in poor weather conditions to Norrköping in the south, where Count von Rosen had his castle. It was a wonderful place by a big lake, surrounded by forests which were deliberately left untended in order to encourage the game, and which were said to be full of elks.

Göring's first wife had been Countess Karin von Rosen. It was a strange world we came into. Every modern comfort and convenience was deliberately avoided, and Count von Rosen and his family lived exactly as their ancestors had lived for many generations. There was no electric light or central heating, and everyone ate and drank from pewter plate. The oddest thing to my way of thinking was that the only water-closet in the place was in the servants' quarters. And every summer, it appeared, the Count and his family would withdraw without any servants at all to a sort of blockhouse in the heart of the forest, and there they would live for a fortnight completely alone. In the evenings the

Count would sit with his wife and children in front of the great open fireplace in the hall and sing English songs, accompanying himself on the guitar.

From there we went to visit the famous Swedish explorer Sven Hedin, who was a lifelong friend of Germany. And then we returned to Berlin.

Before Hitler actually came to power the relationship between him and Reich President von Hindenburg was not too good, although Hitler had a tremendous respect for the old Field-Marshal, to whom he always referred as 'the old gentleman'. It was only after Hitler came to power that the relationship between the two men improved, and then it quickly became warm and even friendly, particularly when the vigorous and determined younger man freed Germany from the scourge of unemployment. During these years, therefore, Hitler often flew to Marienburg and drove from there by car to Neudeck, where von Hindenburg had his estate.

By this time there was only one point on which they still did not see altogether eye to eye: the Wehrmacht. Hindenburg was very apprehensive in this respect, and feared that Hitler would take some radical step, which, in his heart, he knew he would find it impossible to prevent. Again and again he made his point of view clear to Hitler: 'Politics – that's your business; the army – that's mine.' As a matter of fact, Hitler was careful to do nothing that would have displeased 'the old gentleman'. He knew that time was on his side, and that he could afford to wait. And the radical step he did take in the year following the old President's death would certainly not have displeased Hindenburg.

On 16 March 1935, Hitler informed the German people that he had severed the last of the slave chains imposed on them by the Versailles Treaty, and had reintroduced the old Wehrmacht. And the very next day he flew to Munich to take the salute at a great military parade.

As we touched down, a salute of twenty-one guns was fired. Detachments of the Reichswehr, the police, the SA, the SS, the Labour Service and other uniformed bodies were drawn up waiting for inspection on the Oberwiesenfeld. Hitler was greeted by General Ritter von Epp, Reich Governor of Bavaria, on behalf of the Bavarian people. With von Epp were old Field-Marshal von Mackensen; Admiral Raeder, the head of the navy; General von Blomberg, the leader of the Reichswehr; and Göring. Hitler was tremendously impressed by his reception and by his subsequent triumphal progress through wildly cheering crowds in the streets of Munich, and on the flight back to Berlin he could hardly talk about anything else.

It was in the spring of this year that we were equipped with our first Condors, which had two cabins and could carry eighteen passengers. They were the last word in design and construction, and they were capable of a cruising speed of a hundred and eighty-five miles an hour. Amongst the many ultra-modern features they possessed was the new retractable undercarriage. On Hitler's plane the first cabin was for him and the rear cabin for anyone who happened to be flying with him. In Hitler's cabin there were a table, an arm-chair, a small couch, and a safe for documents. There were pantry arrangements for the service of food, and provision for a stewardess, our first. She was a certain Fraulein Diem of Augsburg, and she stayed with us until the beginning of the war. Hitler always preferred to be waited on by this stewardess, who was an attractive little thing, rather than by his own manservant, and he made no secret of the fact.

'I can never understand the Berliners,' he would say. 'They always want waiters to serve them. I think it's much more agreeable to be waited on by a pleasant and attractive girl.'

Our new machine, the Condor, took over our old number D-2600 and was named 'Immelmann' like the other. It had a special visitors' book in which everyone who ever flew in it signed his name, and after a while it became a truly wonderful collection of autographs. Unfortunately it was destroyed later on during an air-raid on Schleissheim.

Owing to the considerably increased speed of this powerful and comfortable machine, our flying times were quite materially reduced; for example, for the Munich–Berlin journey we needed only an hour and thirty five minutes. As Hitler was always greatly interested in flying times and always insisted that the landing should be as punctual as possible, special dials were built into his cabin from which he could see at a glance what he wanted to know, as well as a speedometer, an altimeter, and a clock. This clock was chronometrically adjusted before each flight, and I always had to tell him the approximate time on which I reckoned to touch down in the prevailing wind and weather conditions. My forecasts were something like ninety-eight per cent accurate.

At first Hitler didn't much care for the Condor – he had grown attached to the old Ju.52 – and an incident that occurred on a visit to Hamburg reinforced his opinion. He inspected several companies of SA men on the airfield at Fuhlsbüttel before leaving for Berlin, and then he came up to me to ask about the weather forecast for the return journey, as he usually did before we set off. As we stood there a new Ju.190 came in and circled round once or twice before landing. I noticed at once that the pilot had forgotten to put down his undercarriage, with the result that he unwittingly made a pancake landing and slid and bumped along the ground clumsily before finally coming to a stop. No great damage was done, but the propeller was broken. The pilot and the passengers got out, very white in the gills – no doubt they had been badly shaken up.

'You see, Baur,' exclaimed Hitler excitedly. 'What did I tell you! That's the sort of thing that could happen to us in the Condor.' I pointed out that our machine was equipped with an automatic warning signal. As soon as I cut out to land, a hooter began to sound to warn me to put down the undercarriage, and in the ordinary way it went on sounding until the undercarriage was down. You could switch off the hooter, it was true, but I never did, despite the disagreeable noise it made. But Hitler wasn't altogether pacified.

'At least nothing like that could happen with the old Ju.52 with its rigid undercarriage,' he declared obstinately.

In the end, however, he got used to the Condor with its many new gadgets.

For quite a while Hitler was a fairly regular guest in the Hotel Kaiserhof. Three or four times a week he would go there with a small party to have tea and listen to its excellent Hungarian band. Goebbels had first drawn his attention to these very fine musicians, and suggested that at the same time it would give him an opportunity of mixing with ordinary people. A special table in the corner was always reserved for Hitler, and from there he had a good view over the hall. Naturally, as soon as the news got round that Hitler made a habit of going there the place used to be full almost to bursting-point.

After a while Hitler noticed that the tables around him were invariably occupied by the same old ladies. 'With all due respect to elderly ladies,' he grumbled on one occasion, 'I'd really prefer young ones.' And he instructed his Chief of Police to find out how it came about that these same old ladies were always there. It turned out that they paid regular bribes to the waiters for table reservations. Another thing that came out as a result of these same enquiries was that as soon as he left, the cups, saucers and other utensils he had used were collected and sold at high prices as souvenirs. After that Hitler wouldn't go near the place, and he expressed astonishment that such things could happen in a good hotel like the Kaiserhof. He sighed: 'Life is full of disappointments, Baur.'

Naturally, Hitler had to have some recreation, and film performances were amongst his favourite pleasures. Every evening when he was there, films were shown in his rooms in the Reich Chancellory. The German film industry just didn't produce sufficient films to meet such a steady demand, and so large numbers of American, British, French, Swedish and Czech films were also shown.

By this time most foreign governments had philosophically accepted Hitler as Germany's ruler, and were doing their best to establish friendly relations with him. In consequence there was a good deal of important coming and going in the air, which kept me busy.

On 18 June 1935, I flew to Munich to pick up the Hungarian Premier, Gömbös, who had been invited by Hitler on a state visit. Gömbös arrived in Munich by special train at 07.30, and was welcomed by Hitler's adjutant, Brückner. After breakfast Gömbös came to the airfield and inspected my machine, showing a keen interest in its up-to-date equipment. We took off at 08.30 and at my invitation he sat in front next to me, where he could get an excellent view of the towns and the countryside over which we were flying. When we touched down in Berlin, Hitler himself was on the airfield to greet him.

Before leaving the airfield Gömbös thanked me warmly for a wonderful flight. After a tour of inspection through Berlin a state banquet of four courses was held in his honour that evening. When the moment came to drink the toast of the honoured guest, champagne was served as usual. Hitler had a champagne glass in his hand too, but it was filled with Appolinaris mineral water instead, and – as a lifelong abstainer – Hitler drank his guest's health in this. Gömbös remained for a few days in Berlin for talks and then I flew him back to Munich, from where he went on to Budapest by train.

This was also the year of the great Paris exposition, and Hitler was very anxious that Germany, who had a pavilion of her own, should be properly represented. On several occasions I had to fly the architect, Speer, who was in charge of the preparations, to Paris to supervise and inspect the work. When the exposition was opened, Hitler insisted that as many people as possible from his own intimate circle should be present, and he allowed them sufficient foreign currency to spend a very comfortable if not luxurious week in Paris. I flew them to Paris and I was with them at the opening of the exhibition. It was quite clear that the two pavilions that attracted most interest were those of Germany and Russia, which vied with each other. On our return to Berlin we all had to report in great detail to Hitler concerning everything we had seen, and give him our general impressions. He keenly regretted that his position had prevented him from going in person.

It was often impossible for Hitler to do what he would have liked to do. In the summer months he would usually walk in the garden of the Reich Chancellory on Sundays, and frequently I was his only companion. One day I asked him outright whether he didn't find it a bit boring always to be on his own, except for me or an adjutant, when, outside, every door stood open to him.

'Baur,' he replied earnestly, 'I know that every door is open to me, but the fact is that where I'd really like to go I can't go any more; whilst the places where I could go, I don't want to go. You see, when I do go as a guest somewhere it isn't long before my hostess asks me for some favour or other. As her guest it isn't easy for me to refuse whatever it is she wants, but very often my conscience makes me. So on the whole I prefer not to put myself in such embarrassing situations in the first place.'

He was silent for a moment or two, and then he went on: 'Now there's one place in particular I'd like to go to again. But I can't now. During the early days of my struggle I lived with an old woman in Munich who had a small stall in the market. When I came home in the evenings she would be at her sewing-machine, and she always wanted to know whether I'd had any supper. Very often I hadn't, and then she'd get up and find me something: a glass of beer, and some bread and cheese, or something of the sort. 'I know you mean well,' she used to say, 'but you ought to give up all that politics business and get yourself a job, and then you'd be able to eat properly.' Very often I wouldn't even be able to pay her the rent on time, but she'd still give me something to eat. Now that's someone I'd very much like to go and visit again, but as Reich Chancellor I can't.'

It was typical of Hitler that he was always impulsive and would do a thing immediately it came into his mind, and now he sent for his adjutant Brückner.

'I've just been telling Baur about an old woman who was kind to me years ago when she let me a room in Munich. I expect she's an old-age pensioner by this time – if she's still alive. I want you to find out about her and arrange for her to have a modest allowance.'

Hitler was essentially a man of simple tastes, and he disliked luxury and show. I remember when Göring suddenly presented him with a new plane for his private use, a Ju.52. It had been built according to Göring's special instructions. Hitler and I inspected it together. It was luxuriously equipped and it had every possible comfort; for example, all the seats were upholstered in green suede.

'Wonderful, Göring, wonderful! Very beautiful indeed,' exclaimed Hitler, winking surreptitiously at me. Afterwards when we were alone he said: 'Now that machine would suit Göring very well, but it doesn't suit me. I don't care for that sort of thing. We'll stick to the old simple, well-made things. What would my friends think if I started flying around in a luxuriously equipped plane like that! No, Baur, don't you let anyone mislead you into doing anything of that sort. It isn't my style at all.'

Whilst we were in Munich one day Esser appeared and asked Hitler on behalf of Dr Dornier, the constructor of the famous flying-boat Do. X, to make a flight in it. As I have already recorded, Hitler had previously inspected the gigantic machine in Warnemünde and he had not been greatly taken with it.

'I haven't much time,' he answered, and then he turned to me: 'What do you think about it, Baur? Is it all right? Can you fly safely in a thing like that?'

I replied that in my opinion there was nothing to fear, and that, really, he might do Dr Dornier the honour; upon which he seemed reassured and agreed to make a short flight. They were flying around overhead for a good hour and I took advantage of the situation to rush home.

Incidentally, this absolute trust Hitler had in me as a pilot was always a little awkward when I wanted a holiday, which I usually took in the winter months, when there wasn't so much air travel going on, and when I could enjoy my favourite sport – skiing. I always had to ask for leave two or three times before I finally got it, and then he would always try to make me promise not to go skiing, because he thought it was too dangerous. When I would point out to him that as a good Bavarian I had skied since I was a little boy and could really be regarded as quite good at it, he would say:

'That's all very well, Baur, but even the most experienced skier can meet with an accident. I don't want you laid up for weeks, and perhaps even months, with broken bones.'

But that was one point on which I wouldn't give way, and it was always he who had to; and so for a couple of weeks I would get out into my beloved mountains and ski to my heart's content in preparation for the new onerous round of duties that would be awaiting me when I returned.

At the end of Hitler's successful flight with the Do. X, Dr Dornier invited him to fly with the machine to Passau the next day, where he proposed to come down on the reservoir of the Kachlett power-station; but this Hitler refused to do, pleading that he was overburdened with work. Dr Dornier made the trip with Major Hailer, and on setting down, something went wrong. The tail of the Do. X was torn off and everyone got a bad shaking and a thorough soaking – probably the pilot had set the Do. X down at too steep an angle.

'You see, Baur,' declared Hitler, 'I was right. I just had a feeling in my bones that there was something wrong with that monstrous thing.'

* * *

On 19 June 1937, I was forty years old, and Kannenberg was given special instructions by Hitler to prepare my favourite dinner: roast pork with potato dumplings. Now Hitler was, of course, a vegetarian, and how he came to know about my non-vegetarian fancies was rather funny.

'Baur,' he said one day, 'you know the best thing for you would be vegetarian food such as I eat. It soothes the nerves and it's very good for you. You really ought to become a vegetarian. You'd be very healthy.'

'I'm already very healthy,' I replied, 'and my nerves are all right too. And I'll tell you something else: I'm not one of those hypocrites who come here and eat a vegetarian meal with you and then go over afterwards to Kannenberg and have a proper meal. I'd sooner have one good meal of roast pork with potato dumplings than all the nut cutlets in the world. You'll never make me a vegetarian.'

Hitler laughed at my forthrightness and my determination to stay a meat-eater, and after that Kannenberg received orders always to have roast pork and potato dumplings ready for me on my birthday.

On this particular birthday, when Hitler had congratulated me he added his warm thanks for having flown him safely for six years. Herr Werlin, the General Director of the Mercedes Works, was with us at table that day, but I thought nothing of it. Hitler was finished first, as he always was, because he ate less than anyone else. As soon as I had finished he excused himself to the others who were still eating, saying that he couldn't wait any longer to show me my birthday present, and getting up from the table he led me through the conservatory and out into the garden. I was wondering what sort of a present he was going to give me – perhaps something for the garden of the new house he had recently had built for me? But when we got outside, standing there on the gravel path was a wonderful Mercedes limousine. It was my birthday present, and at first I stared at it almost open-mouthed.

When I recovered sufficiently to thank him, he told me how it had come about. He had first discussed possible presents with his intimate circle, Bormann and the others; but none of their suggestions had pleased him, and then he had had his own idea. From the airfield at Munich to my house at Pilsensee was about an hour's drive, and one day he got the idea of following me in his own car without my knowing it, in order, as he said, to find out whether I drove like a madman, as – according to him – most flyers did. Well, I didn't – I have as much respect for my bones on the ground as in the air. But what he had noticed was that I drove an American car, a Ford; and he didn't think that right for his flight captain – hence the Mercedes.

I got permission from him to drive it to Munich that night. I was tremendously pleased with it, and when I got home to my wife and family I couldn't help thinking that I was a pretty lucky man. My wife and I agreed that with this grand car we had most things we wanted. If I had another wish it was just that it should always stay that way. But that was obviously too much to ask. I drove that car to the end of the war, and then the Americans confiscated it and I never saw it again – but, by then, that was the least of my troubles.

Hitler was invited to pay a visit to the Italian court as the personal guest of the King of Italy. Unfortunately the meteorological reports were very unfavourable, so Hitler decided to go to Rome by special train. I was to lead a flight of three Condors. In Rome I put up at the hotel I had always used there, the Massimi Daceglio. I had stayed there on innumerable occasions as flight captain of the Lufthansa, and its Bavarian proprietor, Herr Kiesel, had become my very good friend. I then reported my arrival to Hitler, who had been given a suite of rooms in the Quirinal. The first thing he said to me after his greeting was:

'Just imagine it, Baur: as soon as I got out of the station' (which, incidentally, had been built specially for him and was like a bower of flowers), 'what should I find but prehistoric animals to drag me away in an antediluvian state-coach! What a conveyance for a modern man! But there you are, Baur; that's the royal tradition, so I had to put up with it. But I didn't feel comfortable, I can tell you.'

The reception they had prepared for Hitler was tremendous, and must have cost a pretty penny. At the parade the next day I noticed that Hitler spoke a good deal to Mussolini, and hardly more to the King than politeness required. Incidentally, he said more than once that he regarded the King as a hindrance to Mussolini, and an obstacle to the carrying out of his plans.

This time the march-past of the Italian Fascist organisations was distinctly better: they had obviously been in stricter training in the meantime. As a flyer, I was of course interested in what the Italian Air Force had to show us. Big stands had been erected in Furbara facing the sea, and everyone who was anyone in Rome was there. The aerobatics the Italian flyers showed us were first class, and I was particularly impressed by their formation flights. Then came bombing demonstrations. Medium bombers dropped small bombs on land objectives, and the aiming was fairly good. Then heavy bombers attacked two ships out at sea in full view, and sank both of them – or appeared to, for I heard it whispered afterwards that they had really been sunk by charges electrically detonated from the shore, though I can't say anything one way or the other about that. It looked good, and, on the whole, the performance of the Italians in the air was quite impressive.

That evening we attended an open-air performance of *Aïda* in the Mussolini Forum. Hundreds of actors and actresses took part in it, and once again Italy's leading opera-singers gave us their best. Altogether it was a very enjoyable evening.

The next afternoon there was a state banquet given in Hitler's honour. I was waiting in the anteroom together with about two hundred other guests for the arrival of the King and Queen and the guest of honour, Hitler. After a while two great doors were opened and a chamberlain announced the imminent arrival of Her Majesty the Queen of Italy, and Herr Hitler, Chancellor of the German Reich. The two high personages appeared, the Queen, a big, handsome woman, on Hitler's arm. As they entered the hall all the Italians bowed low – some of them even went down on their knees. And as the two passed through a narrow lane between the waiting guests, many of them took the Queen's gown and kissed it. Hitler was obviously highly embarrassed by the whole business: the low bowing, the kneeling and the kissing of the Queen's hem. With a flushed face he almost dragged her along so as to get it over as quickly as possible. We thought he was going to have a stroke, but he managed to get the Queen through to the hall where the banquet was to take place.

I referred to it that evening when we were alone, and he said: 'Baur, it was terrible. These court ceremonies upset me. I shall never get used to them. When I saw those Italians on the ground I thought it so humiliating that the only thing I could do was to get it over as quickly as possible.'

He loathed all such obsequious ceremonies.

During the visit, Mussolini showed his fleet in Naples, and Hitler was certainly very much impressed by that, particularly by about eighty or ninety submarines which submerged and surfaced in formation with extraordinary accuracy. After that, Italian tanks did firing exercises with live shells, but Hitler was not particularly impressed by their performance.

That evening deputations arrived in costume from all the Italian provinces and performed their local dances. This otherwise pleasant evening was spoiled for Hitler by his annoyance at the way Mussolini was kept in the background by the King; and several times, pretending that there was something he wanted to say to him, Hitler took Mussolini by the arm and led him to the front with the King and Queen.

Quite generally, Hitler did not care much for the Italian Royal Family, and this was particularly true of the Crown Prince Umberto. In the summer of 1938 the Crown Prince and Princess were invited to Berlin, and Hitler instructed me to fly them back to Milan afterwards. As we flew over the Alps I kept them informed the whole time of our position and height, and I pointed out each important peak and valley, for I knew the Alps like the palm of my hand. We landed without incident on Taliedo airfield near Milan, and both my passengers thanked me warmly for having made their flight so interesting. A few weeks later, through the Italian Embassy in Berlin, I received an inscribed photograph of the royal pair in a silver frame. When I reported back to Hitler that I had flown his guests safely to Milan he nodded, and then said that he was sorry for the poor woman; she must have a good deal to put up with, and the marriage didn't seem to be a happy one.

Now that there was a proper German Army again, based on compulsory military service, instead of the small Reichswehr, Hitler was often at Krupps in Essen for discussions on various armament questions, and the latest weapons were always demonstrated to him. After such visits we usually went on to Bad Godesberg, where Hitler would stay, as always, in the Hotel Dreesen. That evening a big Rhine salmon, which we were shown still alive, was prepared for our dinner. It weighed over fifty pounds, and I for one was looking forward to it. We were all in the dining-room actually with our hands on the backs of the chairs preparatory to sitting down as soon as Hitler did, when von Puttkamer, Hitler's naval attaché, was called to the telephone.

Hitler immediately declared that we would wait until he returned before sitting down to dinner; but when von Puttkamer did return it was to inform Hitler that Admiral Raeder wished to speak to him. This in itself was unusual. It was very seldom that anyone asked for Hitler to be called to the telephone. Whatever it was, it was obviously a matter of some importance, and in the meantime that gigantic Rhine salmon had to wait. After about ten minutes Hitler reappeared and strode up to me at once.

'Baur, what is the earliest possible moment we can start for Berlin?' he demanded.

Actually we took off at 21.00 hours, and I flew him to Berlin on an empty stomach – mine in particular; he didn't mind so much. The Spanish civil war was going on at the time, and apparently the German battleship *Deutschland* had been fired on. A number of sailors had been killed and wounded. We landed in Berlin at 23.00 hours, and half an hour later I arrived in Hitler's apartment in the Reich Chancellory. He was waiting for the morning papers, which were always brought to him as soon as they came off the press. As I came in he had the first of them in his hands.

'Hallo, Baur,' he greeted me. 'You here already!'

'Yes,' I said, 'I am, and I'm starving.'

'Well, go into the restaurant and get a meal.'

I did so, and after a while he joined me.

'The Russians have fired on the *Deutschland*,' he said, 'and I've had to act quickly to prevent such things from happening again. You see, Baur, how important it is that I should keep you always with me. You never know what's going to happen next. Because we were able to get to Berlin quickly I was able to settle everything immediately, and things are already moving. What a terrible loss of time it would have been if I'd had to take a special train to Berlin!'

It appeared that as a reprisal for the bombardment of the *Deutschland* Hitler had ordered the bombardment of the Spanish coastal town of Almeria. He declared that it would just have been a waste of time to use diplomatic channels. The only thing to do was to act, and act quickly. The German warship nearest to Almeria would open the bombardment at dawn the next day. Hitler had discussed the matter with the naval authorities, and was quite convinced that he had acted correctly.

A few days later he returned to the subject and told me that the foreign press had remained relatively calm in face of the German reprisals, and that no one had even seriously disputed his right to act as he had done.

* * *

In the first few days of March the newspapers sold like hot cakes all over Germany, because there was great excitement on account of the situation in Austria, on whose frontiers German troops were massed. On 12 March at 08.10 we took off from Berlin, and landed in Munich at 10.30. That morning German troops had already crossed the border into Austria, and Hitler now followed them by road. I flew to Vienna and reported to the Hotel Imperial where Hitler had already made his headquarters. Early on 13 March Cardinal Innitzer came to see him. There was a tremendous mass of people gathered in front of the hotel when the car containing the Cardinal and his retinue drove up. Hitler had a suite on the first floor, and I and others stood on the landing to see how Hitler would receive the Cardinal. Hitler went to the door to meet him and bowed deeply, a thing I had never seen him do before. The meeting was polite, and Cardinal Innitzer seemed determined to keep the interview agreeable. When their discussion was over they parted on obviously friendly terms.

Hitler was clearly satisfied with the upshot of the discussion, and he declared gleefully that he had succeeded in ensuring peace between Church and state in Austria. He had given certain assurances, and Cardinal Innitzer had deemed them adequate. Thus, although Hitler's arrival in Austria was not desired by the Church, it was not positively opposed.

In the afternoon great demonstrations took place in the Burggarten, and the enthusiasm of the masses was indescribable. Hitler had a number of meetings with various other prominent personalities in Austria, and then we flew back to Berlin.

The Czech crisis boiled up next, and there was once again great excitement in Germany. We could sense that everything was at stake, and that at any moment the die could fall. I flew Hitler to Godesberg, where he was to meet the British Premier, Chamberlain. In the Hotel Dreesen there is a smaller room off the entrance hall, and you can see into it through a glass door. It was here that Hitler and Chamberlain had their discussion, whilst we all stood outside as spectators. It was like looking at a silent film – but without titles to help you. We could see the two statesmen talking and see their gestures, but only guess at what they were saying.

They greeted each other politely; then the discussion began, and during the course of it a map was produced and laid out on the table. It was from this moment on that the discussion began to get lively, and it was quite easy to see that Chamberlain was not at all in agreement with Hitler's proposals. But Hitler went on talking uninterruptedly, gesticulating again and again to the map. We could see that he was speaking very energetically. From what we could judge of the business it didn't look as though the discussions were going to lead to any agreement.

The next morning Chamberlain didn't turn up at all, and let Hitler know that he was indisposed. Hitler immediately offered him his own physician Dr Morell, but although he was thanked for this kind offer, it was refused. In the afternoon Chamberlain came down from where he was staying on the Petersberg, and the discussions were resumed. It is now a matter of history that they ended in the famous Munich agreement.

Hitler was delighted, and he kept telling us what clever politicians and diplomats the English were. His discussions with Chamberlain had made him more than ever determined to press on with his favourite plan to win both Britain and Italy as friends of Germany. One thing he said again and again was: 'If we can get an alliance with both the British and the Italians then we can arrange matters in our own Reich just as we please.' And whenever he had British visitors he was never tired of stressing that if only Britain would leave him a free hand in Europe she need not fear that he would do anything whatever to weaken her world position. No doubt the Naval Agreement, the many discussions with leading British politicians, and a number of steps taken through mediators were all designed to bring about the same consummation. And Hitler stressed in particular that he had no ambition for Germany to possess the strongest navy; all he wanted was sufficient naval strength to defend her shores and keep open the routes to her colonies – which he hoped that Britain would soon return.

During discussions at table, too, Hitler often expressed his admiration of British international diplomacy, and the idea of friendship with Britain cropped up again and again as a sort of sheet-anchor in his conversation. For my part, I believe that he was perfectly sincere in this desire.

Later on, of course, Hitler had to abandon these ideas, and today there is not much point in speculating as to what might have happened if he had succeeded in establishing the friendly relationship which he so much desired. It is enough to say that a good many things would be different now. The unfortunate truth seems to be that when you have two big powers both anxious to play a leading role in the world, their interests collide at so many points that any fundamental agreement for joint action is impossible. Aren't we witnessing the same thing all over again?

Soon after the occupation of Austria, Hitler began to talk about the way in which Czech territory drove like a wedge into the new German Reich, and to say that something must be done about it. After a certain amount of preliminary negotiation Hitler sent for the President of the Czechoslovak Republic, Hacha. When Hacha, an undistinguished and rather pathetic little man, arrived in Berlin he gave every sign of being very ill at ease, knowing no doubt that the negotiations between him and Hitler were going to be very difficult.

Hitler wasted no time, but immediately demanded that Hacha should agree to the incorporation of the Czech Republic into the German Reich. At first Hacha desperately refused to agree, but when he saw that Hitler was quite determined and that resistance would only mean useless bloodshed, he surrendered. When it was all over he had a seizure, and Morell, Hitler's personal physician, gave him several injections. Morell told me afterwards that he had been afraid Hacha would die on the spot. Fortunately he recovered sufficiently to be able to leave the Reich Chancellory.

German troops were already concentrated on the Czech frontiers, and Hitler now gave orders for the invasion. He then boarded a special train so as to be with his troops in Prague, if possible even before Hacha got back. I was to fly to Prague to be on hand for further instructions. When I touched down on Prague airfield Hitler was already in the Hradschin, the ancient castle on a hill overlooking Prague which was the seat of the Czechoslovak Government.

When we arrived, Hitler explained 'the historic role' which the Hradschin had played in German history, and declared that it was now to play that role again.

The Czechs had hastily evacuated the Hradschin, and there was very little furniture left. The staff had gone, too. German personnel soon got the kitchens going and provisionally put the great dining hall in order. After the formalities connected with the formal incorporation of the Czech Republic into the Third Reich, Hitler flew back to Berlin.

The German Labour Front under Ley had built a couple of 26,000-ton vessels for its 'Strength through Joy' movement, to serve as holiday-ships. Ley himself had several times asked Hitler to come on board for a cruise, and Hitler had always refused on account of pressure of work; now he agreed, and I flew him to Bremerhaven, where he boarded one of these vessels, the *Robert Ley*, which was about to make her maiden voyage with a thousand passengers on board.

Hitler inspected the whole vessel, which was splendidly equipped with several big dining-rooms, gymnasiums, auditoriums, dance halls, swimming-baths, a library and fine promenade decks. On the way to Heligoland we were escorted by two fast destroyers, and at one time a submarine surfaced near us, the crew tumbling out of the hatchways and lining up on deck to greet us.

When we were on Heligoland Hitler's chief interest was in the deep excavation work which was being carried out to fortify the island and install big naval guns. And this was typical of the shadow that was now rising over us all. When I look back at my life, I can see that by this time I had already had my heyday. I had been privileged to play an active part in the beginnings of flying, and I had done my share to help build it up to what it had already become by that time. The old 'kites' we had flown in the beginning had now given way to masterpieces of technical ingenuity, and my comrades were flying passengers over dozens of routes which linked up all big towns, and all important countries – and even continents. Our Lufthansa had already earned the highest possible reputation in the world. All in all, therefore, I think we had every right to be proud and satisfied, for the development of civil flying from the first post-war years until 1939 had been truly enormous.

We were airmen, though, not politicians; and we thought Germany was enjoying a period of great constructive progress. But a change was taking place. Flying was being pressed into the service of war; its aim was no longer to carry passengers and freight quickly and safely, but to carry and drop as big a weight of bombs as possible. 'Flying fortresses' were what was wanted now, not fast and comfortable passenger planes. In the meantime we continued to fly. We could not see the whole game, and we went on flying until, with the outbreak of the Second World War, the whole character of flying changed.

PART FOUR

The Second World War

I HAD BECOME used to surprises by this time, but I must confess that even I was shaken when one day Hitler calmly said to me:

'Baur, get ready to fly Ribbentrop to Moscow in a few days' time.'

A party of thirty-five was to be flown to the Russian capital, and as our Focke-Wulf Condors could carry up to twenty passengers, that meant two planes. Late in the afternoon on 21 August 1939, I landed on the Reichenhall-Aiming airfield to pick up Ribbentrop, who was with his staff on his country estate at Fuschl. Shortly afterwards he and the others arrived in cars, with two lorries bringing up the rear with their baggage. We managed to pack it all away, but it meant that we were heavily loaded, and it wasn't too easy to take off from that small airfield. We flew to Königsberg and spent the night there. I and my crews were up early in the morning getting our machines ready, and I was studying the route the Russians had laid down for us, which was not, to my surprise, the direct one. We were to avoid Polish airspace and set course Dunaburg–Veliki-Luki–Moscow, arriving at the 'Aero-Port' on the River Moskva in four hours and a quarter after the take-off. As I circled the airfield before touching down I realised that a big reception had been arranged. There were Soviet red flags with the hammer and sickle, and German red flags with the black *Hakenkreuz* on a round white ground, flying everywhere. There was a guard of honour drawn up, and a military band with shining brass instruments.

Ribbentrop was the first to get out of my plane, and he was heartily welcomed by the Soviet Foreign Minister, Molotov, whilst the military brass band played first our national anthem and then theirs whilst everyone stood at the salute. Ribbentrop then marched along with his arm raised in the Hitler salute whilst he inspected the guard of honour. 'My God!' I thought. 'Wonders will never cease!'

Ribbentrop and his party and the Russians then drove off in a fleet of cars into the town; Ribbentrop stayed with the German Ambassador, Schulenburg, whilst those with him were quartered in hotels. I remained on the airfield for the time being, where our planes were the centre of a great deal of attention. The Focke-Wulf Condor was famous throughout the world by this time because of its non-stop flight from Berlin to New York, a sensation for those days, and its non-stop flight to the Far East. The machines looked good too; aerodynamically they were excellent, and undoubtedly they were not only amongst the most powerful but also the most beautiful planes in the air before the war.

The Russian experts made no secret of their admiration. The Russian foreman had at one time worked on the Königsberg–Moscow line and he spoke quite good German; he produced the necessary mechanics and so on, and work started at once to prepare our machines to take off again the following day.

As usual at the end of a journey we had a good deal of food and little luxuries of various kinds over: white rolls, cake, biscuits, chocolate and so on, all neatly packed. As a general rule we had no difficulty in getting rid of them to make room for our supplies for the homeward journey, but this time my mechanic informed me that the men engaged on our engines and the women who were cleaning out the inside of the planes all refused to accept them. I got hold of the foreman who spoke German, and asked him what was the matter. He smiled and said that Russians had enough to eat. I replied: yes, of course, I was quite sure they had, but that wasn't the point. It wasn't a question of charity, or feeding the hungry: we just didn't want good stuff wasted. He still smiled and said no; it was forbidden. I then told my mechanic to put the baskets with the stuff on a bench in the hangar and leave them there. The next morning when our fresh supplies arrived those baskets were all empty. There are more ways of killing a cat . . .

A little later a squad of photographers arrived, complete with small ladders. They were pretty poorly clothed, and they wanted to know whether they could take photographs of our Condors. 'Carry on,' I said. And at that they photographed our planes from every possible angle. They all seemed very surprised that they were allowed to take photographs at all, and astonished that they could go anywhere. Even so, they really couldn't believe that they would be allowed to photograph the engines, and their leader came specially – and very doubtfully – to me to know whether they might; and when I said yes he looked at me in vast astonishment.

When everything had been settled and the work was well under way, Liehr, the pilot of the second machine, and I decided to go into Moscow itself. Our crews were to live in the machines, get their food there and generally keep an eye on things, because, naturally, we were alive to certain possibilities . . . But, in fact, the Russians intervened.

Whilst we were preparing to leave, a man in civilian clothes came up to me and addressed me in excellent German, informing me that he was in charge of the GPU, the Russian secret police. He had been instructed to guard our machines. I told him we preferred to do it ourselves. Oh no, he said, that was impossible. He had strict instructions: a hangar had been made ready for our machines. They would be rolled into it and locked away and the key handed to me. GPU troops would then undertake the outside watch.

We were guests of the Russian Government, and it was difficult for me to object to this arrangement, which seemed all right, so I agreed. When everything was ready the two machines were trundled into the hangar, the doors were closed and locked, and I was given the key.

A messenger from the German Embassy then handed us two hundred roubles each, declaring that we probably shouldn't need any money, but it was better for us to have just a little. It did seem a little to me so I pointed out that the possibility of being able to tip freely was a great lubricant when you wanted anything done quickly, and that I had always been allowed to do what I thought best in that respect. How was I going to get on with two hundred roubles? I was then informed that tipping had been abolished in Russia. I wondered, but gave it up. After that we all drove into town. Liehr and I were quartered with the German military attaché, Herr von Köstring, whilst our crews were given rooms in the Hotel National, an Intourist establishment.

When we had washed and changed we went down to dinner. Nothing about it seemed very Russian, but von Köstring immediately explained that it had all been brought in at Embassy instructions from Poland and Sweden – it was cheaper that way. After our meal we naturally wanted to see the town. We were given a German Baltic girl as an interpreter, and we set off with her in a car provided by the Russian Government.

As we left the building she pointed out the GPU post whose job it was to watch all comings and goings. A man would now telephone to GPU headquarters to inform them that a car, number so and so, containing so and so many people, age, sex, and so on, had just left, going in whatever direction it happened to be – and giving the names of the passengers, if they happened to be known. After that, our interpreter explained, another car would tack itself on to us and follow fifty yards or so in the rear, and wherever we went and whatever we did, the GPU would be on our heels.

Once again we were urgently warned that the taking of photographs was strictly forbidden, and that any attempt to use a camera would get us into serious trouble. I had already discovered this at the airfield when Zintl and I had taken our Leicas with us.

'For heaven's sake, Captain Baur, don't attempt to take any photographs!' the representative of the German Embassy had said. 'Best of all, leave your cameras behind altogether.'

'I know better than to take photographs on an airfield,' I said, 'but surely in the town a visitor can snap this or that interesting building.'

But no, this wasn't so: no photographs at all, or else . . .

We assured the girl that we wouldn't dream of taking photographs – we hadn't even our cameras with us. After looking at the Kremlin we drove out to a hill from where we had a wonderful view over Moscow. After having driven to see all the sights we returned to the German Embassy and stayed there until well past midnight. Heinrich Hoffmann, Hitler's official photographer, was then called to the Kremlin to take pictures of the final scenes at the discussion between Stalin and Ribbentrop. He returned full of enthusiasm. Early next morning, Liehr and I and our crews were back on the airfield to take our machines up for a trial flight before flying Ribbentrop's party back to Germany.

We had found no opportunity of buying anything during our short stay in Moscow, and everyone else gave the money back, but I thought it would be a shame, so I asked our girl interpreter to give it to our Russian driver, who had driven us around all day and half the night. She was sure he would refuse it, but I said that he looked as though a couple of hundred roubles would come in useful and I urged her to try. So when we came to the airfield she leant forward and offered him the roubles. At that there was an explosion. The man was furious; he wanted to know whether this was the thanks he got for having done his best for us – to get him into prison; we knew perfectly well that it was forbidden to take tips! And so on. We did our best to calm him down, and in the end we parted good friends – and I too gave my roubles back to the Embassy.

Soon after that, our machines were waiting ready on the tarmac to take off. Ribbentrop arrived with his party and the Russian Foreign Minister, Molotov, who was all smiles and said good-bye to Ribbentrop with great friendliness. Before the take-off we were in touch with Berlin and received instructions not to fly to Obersalzberg, where Hitler was at the time, but straight to Berlin – he would fly there in the meantime to meet Ribbentrop on his return. We made a short intermediate landing in Königsberg, and soon after that we touched down in Berlin, where Hitler was anxiously waiting to hear Ribbentrop's report.

For weeks after that I listened to discussions at table in the Reich Chancellory concerning the results of the negotiations in Moscow. As there were new guests constantly, Hitler had occasion to deal with the matter again and again. He was very satisfied with what had been obtained, and he said so frequently. In addition, his opinion of Stalin had changed, and this astonished a good many people. For example, Hitler once remarked that Stalin's career had really been rather like his own. Stalin had come from below to the top; and he, Hitler, knew better than anyone what it meant to have worked your way up from being an unknown man to being leader of a great state. At that some shocked guest declared:

'But my Führer, you really shouldn't compare Stalin with yourself. Why, he was a bank-robber!'

Hitler brusquely rejected the observation and declared that if Stalin had actually robbed any banks, then it had been not for himself but for his party and his movement – which was a very different thing, and not to be regarded as bank-robbery in the ordinary way.

Another result of Hitler's changed attitude towards Stalin was that the Eher Verlag, his own big publishing house, and all the others, were given instructions to pulp their stocks of anti-Communist material – an order which gave rise to a good deal of doubtful head-shaking.

The negotiations with Poland did not have the desired result, and Germany invaded Poland. In my opinion Hitler ventured that far only because he felt sure that Great Britain and France would not intervene. I can well remember the morning on which the ultimatum was handed to the Polish Ambassador. Hitler and Ribbentrop, with a number of other people, were in the smoking-room at the Reich Chancellory, and Hitler declared positively:

'I can't imagine the British and the French going to Poland's assistance. They're bluffing, Ribbentrop; you'll see, they won't come in.'

Ribbentrop didn't agree with him, and said so. He also added that all his information suggested that the British and French were serious and would come in. Hitler remained unconvinced. And when the British and French declarations of war were handed over he consoled himself with the thought that war with them would have been unavoidable in the long run anyway, so it was better that it should come now since it would free his hands to carry out his plans for strengthening and consolidating Germany.

Several times he declared positively that the war could not last more than a couple of years; and he was so firmly convinced of this that he told Speer not to reckon with much more than two – or at the utmost four – years for the various industrial buildings and plants made necessary by the war.

With the war a new routine life began for us. I flew Hitler to Krössinsee, the ancient monastic stronghold in Pomerania, where there was an airfield, and from there he made short flights to the front. A little later our base was pushed forward to Oppeln in East Prussia. On our flights over Polish territory we often had to land on ordinary fields and meadows, which made things difficult for our escort of fighter planes – we usually had six with us – and splinters were common. The fighter planes were so fast that ordinary fields just weren't big enough to provide the necessary run. Sometimes it happened that we had only a couple of fighters to escort us on the way back – the others had suffered such damage in landing that they were unable to take off again.

When the German troops were at the gates of Warsaw we landed about eighteen miles away in a stubble-field. Hitler was to arrive by car. A concentration of about five thousand guns had already opened the final bombardment of Warsaw, and Hitler wanted to see the effects from the air. He hoped that it would lead to the surrender of the town. Soon after he arrived with his staff the order to take off was given.

Everyone except myself was already on board, the engines were running, and I was just about to climb into my seat when an army car raced up. An officer jumped out and declared that he had an urgent message for Hitler. I reported to Field-Marshal Keitel, who informed Hitler, who then got out of the plane and received the message in person. I was standing just behind him when the officer declared that he had the sad task of informing the Führer that General Fritsch had been killed in action. He had gone forward with a company against a Polish position and been shot down by machine-gun fire. A bullet had ripped open an artery in the thigh, and the General had bled to death within a few minutes. Hitler briefly expressed his regret, and then got back into the plane and gave the order for the take-off.

With a fighter escort we now flew over the front lines at a height of between six and seven thousand feet, and we could easily see the devastation being caused in the suburbs of Warsaw. After cruising around over Warsaw for about thirty minutes we returned to our landing-place, and shortly after that Warsaw offered to capitulate. A few days later, Poland as a whole surrendered.

A great victory parade was to take place in Warsaw, and I flew Hitler to Warsaw airfield. A great number of high officers were present to receive him, and discussions took place on the spot, with large quantities of maps. After about an hour Hitler got into a car and was driven into the centre of the town to take the salute at the parade.

I waited behind on the airfield with my crew, and food for about a hundred was simmering in field-kitchens. When it got to 15.00 I asked the major in charge of the catering to give us our food, because when Hitler came back we should probably have to get away quickly and the last-minute preparations would probably not allow us time to eat. Tables had been laid in an empty hangar, which had been specially brightened up for the purpose: there were white table-cloths, and even flowers on the tables. In fact, it all looked very attractive. But there was Hitler's well-known puritanism – which was narrower than ever in time of war – to contend with, and I communicated my doubts to the major about his spread, telling him that I didn't think he'd get any thanks from Hitler for his quite extraordinary performance. However, the major declared that it was impossible to ask Hitler to sit down and eat at a table without a table-cloth, so I made no further objection.

The great column of cars arrived from the centre of the town at 16.00, and Hitler marched into the hanger with his retinue, including Field-Marshal Keitel. He gave one look at the festively prepared tables and demanded who had given orders for a state banquet in time of war. Keitel didn't know, and enquiries had to be made to discover the culprit. Hitler was furious, and turning to me he snapped: 'Is everything ready for the take-off, Baur?'

When I told him that it was, he marched off to take his place in the machine, leaving the prepared tables behind, and forcing his retinue to do the same. Field-Marshal Keitel and the others were hungry, and now they were furious, but there was nothing they could do about it. They didn't get anything to eat until we landed some hours later in Berlin.

In the autumn I flew Ribbentrop to Moscow a second time, once again with two Condor machines. This time I and my crew were quartered in the Hotel National. In honour of Ribbentrop, who sat in the former Tsar's box, which was now Stalin's, the Moscow Opera Company staged a ballet evening, which included the famous 'Dying Swan'. The Russians had naturally spared no pains to make the evening a success, and from the artistic standpoint it certainly was, but what we found astonishing was the audience. Some of the ladies had done themselves up as well as they could, but their clothes looked as though they had come out of grandmother's rag-bag. And as for the men, you would have said that they had just come from the work-bench. They didn't even wear ties, and none of the ladies seemed to have hats. Of course, the Russians had more urgent matters to attend to at the time than developing their textile industry. Later on – when I was their prisoner of war – I noticed that the secretaries of high officers and so on, did have good clothes – and hats! But not in the autumn of 1939.

After the opera Ribbentrop met Stalin for the final discussions. Hoffmann was once again asked to the Kremlin to take photographs, but the rest of us stayed in our hotel. When we had gone to our rooms I remembered something I wanted to say to my mechanic, Zintl, so I went out into the corridor to go to his room – and I found that each of our doors was guarded! Perhaps it was for our protection, and it certainly meant that no one could get anywhere near us unobserved. The next morning we had breakfast in the hotel and drove straight out to the airfield. This time, too, Molotov accompanied Ribbentrop to his plane.

As before, the main item of discussion at table in the Reich Chancellory after this visit was its results, and once again Hitler seemed very well satisfied; in fact, he declared quite frankly that, but for this new agreement, food would have become short in Germany. And politically he hoped that the conclusion of the agreement would have some effect on the British.

Ribbentrop and Hoffmann had to tell Hitler about their experiences and their personal impressions in Moscow. Ribbentrop declared, amongst other things, that Stalin had drunk so much vodka that at first he had been sure that only water was in his glass, but later on he had been given an opportunity of seeing for himself that it really was vodka. This wasn't the first time – and it wasn't to be the last – that the Russians demonstrated their simply fantastic qualities as consumers of hard liquor. The only man in the German party who had been able to keep up with them was Hoffmann who was a mighty consumer of strong drink before the Lord; even Stalin had noted his performance with appreciation, and had drunk a personal toast to him.

On 8 November I flew Hitler to Munich for the traditional 9 November celebrations in the Bürgerbräu Keller. Shortly before we touched down, Hitler asked me whether it would be possible for him to be back in Berlin at 10.00 on 10 November, because there was an urgent discussion which he was unable to postpone. I pointed out that November was the month of mists and fogs, and if there happened to be one the next day I couldn't guarantee anything, as it could easily postpone our take-off for hours. In that case, he said, he would return to Berlin by train. At this time he had no special train of his own, and a special carriage was coupled to ordinary time-table trains for him. And as it happened, in order to catch a suitable train he had to leave the Bürgerbräu Keller much earlier than he would otherwise have done. Less than an hour after his departure a bomb obviously intended for him exploded, causing damage and a number of fatal casualties.

Hitler spoke as usual from the same spot where, on 9 November 1923, he had fired that famous shot into the ceiling. The would-be assassin had laid his plans, and made his preparations with this in mind. At first the police investigations came up against a blank wall, but a man had been seized on the frontier at Constance just when he was trying to climb over the fence into Swiss territory. A German frontier guard had seized him by the feet and hauled him back.

The arrested man gave his name as Müller [his real name was Georg Elser – ed.], and said he was a mechanic. In his pocket they found a piece of bronze which proved to be identical in kind with the alloy used in the manufacture of the Bürgerbräu Keller time-bomb. Asked why he was trying to get into Switzerland illegally, the man declared that his reasons were purely personal; questioned concerning the explosion in the Bürgerbräu Keller, he denied all connection with it. However, he had a sister living in Munich, and he had been living with her. A search of her flat at first produced nothing sensational. But on the wall there was a traditional Schwarzwald cuckoo-clock. A detective noticed that it was not going, and remarked that with a mechanic in the house it ought to have been easy enough to put it right, whereupon the woman said that her brother had, in fact, worked on it, but without success. The clock was then taken away and examined, and it was discovered that a number of wheels were missing. Amongst the bits and pieces collected from the infernal machine were those very wheels. There was no longer any reasonable doubt as to where that machine had come from and who had put it there; in fact, when faced with the evidence the man confessed. The questioning of his sister produced the fact that Müller had said that he would soon be going to Switzerland, where he would be able to earn a lot of money working for a Frenchman.

Himmler appeared in the Reich Chancellory with a film of the whole investigation, but Hitler refused to look at it, saying that he 'didn't want to see the swine'. However, Himmler showed the film, and I was amongst those invited to see it.

Müller had insisted under examination that he had made the whole ingenious piece of apparatus himself, and the Gestapo was very anxious to know whether this were true or not; so Müller was provided with the necessary materials, and did in fact, make working diagrams and then build an exact copy of the infernal machine which had gone off in the Bürgerbräu Keller.

Under examination Müller declared that he hated Hitler and had determined to put him out of the way. He knew, of course, that he would find it very difficult, if not impossible, to get anywhere near him in the ordinary way; so a time-bomb set to explode at the traditional celebration in the Bürgerbräu Keller on 9 November seemed the best solution of the problem, particularly as the exact place where Hitler would be standing was known, and also the time at which he would be there. The Bürgerbräu Keller was not guarded particularly, and he had found an emergency exit through which he could get into it easily without attracting attention.

Weeks ahead Müller had manufactured his bomb and prepared where it was to go, quite close to the spot where he knew Hitler would be standing. For this he prised off wooden boarding and took out a brick or two behind it, replacing the wood over the cavity and sweeping up everything when he had finished, so that things looked exactly as they had done before. On 8 November, the day before the meeting, he got into the hall again and placed his infernal machine in position in the hole he had made for it, setting the mechanism to explode for the time when in the ordinary way Hitler would have been there. Then he put back the wood boarding, and walked out of the place, leaving absolutely nothing out of the ordinary to be seen. Before the meeting the Gestapo naturally searched the hall as a precaution, but Müller had been too clever for them, and nothing was found.

At first Müller was to have been brought before the Volksgerichtshof, or People's Court, and publicly tried, but Hitler decided against this, and in the end the man was secretly executed.

In November 1939 I was instructed to fetch King Boris from Sofia, and I landed there with my Condor on the ordinary civil airfield. My journey was secret, and I had a passport made out in the not very imaginative name of Schmidt. In accordance with the instructions of the German Foreign Office I presented myself to the German air attaché, Colonel Schönbeck, who looked at me suspiciously and said immediately: 'Schmidt? You're name's not Schmidt. I've seen you somewhere, but I just can't place you for the moment.'

Of course, I had to insist that my name really was Schmidt, but just at that moment my mechanic, Zintl, came up to tell me something, and addressed me as Baur! After that I had to explain the whole thing to Colonel Schönbeck, telling him who I really was, and why I had come – adding that King Boris's departure was to be kept secret. It wasn't a very good start, but at least I had played my part properly.

Shortly afterwards I received instructions from the German Embassy to leave the civil airfield and land on a military airfield not far away, where the machine was to be looked after for the night. I did my best to carry out those instructions, too, but when I tried to take off I discovered that the ground was too soft – it had rained a good deal since I had landed. I just couldn't move, and nothing I could do made any difference. Fifty soldiers were mobilised with spades and boles of wood; even then it took hours, but in the end a tractor pulled the Condor out of the mud. Then at midnight it started to freeze, and that was my salvation.

I took off at dawn and flew to the military airfield. At 08.00 King Boris appeared, accompanied by his brother and a general of the Bulgarian Air Force. Nothing moved on the airfield; everyone had been given instructions to stay out of sight, and the big field looked absolutely deserted. King Boris was in civilian clothing, and he recognised me at once, for I had already flown him from Zürich to Vienna. He asked all sorts of questions about the weather forecast and so on, and showed great interest in various technical details – when he travelled by train he would often go into the locomotive cabin and drive the train himself.

He knew nothing about flying, but he asked me if he could sit up in front. My mechanic gave up his seat next to me, and we started off in the direction of Berchtesgaden. The weather wasn't bad, and as the King was so keen I gave him his first flying lesson, showing him how the machine reacted to gusts of wind and how deviations could be corrected. He was astonished at the readiness with which the great plane answered to the slightest movement of the controls. On a quiet stretch I actually let him fly the plane himself. He was a very good pupil, and by the time we had landed at Ainring airfield near Reichenhall he had learned quite a bit and was looking forward eagerly to the flight back.

He was received by Hitler, spent the night in Schloss Klessheim near Salzburg, and the next morning I flew him back to Sofia, during which time he had another lesson. He thanked me warmly before he left us at Sofia, and assured me that we should often be flying together in the future; this turned out to be true, for I flew him on many occasions during the war.

In December 1939 we flew into the Saar district, and from there Hitler made flights to various parts of the front. At that time, of course, the offensive in the west had not begun, and with the exception of one or two spots all was quiet. Just before Christmas, Kannenberg, who was in charge of the household at the Reich Chancellory, made up Christmas parcels for the men of Hitler's bodyguard and for those in his immediate circle. I knew how gladly Hitler liked to give, and how particularly delighted he was when his gifts were appreciated, and he happened to say to me that it was a shame that he couldn't go out shopping and choose the presents himself. I said that he ought to do what Göring did: go to a shop after closing hours and have the whole staff waiting on him. Hitler laughed and said that such a method of shopping no doubt suited Göring, but personally it didn't appeal to him.

After Christmas visits to various parts of the front we flew back to Berlin. Before the launching of the offensive in the west, the famous Organisation Todt built headquarters for Hitler on the Ziegenberg in the Taunus. Reich Minister Todt arrived in the Reich Chancellory to lay plans and photographs before Hitler. As he looked through them, however, Hitler grew more and more dissatisfied.

'This is supposed to be a military headquarters,' he snapped, 'and yet I see there are wood-carvings, wrought ironwork decorations and thick carpets on the floors. Do you really think I'm going to occupy a headquarters like that? Later on, thousands of German citizens will visit this place. Would any of them possibly understand how I could live in such luxury in wartime?'

Todt defended himself and said that the Reich Chancellor had certain representative duties, so that in the circumstances the installation was not unnecessarily luxurious. But Hitler refused to be persuaded.

'You can do what you like on the Ziegenberg,' he declared bluntly. 'I won't be there.'

With that, a feverish search started up for a new headquarters. A suitable spot was eventually found in the Eiffel, and this headquarters was called 'Felsennest' or rock eyrie. The blockhouses were bored into the solid rock, and a special airfield was laid out near Euskirchen, about eight miles away. Hitler moved in just before the opening of the offensive in the west.

In the meantime the Chancellory was a hive of activity. High naval and military officers were constantly coming and going, and it was quite obvious that something big was in the offing; but what it was I didn't know, and didn't learn until the invasion of Norway had actually started. For a while after that all the table-talk at the Reich Chancellory was about General Dietl and the difficulties of keeping him supplied, for shipping losses were heavy, and, in fact, for a while it seemed touch and go. But finally it became clear that the invasion was a success, and then everyone breathed again. Hitler was delighted at the way Dietl and his men had carried off the daring coup, and he was convinced that their deed would stand out in history. Also, he was overjoyed when Intelligence informed him that the German invasion had forestalled the British by only twenty-four hours.

When the fighting was over, Terboven, Gauleiter of Essen, was appointed Commissar for Norway, and I was instructed to fly him to Oslo. On the day of the flight the weather was very unfavourable, and the landing was particularly difficult. Oslo airfield is a rock plateau hewn out of solid granite. As far as you can see, there isn't a blade of grass: just rock, and nothing but rock while behind it the town rises up still higher. It was no joke landing a big four-engined plane there, particularly as the actual landing-strip was narrow and little more than a thousand yards long. And to encourage any pilot coming in to land was the sight of plane-wrecks to left and right of him as he touched down. The least deviation from the straight and narrow would have meant the destruction of the plane. I managed it all right, but I breathed a sigh of relief when we finally rolled to a halt safe and sound. The next day I flew back to Berlin, and reported to Hitler that Oslo airfield was quite unsuited for normal Luftwaffe use.

One morning I was ordered to take three Condor planes to Hamburg that same evening. Hitler was to come on afterwards by train. The flight was to be kept secret, and in Hamburg I was to arrange for a sufficient number of life-jackets to be taken on board. Everything was to be ready for a take-off at six o'clock the following morning. When I arrived in Hamburg I had some difficulty in getting hold of fifty life-jackets, but I succeeded, though not without making it an open secret that Hitler was flying to Oslo to visit his troops in Norway.

I stayed the night in a small hotel in Fuhlsbüttel, and I was up very early the next morning. At 04.30 I was sitting down having my breakfast when I was called to the telephone. It was Hitler's Luftwaffe Adjutant, von Below.

'Just a moment,' he said, 'the Führer himself is coming to the telephone.'

Hitler wanted to know whether everything was ready for the take-off and whether the life-jackets were safely on board. I was a bit puzzled at this, because when I was given instructions to do a certain thing it was usually assumed that I would do it; no one, and certainly not Hitler himself, ever rang up to enquire whether I had in fact carried out my instructions.

But then Hitler said: 'I know I can trust you, Baur. You've done everything you were told to do, but in the meantime one or two things have changed. I want you to come to me at once.'

'Where to?' I asked.

'To my Felsennest headquarters. Touch down at Euskirchen. The fact is that the western offensive started this morning. You were sent to Hamburg to make all those preparations in order to mislead enemy intelligence. But come straight away now. I need you urgently.'

I took off very early and flew to Euskirchen. The offensive in the west was going forward rapidly. There wasn't, in fact, a great deal for me to do with my Condors, but my Fieseler Storch planes were kept very busy taking Hitler's military adjutants backwards and forwards from his headquarters to the various command centres. When difficulties arose, Hitler's opinion was taken direct to the commanding general in this way.

After a few days I began to fly Hitler more and more often into French territory, where we landed for him to discuss matters with his generals on the spot. We always set off from his Eiffel headquarters and returned there, but by this time it was really too far away from the fighting, which had rolled deep into France. Hitler therefore ordered a more suitable place to be found as quickly as possible. I flew Colonel Schmundt, the Adjutant-in-Chief of the Wehrmacht, into the Ardennes on this quest, and we landed in a field not far from Rocroy. It had been decided that the new headquarters should be established in some out-of-the-way village, and in Rocroy we found a small hamlet of about ten cottages on the verge of the Ardenne woods, which, we decided, would do very well. The church tower was taken down and put to one side, with the intention of putting it up again when hostilities were over, and the whole building arrangements were carried out by the Organisation Todt within a matter of days. A special underground concrete shelter, or bunker, about ten feet down, was built for Hitler.

Most of the inhabitants of the little village had already fled into the interior, and those few who were left we moved away. The new headquarters was occupied by Hitler as soon as it was ready. The nearest airfield was about three miles away on French territory, and my crews were quartered in a small village in the neighbourhood, but the headquarters itself was on Belgian territory.

When not actually in use our machines were kept under camouflage netting in the nearby woods. We had our own wireless station, storage bunkers and recreation huts for us to stay in during waiting periods, quickly run up by the Organisation Todt. From here we were constantly flying to Rheims, Charleville, Lille and so on. I flew Hitler into Lille immediately after the town was taken, and the fact that he appeared so soon after the fighting certainly made an impression on the civilian population, which was precisely what he had aimed at. He ate all his meals from field kitchens like the men, though in his case the meat had to be removed first. Made wise by the story of the over-zealous major in Warsaw, which spread like wildfire, no one again tried to present any improvised banquets for Hitler in the field.

Our most successful fighter wing was stationed in Charleville at the time. I flew Hitler there to inspect it, and he personally decorated Galland, its commander. Göring happened to be with Hitler at the time, and whilst he was waiting – being greatly interested in food – he casually asked a cook in charge of a field kitchen what he had been in peacetime. The man replied that he was a smith by trade! Göring was furious. He sent for the catering officer and dressed him down: 'I see you make smiths cooks; so I suppose you make cooks smiths, and mechanics bakers, and bakers mechanics!'

We hadn't heard much about 'the Führer's Deputy', or, in other words, Reich Minister Rudolf Hess, but after we had been in our new headquarters a few days he arrived in a Ju.52 flown by Captain Doldi. I happened to be at the airfield in a small army car, and Hess got in beside me and drove straight to Hitler, who met him in the local school building. Apparently Hess wanted to be allowed to make a tour of the front, but Hitler refused, declaring that it was essential that he should always have someone in Germany in his absence on whom he could rely absolutely. Hess must therefore take no risks at the front, but return at once to Munich. Hess was obviously depressed at Hitler's decision, and the next morning when I drove him to the airfield he relieved his feelings to me.

'So you see, that's how it is with me, Baur. But I'd sooner be a company commander at the front than a Reich Minister at home. In wartime an able-bodied man ought to be at the front, not miles away stuck in some office. When I think of my job at the moment: listening to and arbitrating in endless Party disputes . . . I wouldn't mind it so much in peacetime, but now – in wartime!'

He inspected our installation – we had about forty machines at the time – and then climbed into his own Ju.52 and flew back to Munich as he had been ordered.

When Paris fell and the tide of war rolled southwards beyond it, Hitler decided to visit the French capital. On the morning fixed for the flight our airfield was shrouded in a thick mist, and I had to take off blind, but as I knew every inch of the airfield by this time there was very little danger. We landed at Le Bourget at five o'clock in the morning, because Hitler wanted to get his visit over and done with before the Parisians were on the streets. I went along with him on his tour through the town. Workmen were tramping along going to the factories; the street-sweepers were just starting their jobs; and the concierge were beginning to open up the front doors.

From the airfield we drove along the Champs Elysées to the Arc de Triomphe and the grave of the Unknown Soldier. Then we visited the Louvre, the Trocadero, the Eiffel Tower, the Paris Opera and, finally, the Invalides, where Hitler was particularly interested in the tomb of Napoleon. By six o'clock we were back again on the airfield. The take-off was delayed because the air had gone out of the tail-wheel tyre, and whilst he waited Hitler stood and talked with a group of Frenchmen, mostly workmen and mechanics. On the way he had been recognised now and again, although very few people were on the streets at that early hour.

So far the campaign had proceeded exactly according to plan. Then France surrendered altogether, and Hitler enjoyed a triumph over 'doubting Thomases', who seemed to have been wrong after all – they weren't, though! Shortly before the campaign ended, and when it was already quite clear that Germany's victory would be complete, Mussolini came in. Hitler was not at all impressed by the showing of the Italians. He said contemptuously that they had come in only when they were quite sure everything was going to be all right, and even then the French had given them a thrashing in Savoy. But now they were making ridiculous claims; for example, they wanted Tunis.

As the crown of his western campaign Hitler now had a special titbit in mind. The railway carriage in which the German plenipotentiaries had signed the armistice agreement in 1918 was still standing as a showpiece in the forest of Compiegne, and Hitler had long decided that the French should now accept and sign the German terms in that same carriage. This was done, and Hitler then declared with satisfaction that the last remnants of the Versailles Slave Treaty had now been wiped away. As a result of 'this historic act', Germany's honour was restored in full.

We now left France, and after a short stay in his new headquarters in the Black Forest, Hitler flew back to Berlin. We were now equipped with new Condor machines, armed with four machine-guns, two above and two below, so that there were no blind-spots anywhere. The same type was introduced into the Luftwaffe. They had four engines of a thousand horsepower each, and they could stay in the air for fifteen hours at a time, long enough to allow them to fly far out into the Atlantic from Bordeaux and return around the north of Scotland to land in Norway. Inside they were much the same as our old Condors, except that now each seat was provided with a built-in and unobtrusive parachute. By Hitler's seat there was an emergency lever with a red handle. When pulled it opened a space beneath him which could be used to leave the machine by parachute in the event of urgent danger.

We had unexpected trouble with the first of our new Condors, though they were splendid machines. I had flown it to Berlin from the Focke-Wulf works at Bremen, and I wanted to make a number of test flights, particularly to try out the new wireless equipment. The machine was ready to start on the first of these trips, and I was just about to climb into the cabin when suddenly the whole thing collapsed with a loud crash and lay there on its belly, looking somehow very forlorn. A white-faced Zintl appeared at the cabin door and looked out at me in horror. I wondered what on earth had happened. The arrangement of the various levers was different from that in our old Condor, and Zintl, not knowing this, had pulled the lever which in our old Condor removed the brakes from the wheels in readiness for the takeoff, but which in this new Condor drew up the retractable undercarriage!

Fortunately no one happened to be standing underneath at the time, or there would most certainly have been a fatal accident. A certain amount of superficial damage was done, which meant that the machine would be out of commission for a few days, and as Hitler wanted to use it quickly I had to report the matter to him. Fortunately he didn't blame Zintl, but the Focke-Wulf people for changing the arrangement of the levers.

Discussions were necessary from time to time with Laval, the Prime Minister of the Vichy Government, and I would fly to

Baur aged 21 during the First World War. One more air victory would have qualified him for the *Pour le Merite*, but the war ended shortly after his 9th kill

A Lufthansa pilot

At the controls of the Führerplane

A General in the Second World War

Warm greetings in 1932

Baur briefing Wilhelm Brückner and Hitler on flight plans in 1932

During the 1932 election flights: (left to right) Dr Hanfstengel, Hitler, Julius Schaub, Heinrich Hoffmann, Baur and Wilhelm Brückner

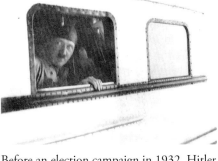

Before an election campaign in 1932. Hitler peers pensively from the chartered G-24

Hitler relaxes during a flight over Germany in 1932

Baur's wedding day on 13 May 1936 at the Führer's Munich apartment. Hitler was best man. Baur's 12 year old daughter by his first wife is on the right of the picture in BDM uniform

On 28 March 1936, on the eve of the election, Hitler meets with his closest advisers. Baur is at the left of the picture with Hess.

A youthful admirer in Berlin gets Baur's autograph

King Boris of Bulgaria with Baur after a flight

Hitler, Baur and Bormann visit a military field hospital

Hitler and Baur return the salutes of welcoming troops

Baur flies Mussolini to the Russian
Front in 1942

Baur in discussions with his escort
pilots and security personnel in
Vinnitsa, Ukraine

Field-Marshal von Manstein presenting Baur
with a bottle of champagne in the Crimea

At the controls of the Condor Fw-200 in 1942

Views of the interior of Hitler's Ju.290

Hitlers
Flugzeugführer

Elgener Bericht
Hamburg, 17. August

Der ehemalige Flugzeugführer Hitlers, Flugkapitän B a u r , befindet sich nach Mitteilung eines Rußlandheimkehrers mit anderen Prominenten des NS-Regimes in einem MWD-Lager östlich Moskau. Baur hatte bei den Kämpfen an der Waidendammer Brücke in Berlin, an der auch Bormann und Hitlers Kraftfahrer Kempka einen Ausbruchsversuch unternahmen, ein Bein verloren. Die Behandlung in dem vollständig von der Außenwelt abgeschlossenen Lager des MWD (russische Staatspolizei) soll sehr streng, die Verpflegung mangelhaft sein.

Newspaper article written two years before Baur's release reporting that he had lost his leg attempting to escape from Berlin and that he remained a prisoner of the Russians

Baur being interviewed at Camp Friedland following his return from Russia in October 1955

Baur at home with his mother after a decade of Soviet imprisonment

Dijon, pick him up there, and fly him to Obersalzberg. After the discussions with Hitler I would fly him back to Dijon, from where he would return to Vichy by train. But one day I was told that the rest of France was now to be occupied, and that this time I was to take Laval on from Dijon, where fighter protection would be waiting for us, to Vichy. I was warned in particular to be on my guard against any attempt to detain me.

When we got to Dijon the fighter escort hadn't turned up, but fortunately ground mist was reported from Vichy, so that Laval had no idea what was really causing the delay – which was a good thing, because it was essential that he should not learn prematurely that we distrusted him. Our fighter escort turned up half an hour late, and I arranged with the squadron leader that when I landed the fighter escort should circle round over the airfield. I would keep my engines running, and take off again as soon as Laval and his companions had left the plane. In the event of trouble I was to fire signal rockets. Shortly before midday it was reported from Vichy that the ground mist had cleared, and we were able to set off – with fighter escort. Before leaving the plane Laval asked me if I could stay for a while, as he would be very happy to have me to lunch, but mindful of what had been said to me I excused myself by saying – truthfully! – that I had been given orders to return to Berchtesgaden at once. Laval expressed his regret, thanked me for my services and got out to inspect the guard of honour which was drawn up to greet him, whilst I took off at once. I flew back with the fighters as far as the demarcation line, when they turned away to return to their base, leaving me to fly on alone.

German bombers were over Belgrade, and the German drive against Yugoslavia had begun. Throughout the campaign, which did not last very long, Hitler's special train stood about fifteen miles outside Wiener-Neustadt, with its locomotive constantly under steam so that in the event of an air-raid the whole train could be quickly drawn into the safety of a nearby tunnel. The neighbourhood was so mountainous and broken that it was impossible for me to find a suitable landing-place anywhere near, so we had to stay in Wiener-Neustadt and maintain a shuttle service with Mönchskirchen, which was the nearest village, using the small Fieseler Storch planes. Hitler stayed in his special coach the whole time, even celebrating his birthday there.

Shortly before the victorious ending of the Yugoslav campaign I was sent to Sofia to pick up King Boris and the Bulgarian Premier. Usually the King was in civilian clothes, but this time he had put on uniform. We landed in Wiener-Neustadt at 09.00, and from there King Boris went by car to Hitler's special train. Before he left I told him that if he wanted to return to Sofia that day, 17.00 would be the latest time for the take-off, as otherwise we should arrive in the dark and perhaps be mistaken for British planes and be fired on by his own ack-ack. Hitler, I said, had given me strict instructions not to fly him after dark.

The time I had mentioned came and went, and King Boris hadn't turned up. I waited for half an hour, and then I ordered the planes to be rolled into their hangars. King Boris turned up at 20.00, and pretended to be very surprised that no planes were ready for him.

'We must fly to Sofia at once, Baur. It's most urgent. I want to announce on the wireless in Sofia this evening that Hitler has promised me Macedonia and the Mediterranean harbour of Burgos.'

I reminded him of what I had said that morning: Hitler had absolutely forbidden me to fly him after dark, though, if he cared, I said, I would be perfectly prepared to fly the Premier and the other gentlemen back. During the subsequent conversation I discovered what had delayed him. On the way to Hitler he had sighted a castle that had belonged to one of his great-aunts, a place where he had spent a part of his youth; a sentimental feeling had made him want to visit it again and see what the old place looked like. I then suggested that he should drive back there now and spend the night, and drive in again early in the morning to fly to Sofia.

'I can't do that,' he said. 'The old lady got hard up and sold it long ago. It belongs to someone else, and I don't know a soul there now.'

In the end it was arranged that the King and his companions should spend the night in the Hotel Imperial in Vienna. We were to take off the following morning at 09.00, and at 08.30 the engines were running; but then a telephone call came from the Hotel Imperial postponing the start until 11.30 – the King, it appeared, had had a wonderful night in wartime Vienna . . .

'My Bulgarians won't mind my having had a bit of fun,' he said when he finally arrived. 'Not when they hear what I've got to tell them. And it was wonderful for me to be able to behave like an ordinary citizen for once.'

The return flight to Sofia went without incident, and then I returned and reported as usual to Hitler, telling him at the same time about the King's delight with what he had achieved – 'though he said he would sooner have had Salonika than Burgos,' I added.

Hitler smiled at that: 'I dare say he would, Baur. But we've earmarked Salonika for ourselves. When the war is over we shall need a port on the Mediterranean. Trieste, the former Mediterranean port of the Austro-Hungarian Empire, is in Italian hands, and the Italians are our friends, so I don't want any dispute with Mussolini.'

The Regent of Hungary, Admiral Horthy, was another one who was in at the share-out, and Hitler promised him the Banat frontier province, Carpathian Ukraine and a part of Galicia. I flew him from Budapest to Wiener-Neustadt and back, and after the flight he decorated me with a Hungarian order, the Comptur Cross, to be worn on a ribbon round the neck. Incidentally, King Boris also presented me with an order – to be worn on a ribbon round the neck. I wore those orders only when I happened to be flying the gentlemen who had given them to me.

The generous hand-out of territories naturally didn't please everyone – for example, the people who lived in them; and once at table in the Reich Chancellory, I heard Hitler saying that he had received a deputation of Carpathian Ukrainians. They had, it appeared, begged him not to let their country be swallowed up by Hungary, declaring that they had nothing whatever in common with the Hungarians, historically, culturally or otherwise. In fact, they regarded the measure as nothing short of a national disaster, and they begged him to incorporate their country in the German Reich instead.

In his heart Hitler agreed with them, and he was well aware that the measure would do a great deal of harm to Germany's prestige in Ukraine, but he told us that he had been compelled to send the deputation away disappointed. He had told them that at the end of the war Congress Poland would become an independent state again with her own government. Germany would want only the 'Warthegau' and the territory of the former Polish corridor through East Prussia; therefore to incorporate Carpathian Ukraine into the German Reich would mean to create a new corridor, and in the event of hostilities in the east the Carpathian Ukraine would be lost at once.

Hitler told us that the deputation had left him with tears in their eyes, but that although he had every sympathy with their point of view, he had been unable to take back his word to Horthy.

The thing that struck me afterwards was that if at the time Hitler had harboured any intention of attacking Soviet Russia, his decision with regard to Carpathian Ukraine would have been different.

The everyday routine of the Reich Chancellory was agreeably broken by a report from Hitler's naval attaché, Captain von Puttkammer, that a U-boat had succeeded in penetrating the defences of Scapa Flow, had sunk two armoured cruisers there – and made good its escape! Further reports confirmed the first good news, and then it was announced that the submarine in question, which was under Lieutenant-Commander Prien, was returning to its base at Wilhelmshaven. I proposed to Hitler that I should take a couple of Condors to Wilhelmshaven, load the commander and his crew on board, and fly them straight back to Berlin, where Hitler could thank them in person.

Hitler agreed, and I landed on the airfield at Wilhelmshaven shortly before the submarine moored. We waited on the airfield, and the whole crew were brought to us at once, exactly as they disembarked from their submarine, without even being given time to change their uniforms and make themselves spick and span. But before we could take off, the naval authorities intervened and insisted that they could not be flown to Hitler without shaving and freshening themselves up. We spent a night in Kiel before flying on the next day, and in the meantime an official reception had been arranged for our arrival at Tempelhof. By this time Prien and the others were all well-shaven and in their best uniforms. Representatives of the Government and of the municipality were on the airfield to welcome them, and then they were driven straight to the Reich Chancellory, where each man was heartily greeted by Hitler in person. They remained in Berlin for a week, during which they were fêted everywhere and loaded with honours.

In November 1940 Hitler informed me that I was to fly once again to Moscow, this time to fetch the Soviet Foreign Minister Molotov to Berlin for an official visit. All the necessary preparations were made, but then came a telegram from Moscow that our offer was refused – 'with thanks'. Molotov proposed to come with a party of no less than two hundred and sixty-five persons, and therefore it would be better to come by train.

I happened to be in the entrance hall when Molotov arrived in the Reich Chancellory to see Hitler. He was accompanied by three men who were obviously GPU men. Our own people tried to fraternise with them, offering them coffee, cakes and so on, but the three Russians just gave the same stereotyped smile all the time and refused everything – much to the surprise of everyone except those of us who had been in Moscow. Molotov stayed in Berlin for three days, from 12 to 14 November inclusive, and it so happened that the British were bombing Berlin at the time, so he had a good opportunity of discovering something about modern warfare at first hand. Incidentally, Hitler totally underestimated him, declaring that he was a cipher, a typical subordinate bureaucrat.

In Norway at about this time the number of mysterious explosions in planes whilst in the air, resulting in the loss of the machines and their crews, increased to such an extent that there could be no reasonable doubt that the Luftwaffe was faced with very clever sabotage. The British were, of course, suspected at once, and the most searching investigations were conducted. In the end the cause of the trouble was found. It was a very ingenious time-bomb enclosed in a rubber tube. It looked quite harmless, and it was easy to toss it through any one of the many openings to be found on a plane, and there it would lie harmlessly, until . . . until the plane reached a certain height, when it would explode. Most of the planes destroyed in this way had their tails blown off, after which they plunged down to certain destruction.

One of these altitude bombs was handed to me for instructional purposes so that I and my men could know what to be on the look-out for – because, naturally, if there were any one plane more than another that the British would like to fit with one of these little rubber-covered devices, it was mine. The explosive charge was set off by a special altitude device powered by an ordinary small pocket-lamp battery, and as such batteries could be stored for at least a year, the rubber-covered device could lie around for a long time quite harmlessly. But if ever that plane reached the previously arranged height . . . After that, we naturally greatly increased our precautions.

* * *

One day Hitler told me that he would be making a long journey – by rail. It was to meet General Franco on the Franco-Spanish frontier. This meeting took place on 23 October 1940, at Hendaye, and Hitler demanded that Franco should allow his troops to march through Spain to attack Gibraltar. I was given instructions to follow with three Condors, and to do the journey by stages. My first stop was Bordeaux, where we stayed for two days waiting for the arrival of the Foreign Minister, Ribbentrop.

Ribbentrop arrived at eight o'clock in the morning. The weather in Bordeaux was good, but it was reported to be very bad along the route to Tours, where I was to fly him. Cloud cover was between one hundred and a hundred and fifty feet. I told Ribbentrop that the bad weather, plus the fact that I did not know Tours airfield, meant that I could not fly him on my own responsibility. Ribbentrop was very upset on hearing this, and I learned that the meeting between Hitler and Franco had already taken place, and that Hitler was on his way to Tours to meet Marshal Pétain there. It was absolutely essential that Ribbentrop, as Foreign Minister, should be there too.

In the circumstances I agreed to do my best – on his responsibility. I took off all right, and for two-thirds of the way I flew blind. When we approached Tours I got a beam from the station there, and the information that if I decided to land it would have to be at my own risk. When I broke through the cloud I found we had just skimmed a hangar. I landed – safely. A bit of luck.

Ribbentrop drove off at once to the country house where Marshal Pétain was staying, and I received instructions to fly to Belgium and wait there till further notice. After his meeting with Pétain, Hitler went on to Italy to meet Mussolini. When I got back to Berlin I heard Hitler talking about his meetings with Franco and Pétain. The taking of Gibraltar would, of course, have been of enormous importance for Hitler, who had his soldiers in North Africa, and desperately needed the command of the Mediterranean. Hitler had promised that if Franco would let him take Gibraltar he would give it to Spain, and the Spaniards would then be rid of the British 'once and for all'. But Hitler found Franco, as he said, a great disappointment. The Spanish statesman refused to have anything to do with the affair, and Hitler irritably declared that he had 'the manners of a sergeant-major'. On the other hand, Hitler always spoke of Marshal Pétain with sincere respect, and assured us that he had always treated him with the greatest consideration, doing his utmost never to play the role of victor towards him.

One evening I was in Vienna strolling along the Kärntner Ring, when Flight-Captain Stöhr, Messerschmitt's chief test pilot, who was sitting outside a cafe, called out to me. I joined him, and he told me that he was on his way to Tokyo to demonstrate Messerschmitts to the Japanese. In conversation he mentioned that Rudolf Hess frequently came to the Messerschmitt works in Augsburg to try out the new Me.210, the very latest two-engined plane, a very swift job which had not yet become operational.

Everyone knew that Hitler didn't like Hess flying, and had forbidden him to fly alone – he always had to have a full flight-captain with him. However, Hess went to Messerschmitt, who, of course, knew all about the prohibition, and declared that he had a special mission about which he was unable to talk. Now for one thing Hess was Deputy Führer, and for another he might well have a special mission, so Messerschmitt let him have his way; but according to Stöhr everyone was worried to death when Hess flew the Me.210 on his own, because it needed a good deal of handling and no one could be sure from the ground that Hess was experienced enough to fly it.

Hess had a number of changes made in the plane. For example, he had the radar apparatus so installed that he could use it without assistance. Later on I heard from Mortsiepen, his wireless operator, that Hess had begun to show a keen interest in instrument and beam flying. Four weeks after that I happened to meet Hess in Hitler's apartments, and he came straight up to me and declared bluntly: 'Baur, I want a map of the forbidden air zones.' I had such a map for my own use, of course, but I dared not let it out of my hands, because I was sending planes here, there and everywhere all the time, and before every flight I naturally had to make quite certain that they went nowhere near those zones, where they might be shot down by our own flak. Moreover, that map was clearly marked 'Reich Top Secret', which meant that I was not allowed to let anyone else know its contents.

This secret map showed those zones over which even German planes were not allowed to fly, or only at certain definite heights; and as the details changed from time to time you couldn't learn them off by heart once and for all. You had to have the up-to-the-minute supplements. I told Hess that he really needn't worry, because Captain Doldi would always be able to consult the map before any flight he undertook; but this – for reasons that were to become very clear to me later – didn't satisfy Hess: he wanted a map of his own. I told him that the only thing to do was to approach Milch, and this he asked me to do on his behalf. Milch was a bit nonplussed when I went to him and said that Hess wanted the secret map of the forbidden air zones, but after a moment or two's thought he said: 'Well, after all, he's the Deputy Führer, and I suppose there's such a thing as being over-cautious. I'd better let him have it.' And with that map, his training on the Me.210 and his industrious studying of instrument and blind flying, Hess was in a position to fly out of wartime Germany.

Two days after that I flew Hitler to Munich. He went off to his Berghof eyrie in the mountains and I went out to Pilsensee to my wife and children. The weather was absolutely perfect, and I was looking forward to a day or two's fishing, but at eight o'clock on the Sunday morning the telephone rang and I was told that Hitler wanted to fly to Berlin as soon as possible. I knew that he had intended to spend the weekend quietly at Obersalzberg, and I wondered what on earth was the matter now. In any case, I got him off to Berlin that morning just as soon as ever I could, and at one o'clock I was in the Reich Chancellory for lunch. From the smoking-room next to the restaurant you could see out into the garden, and there I noticed Hitler and Göring talking excitedly to each other, so I decided to go out into the garden and see if I could find out what was up. As I came closer I heard Hitler say:

'He must have gone mad, or he couldn't have done a thing like that to me. He's stabbed me in the back – he wouldn't have done that if he'd been normal.' At that moment Hitler spotted me. 'What do you think of it, Baur?'

I didn't know anything about it, and I had first to be told. It appeared that Hess had got into his Me.210 – no doubt with his secret map and his newly-acquired knowledge – and flown, it was supposed, to England. Göring then told me the details as far as they were known at the time. Hess's adjutant had been given a letter to put into Hitler's hands five hours after Hess took off from Augsburg on his flight, which meant that when we set off for Berlin from Munich Hitler had already known what Hess had done – or had set out to do, because no one knew as yet whether he had succeeded: his flight had been plotted up to the neighbourhood of Amsterdam.

As a matter of fact, our experts didn't give him much chance of getting to England. Constant patrols were flown over the North Sea precisely to deal with German planes flying to England, and there was a very good chance that Hess had been intercepted and shot down into the sea. Naturally we now all listened with keen interest to the BBC broadcasts, because we assumed that if Hess did succeed they would make a great propaganda campaign about it. But the BBC stayed mum. Clearly, at lunch that day there was just one item of conversation – Hess and his action.

One theory was that Hess wanted to prevent any further extension of the war. He held the opinion that the war between Britain and Germany was a disaster, and as he had important connections in England he may have hoped to find influential people there to share his views and help him to put an end to the war. He probably also felt sure that if he succeeded in patching things up between Germany and Britain, Hitler would forgive him for his arbitrary action.

Hess – as we heard later – was another man to suffer disappointment. At first the British supposed that he had made his personal escape from the Third Reich, but when they discovered that he was still 'a fanatical Nazi', his undertaking looked merely like an attempt to sow discord in a country at war, and suborn its nationals.

It was, of course, quite impossible to keep the affair a secret in Germany, and a short official communiqué was issued, though it satisfied nobody. The cat was amongst the pigeons now, and there was tremendous excitement. But it didn't last for long; still more important happenings gave people something else to think of.

Shortly after German troops crossed the frontier into Russia I flew Hitler to Rastenburg in East Prussia, and it was here that the 'Führer-Headquarters' were situated for three years. Three massive air-raid shelters, or bunkers, were built, one each for Hitler, Göring and Bormann, who was now in Hess's place as Deputy Leader. Smaller bunkers were built for the headquarters personnel and for the guards. The place could have withstood massive bombing, but, in fact, it was never bombed at all, though on one occasion three Russian bombers were shot down within the outer perimeter. The whole installation was in the woods, and grass and plants were trained to grow on the roofs of all the bunkers and other buildings – so that the installation was practically invisible from the air, even if you knew that it was there.

Rastenburg airfield was unsuitable for our big Condors. Until extension work was carried out we used Gerdauen airfield about twenty miles away, and in the meantime we used Ju.52s to maintain a shuttle service.

At first the German armies drove rapidly into Russia without meeting much resistance, and I was constantly flying

Hitler forward for discussions with his generals in the field, or flying generals and marshals to him and back again for the regular 'situation discussions'. The man I flew most often was undoubtedly Field-Marshal von Kluge, but I also frequently flew von Manstein, Kleist and Küchler.

Hitler invited Mussolini to come to Brest-Litovsk to watch a demonstration of Germany's latest 60-cm fortress gun. I set off with them both in a Ju.52, together with various other people. I hadn't been in the air long before I realised that one of my engines was losing petrol, which was being blown back over the machine. Before long you could hardly see through the windscreen. I didn't know quite what to do: turn back or go on. Finally, as Brest-Litovsk was not far, I shut off the engine in question and flew on with the others. When we landed, and I got out, I could see that my Ju.52 looked like a sardine which had just come out of its tin.

The party, which included Mussolini's airman son, took a meal and then drove off to Brest-Litovsk proper. Hitler explained the effect of the new gun to Mussolini, who inspected the damage it had done. The loss of life amongst the garrison had been particularly heavy because the bombardment with such a powerful weapon had been totally unexpected.

In the meantime my mechanic, Zintl, had been investigating the cause of the trouble in our aircraft. It proved to be in the packing of an oil pump; by the time we got back it had been made good, and the Ju.52 had been cleaned up. As Mussolini wished to visit Göring we put him down on a small airfield near Spitzingsee, where Göring met him. After that he went back to Italy – but he was soon with us again.

A great victory was won near Uman, with hundreds of thousands of Russian prisoners. As Italian troops had also taken part in the fighting, Mussolini decided to take the salute at a victory parade. He travelled in a special train to Grosny in Poland, and his train was halted near a tunnel into which it could be pulled as soon as there was an air-raid warning. I flew with three Condors to Grosny to pick him up, and he was enthusiastic about the great four-engined planes, which he had never seen before. He even asked Hitler's permission to let him fly our plane, and on a quiet stretch he was allowed to do so – with me sitting at his side.

The weather was wonderful, and we flew from Grosny over Vinnitsa to Uman. It was a journey of over six hundred miles, and we did it in three and a half hours. When we touched down, the cars were waiting there to take Hitler and Mussolini to the victory parade. I did not go along, and so I did not witness Mussolini's great embarrassment when on their arrival the German troops were drawn up for inspection – with not an Italian in sight! There had been a good deal of rain and their transport had stuck in the mud. Mussolini's show had to wait until they finally turned up.

They returned to the airfield, and from there we all went on to a gravel pit which was serving as one of the many collection centres for Russian prisoners. There were many thousands of them. Hitler had ordered that all Ukranians should be set free to go home – not unnaturally, there turned out to be an extraordinary number of Ukranians amongst his prisoners. Many of them were lying, of course, and although some Russians may have succeeded in making their way back to their own army, most of them wandered around in our rear until they were picked up again by our men. On the way we came across hundreds of civilians trekking out to the gravel pit to fetch their soldier relatives back.

Afterwards Hitler was very interested to hear from me what Mussolini had thought about the Condor, and I told him that the Italian leader had been enthusiastic. Hitler then said that he would like to give Mussolini one, but he was a bit uncertain about his ability to manage it, as it was not so easy as the Ju.52.

By this time it was autumn, and our troops were still steadily making their way into Russia. Here and there the Russians had tried to make a stand, but they had always been broken and forced to flood back still farther. But matters were not altogether perfect for us either: the Russians were not decisively beaten, and the enormous spaces were swallowing up our strength. As yet, however, success was still with us, and before long German tanks were on the outskirts of Moscow. Vast columns of Russian prisoners moved slowly westwards, and more and more came on behind them. Hitler was convinced that the war in Russia was already decided in his favour, and that it was only a question of time before the Russians formed a new government and offered to surrender.

But then, after a wet autumn, the winter of 1941–42 set in. It proved to be the sort of winter that Russia experiences perhaps once in a hundred years, and before long the whole front lay in the merciless grip of snow and ice, so that almost all movement came to a standstill. Our men suffered terribly, and their material and equipment proved unable to stand up to the extreme cold. Petrol turned to ice; batteries went dead; tanks, tractors, lorries and cars were immobilised; guns were out of action because their breech-blocks froze hard, and even smear oil turned into solid ice.

But the worst trouble of all was undoubtedly the impossibility of keeping our supplies moving regularly. I can well remember Herr Ganzenmüller delivering his daily report to Hitler about how many trains had 'got through'. It was reckoned that sixty-five had to go up daily in order to maintain supplies at a fairly satisfactory level – but very often Herr Ganzenmüller had to confess that only between twenty and thirty had got up. The others had been immobilised – invariably because of the intense cold; perhaps the boiler had burst. Everything possible was done, but nevertheless our men huddled together at the front, in a temperature of ninety degrees of frost, often without warm food in their bellies. A great campaign for the collection of winter clothing was now organised back home in Germany, but it was far too late, and some of it didn't arrive until the following Easter, by which time it was warmer anyway. A scapegoat had to be found, so Field-Marshal von Brauchitsch, the commander-in-chief, was dismissed.

Despite the intense cold we made a number of flights deep into Russia, using the Heinkel 111. This plane could carry six passengers at a cruising speed of about two hundred and twenty miles an hour, which was fast at the time. The Heinkel had one great disadvantage, though: it was very difficult to heat, and most of what heat there was escaped through the machine gun slots.

On one flight to Mariupol on the Sea of Azov, I had Hitler, Major-General Schmundt, his adjutant and a doctor on board. We made an intermediate landing in Kiev, from where the local commander-in-chief was informed of Hitler's coming, and then we flew on.

'Baur, it's shockingly cold in your plane,' Hitler complained. 'My feet are like lumps of ice.'

That wasn't surprising, because he just wasn't warmly enough dressed. I offered to get him a pair of fur-lined flying-boots, but he refused on the ground that they weren't 'an issue' for him. We landed in Mariupol; Hitler was met by Field-Marshal Leeb and Sepp Dietrich, the commander of the so-called Leibstandarte, and they drove on at once to Taganrog, where there were difficulties. In the meantime I insisted on getting him a pair of fur-lined flying-boots, for which he had to sign a receipt – later on when I was in Mariupol I saw that receipt framed and hanging up in the mess.

When Hitler flew with important people he insisted that several machines should carry them, so that in the event of a crash the whole party should not be wiped out. When we flew back from Mariupol, therefore, Field-Marshal von Reichenau, who was with him, flew in another machine. Our baggage machine, a slower plane, had already set off for Rastenburg, but the order now came to fly to Poltava instead. We tried to get into touch with the baggage machine, but the distance was too great, and so we arrived in Poltava without Hitler's effects – and also without von Reichenau.

The pilot of von Reichenau's machine had lost his way, and he arrived only an hour and a half later. I tried to fix up Hitler for the night, but all he wanted was to borrow my safety-razor and a blade in the morning. That night the discussions went on very late, but when we finally got to bed there wasn't much rest – the patriotic Russian bed-bugs saw to that.

When I was in Hitler's headquarters at Rastenburg, which was often, I always ate both lunch and dinner at the common table, and there were always lively discussions on the problems of the day. I recall an interesting discussion about lice. Hitler declared that he could well remember what a curse lice were from his First World War days; and jokingly he declared he would give the Knight's Cross on top of the War Service Cross to anyone who could invent something to save his men from this plague that was tormenting them.

Himmler, who happened to be present, mentioned the well-known fact that cavalrymen rarely suffered from the attentions of lice, but as there were now fewer and fewer cavalrymen, there weren't many soldiers immune from the visitation. Professor Morell was also there, and, as it happened, he was an analytical chemist as well as a physician. He said that as it was obviously the sweat of the horses which kept the lice at bay, the thing to do was to manufacture the ingredients chemically and produce an anti-lice powder.

It wasn't long after this that he reported that he had succeeded, using cheap waste products, and had produced a powder which experiments showed to be effective against lice. Production was now begun, but the disadvantage of this new powder was that it stank to high heaven, and many men said they much preferred the lice. Morell then tried to scent it, and he obtained large quantities of scent from Paris for the purpose, but he could never obtain enough, and so the stink remained.

The epilogue: Professor Morell actually received the War Service Medal and the Knight's Cross as well. For the lice powder?

* * *

Dr Todt, the chief of the famous Organisation Todt which did Germany such tremendous services during the war, often came to Hitler to report, and we all liked him. He was not only a brilliant man, but also a very modest and likeable one. One evening after he had reported to Hitler, I was chatting with him; he told me that he must leave very early the following morning for Berlin, and that Dr Speer would probably go with him. The next morning I drove to the airfield at about 08.30 as usual, and almost immediately I spotted a great cloud of smoke rising into the air. I knew what that was. When I came up I discovered that it was a burning Heinkel – Dr Todt's plane. The Heinkel had just taken on seven hundred and fifty gallons of petrol, so the fire would go on for quite a while. I had long rods brought up, and whilst the firemen clamped down the intense heat to allow us to work, we hooked the bodies out of the wreckage. The remains of a shoulder strap on one of the bodies showed clearly that it was Dr Todt. Apart from him and the three men of the crew, there were two leave men in the plane, but Dr Speer had decided, after all, not to go off so early.

An investigation into the disaster was begun immediately. The weather was very bad, and there was a heavy storm at about a thousand feet with a certain amount of snowfall. The exact time of the take-off had been noted of course; about three minutes later the plane had returned with its undercarriage down. The pilot obviously intended to land, but observers were shocked to note that he was coming in to land with a powerful tail wind – which meant trouble, because the runway just wasn't long enough. When the Heinkel was little more than a hundred yards from the edge of the airfield and coming in fast, a stab of blue flame suddenly shot up from its rump. All observers were in agreement about this, so it could not have been from the petrol, which was stored in wing tanks. The aircraft turned over at about a hundred feet, crashed, and burst into flames.

Of course, the possibility of sabotage was taken into account at once, but no outsider could have got anywhere near the machine;

everyone who had had anything to do with the plane was tried and trusted, and Dr Todt was very popular. A commission of inquiry was appointed by the Reich Air Ministry, and, amongst other measures, every piece of debris was carefully examined – at first without result. Dr Todt's usual machine had been called in for a periodic overhaul and re-check, and in the meantime he had been given another machine, the one in which he had died. It was a Heinkel which had been used as a front-line machine, and like all operational machines it had a built-in destructor device operated by a line with a ring at one end next to the pilot's seat. This device had a three-minute fuse, and it enabled a pilot to let his crew get clear, set the fuse, and then escape himself before the plane blew up – to prevent its falling into the hands of the enemy.

It was known that Dr Todt always sat next to the pilot in the seat normally occupied by the wireless-operator-mechanic. Evidence showed that shortly before the start Dr Todt had walked through the small cabin to this seat. The gangway on this type of plane was very narrow, and Dr Todt had been wearing a bulky combination suit. He squatted down and waited for the wireless-operator-mechanic to vacate the seat after the start; thus he was in the gangway, and it was thought that probably the buckle on one of his flying-boots had caught in the line of the destructor device shortly after the take-off. The burning of the delayed action fuse would have been smelt, and any smell of burning in a plane is an urgent sign of danger, so no doubt the crew hastily tried to find out what the trouble was whilst the pilot lowered his undercarriage and turned back. They probably discovered the trouble to their horror, and then the pilot must have known that he was racing against death, which accounted for his neglecting all normal safety precautions and coming in to land with a strong tailwind – he just had no time to circle and come in against the wind.

The front still went steadily eastwards, and Rastenburg was soon six hundred miles and more away from the fighting. That was much too far, so Hitler's headquarters had to be moved up. A suitable place was decided on in a small wood about ten miles to the north of Vinnitsa in the Ukraine. The work progressed very swiftly. Apart from the usual surface huts, two bunkers were built, one for Hitler and his closer associates, and the other for headquarters personnel. They were considered primarily as air-raid shelters, but in fact the Russians never bombed them, and the only air-raid warnings we ever heard were on account of formations flying past to other objectives.

The local civilian population was called upon to assist in certain tasks. Before long our building supervisors noticed that the Ukrainians were very scared, and they couldn't understand why. In the end, after searching enquiries, it came out. A little while before, headquarters had been built in the neighbourhood for Marshal Timoshenko, and the local civilian population had been mobilised for this too – but at the end of it all the men engaged on the job had just been deported, and their relatives had never heard of them again. The Ukranians were afraid that the Germans would now do the same; and it wasn't easy to allay their fears.

These headquarters were completed by the spring of 1942, and then Hitler moved in. The weather was good; there was a great deal of sunshine; and our relations with the local civilian population were excellent – so good, in fact, that the place was not even surrounded by barbed wire, and remained open on all sides until, much later on, partisans turned up in the neighbourhood of Berdichev, about forty-five miles away. Only then did it become necessary to take special precautions. Our airfield was in Vinnitsa, and from there we flew to various points along the front: Stalino, Zaporozhye, Dniepropetrovsk, the Black Sea, Nikolaiev, Mariupol, the Sea of Asov, etc. As Hitler had issued instructions that VIPs were not to travel by rail, we were kept very busy. In the wet weather we had a good deal of trouble, and those planes which, for some reason or other, we couldn't put away in the hangars, had to be propped up to prevent their wheels from sinking into the ground altogether. After a while we found a more favourable site a little distance away, and after that we used our old airfield merely for emergencies. It sticks in my mind in particular as the place where I first saw wolves outside a zoo. We were taxiing towards the start with Hitler on board, when I spotted a couple of wolves at the edge of the airfield. They didn't seem much disturbed at our approach, and we got quite close to them before they finally looked at us and then loped off into the forest. My mechanic had drawn Hitler's attention to them, and we all saw them very clearly.

There were other headquarters not far from us. Göring had put up his tent about twelve miles from Vinnitsa; Himmler was about thirty miles away, and Ribbentrop was somewhere in the Ukraine too.

In my free time – oh, yes, I had a few hours to myself occasionally – I would fish in the nearby Bug, and my modern fishing tackle and my expert angling methods were always the centre of a good deal of admiring attention. Fortunately I was also able to demonstrate to them that this marvellous tackle really worked, for I landed some very fine perch and pike. But the things that really made the Russians' eyes start out of their heads were our amphibious trucks!

As a keen angler it was impossible for me not to mention, in conversation with Hitler, the fun I got out of angling in my spare time. He wasn't so much opposed to angling, though he had little understanding for it; but he resolutely opposed all blood sports, and was prepared to approve the killing of animals only as a measure of game preservation or to provide people with food. The only blood sportsman he had any respect for was the poacher – he at least, he said, pitted his wits against the gamekeeper as well as the prey, and risked a heavy fine or a term of imprisonment. So during the war Hitler logically released almost all of them, declaring that poachers would make far better soldiers than Sunday-afternoon sportsmen.

A real battle between men and animals, in which the men took risks, appealed to him; he liked certain films sent to him by a friendly Maharajah, and he wasn't in the least disturbed at sequences showing men being torn to pieces by the animals they had set out to hunt. But when we saw films in which ordinary hunting took place he would cover up his eyes and ask us to tell him when it was all over. Quite generally his contemptuous remarks about blood sports and those who practised them used to dismay our enthusiastic sportsmen. Altogether, Hitler's attitude towards dumb creatures, including birds, perturbed a good many of his devoted followers.

Way back in 1933 Gauleiter Hofer of Innsbruck came to me and asked me to help him with a rare and unusual present which he thought would please Hitler very much. It turned out that it was a live golden eagle, a bird which had become very rare, even in Tyrol. I told him that he wasn't likely to get much thanks from Hitler, and I recalled an incident which had happened earlier on. A wonderful pair of golden eagles had their eyrie on the rock face of the Hohe Göll above Obersalzberg. Hitler had always admired these birds as they soared high up over his own retreat. Then one day they were no longer to be seen. An enthusiastic sportsman had shot the male eagle – and to make matters worse he had it stuffed, and then presented it to Hitler!

However, Hofer wasn't to be put off, so we carted the huge cage with its occupant, perhaps the most magnificent eagle I have ever seen, to the Reich Chancellory. Hitler looked at it with admiration, but then he said:

'At least it's alive, Hofer, but it doesn't belong here. Baur will fly you back with it to Innsbruck. Take it to where it was captured and then release it.'

Hofer then had to point out that one claw had been damaged when it was captured, whereupon the director of the Berlin zoological gardens was called to give his opinion. After examining the bird, he declared that it might no longer be able to capture its prey. Hitler then presented the powerful beast with its great eyes and its strong beak to the Berlin Zoo.

Towards the end of the winter of 1941–42 I flew to Bucharest to fetch the Romanian Prime Minister, Antonescu, to Obersalzberg. It was very cold on Bucharest airfield when we started, though of course it was quite warm in our plane. But before long it rapidly got colder and colder, and it was quite clear that for some reason or other the heating apparatus had broken down. To make matters worse, the weather was bad, visibility was poor, and I had to fly very high – thirteen thousand feet and more – over the Carpathians, so that at one time we had fifty degrees of frost in the cabin. Antonescu, who was slim and delicately built, felt the cold very keenly. Fortunately we had plenty of rugs, and we simply smothered him with them until all you could see of him was the tip of his nose.

In the meantime the cabin had become a refrigerator, and the windows were so frozen over that you couldn't see out. It took us three and a half hours to get to Berchtesgaden, but at least I was able to promise Antonescu that it would be warmer on the way back, and it was, because the trouble – a burst pipe – was quickly repaired. In Bucharest Antonescu invited me to dinner and presented me with the Romanian Order of the Crown – 'despite the icy flight'; and when we flew back, there were hampers of good things – food, tobacco, and wines and spirits – for us all.

The son of Admiral Horthy, the Hungarian Regent, was a pilot, and he was killed in a crash on the Eastern Front. From Ribbentrop we learned that young Horthy's mother was working as a nurse in a hospital in Berdichev, only about forty-five miles away, so Hitler instructed Ribbentrop to go to her, express the deep regret of the German Government and invite her to visit him at his headquarters.

I flew her in late that afternoon in the uniform of a Red Cross nurse. Hitler now expressed his sympathy in person and offered her a plane to take her back to Budapest for the funeral, which she accepted; so the next day I flew her to Budapest, together with Ambassador Hewel, who was to lay a wreath on the grave on Hitler's behalf.

We remained in Budapest for three days, staying in the Gellert Hotel as guests of the Hungarian Government. There were very few signs of war to be seen in the Hungarian capital, and one evening we were taken by officers of the Hungarian Air Force to a fashionable restaurant on Margaret Island in the Danube. Everything was as usual: there was no shortage of food; and we were almost the only guests in uniform. And as for ration cards, which Germany had introduced from the beginning of the war, they seemed unknown. A colonel of the Hungarian Air Force had been attached to us during our stay, and he asked me to tell Hitler that he and his friends would very much welcome more fighter planes so that they could play a more active part in the war. On my return to Vinnitsa therefore I passed this on to Hitler.

'No doubt they would like more fighter planes,' he said grimly, 'but to fly around in, not to fight the Russians with. Petrol is scarce, and I've got none to spare for them. I want aggressive pilots, and what the Hungarians have done so far isn't much. No, if I've any fighter planes and petrol to spare, the Croats will get them; they're prepared to use them. Up to now the Hungarians have been a fiasco. They were no good at the front, and when we withdrew them and set them to combating partisans in the rear they were no good either. No, no, I'll keep my fighter planes.'

Hitler's judgments on his allies were often very severe, but there was one shining exception, and that was the Finns. He never mentioned them or their leader, Marshal Mannerheim, without paying them the highest tributes as soldiers.

From the very beginning of the war the German authorities were in touch with the protective powers in an effort to organise an exchange of prisoner-of-war mail with Soviet Russia. Many months passed, and still no answer came from the Soviet Government. Then one day at table Hitler told us that Stalin had at last replied, saying: 'There are no Russian prisoners in German hands. The Russian soldier fights to the death. Should he ever allow himself to be taken prisoner he would thereby automatically exclude himself from the community of Russian people. The Russian Government has therefore no interest in any exchange of prisoner-of-war mail with Germany.' Germany, of course, already held vast numbers of Russian prisoners of war, including Stalin's own son.

One morning it was reported to me that one of my officers, Flight-Captain Schnäbele, had been seriously wounded the night before. I went to see him at once. He was stationed near Berdichev, and the previous evening he had visited a Folk-German* village. It was dark by the time he wanted to go back to his quarters, so for fear of losing the way he asked his host to provide him with a guide. The peasant's two daughters went off with Schnäbele in the car. A mile or so from the village there was a bridge, and when they got there they found it blocked by a tree-trunk. Schnäbele and his driver got out to move the obstacle to one side, but shots rang out. The driver and one of the two girls were killed instantly, and Schnäbele was seriously wounded. The other girl jumped out of the car and managed to make her escape. When help came the two corpses and the wounded man were naked. The partisans had stripped them of every stitch of clothing, and the car had been set on fire. Unfortunately Schnäbele died of his wounds next day. Later on Himmler told me that they had caught the leader of the partisans – Schnäbele's papers had been found on him.

*　*　*

---

*　A village where German peasants had been settled, from perhaps the days of Catherine the Great, retaining all their national characteristics and their German tongue – Translator.

Hitler was in the Ukraine throughout the summer of 1942, and I suppose in that period I flew Field-Marshal Hans von Kluge at least a dozen times backwards and forwards between Vinnitsa and Smolensk. 'Go and fetch me "Clever Hans" from Smolensk,' Hitler would say.

The Sixth Army had pushed forward as far as Stalingrad. German troops were in the Caucasus, and a mountain unit had climbed Mount Elbrus and hoisted the German flag on its summit.

'We'll be in Tiflis soon, Baur,' said General Jodl one day, 'and then you're to fly me there for discussions with our commanding generals.'

But it didn't come off. Disaster gathered over Stalingrad and we withdrew to our old headquarters at the so-called 'Wolf's Lair', or Wolfsschanze, in Rastenburg. Every time I flew back now I would take wounded men with me in our big four-engined Condors; they were usually severe cases, with a chance of survival only if they could be got back to Germany quickly. When we flew in we would bring blankets and medical supplies, which were often in short supply at the front.

One day when I touched down on the airfield at Nikolaiev the wounded were already waiting on stretchers, and whilst we tanked up they were carefully loaded on board with a nurse to look after them on the way. I received the starting signal, and as I taxied forward for the take-off there was a fountain of dirt where the man who had given me the signal had been. At the same time I became aware that my machine was being fired on. Russians were over the airfield, and my big four-engined plane – it was Hitler's own, the D-2600 – must have looked a tempting morsel for them. When I had gained sufficient height I flew straight at one of the Russians. Our plane was completely unarmed and I had twenty-six wounded men and a nurse on board, but at least the Russian could see that my machine was very fast, and he preferred not to wait for me. He turned away and disappeared in the clouds, and all we suffered was a few bullet-holes.

We flew to Königsberg to take the wounded men to a hospital there, and because of the lung casualties we were not allowed to fly above a certain height. During this period we must have flown back many thousands of wounded. And if there happened to be no wounded men we would take leave men on board. One of these men was very grateful, and later on he found a chance of doing something for me.

It was in Krasnogorsk prison camp, and a former lieutenant approached me, saying that he was in the clothing workshop. I had once flown him back on leave, thereby saving him days. Was there anything he could do for me now? In the end he made me a warm cap, which I wore until my release.

One day Hitler ordered me to pick up the Yugoslav Poglavnik in Agram and fly him in for a discussion. I landed on a small German military airfield, and discovered that the neighbourhood was swarming with partisans – so much so that our men could leave the airfield only in force. I had not been there long when the Poglavnik arrived with a column of cars, each of which carried a mounted machine-gun to deal with partisans.

On the flight back to Agram with the Poglavnik I made an intermediate landing in Vienna, and from there I had an escort of six fighter planes. It was evening when we landed in Agram, and too late to start on the return flight, so the Poglavnik invited me to stay with him. We drove into the town escorted by lorries armed with machine-guns, and I had dinner with my host. That evening my collection of Balkan orders was supplemented by a Yugoslav decoration – also to be worn on a ribbon round the neck.

Hitler insisted that he must 'cut Russia's oil artery', meaning the Volga, and he had therefore given orders that the Sixth Army was to hold on to Stalingrad until it could be relieved, but by this time everyone realised that Stalingrad was lost, and that a tragedy without a parallel in German history was unrolling in the ruined town on the Volga.

The mood in our headquarters was very depressed. At table one day Hitler told us that he had discussed with Göring the possibility of supplying Stalingrad from the air. Twenty tons a day would have to be flown in, and Göring had declared that this could be done.

Perhaps in summer it would have been possible, but what Göring had obviously forgotten was that in November and December the possibility of mist and fog has to be considered. The machines had to follow each other into Stalingrad so closely that when visibility was poor the danger of collisions was considerable. In fact, many planes were lost in this way. And there was another disadvantage of poor visibility: our machines often landed their precious loads on enemy airfields.

We afterwards discovered that, through treachery, the Russians had come into possession of various code signals. When the mist was so heavy that a plane could not be landed by sight, the wireless-operator would call for a beam from the ground; a Russian station would then answer him and give him a beam, and the German plane would land on a Russian airfield – usually too late to rectify the mistake. I contributed a number of machines to the Stalingrad air-lift, and one of them did not return.

The last days of Stalingrad shook Hitler deeply, and we realised that for the first time he was beginning to show signs of strain. As far as I can remember, the gist of the last message we had from Field-Marshal Paulus was: 'The cellar in which I have my headquarters with seven other generals has become untenable. Stalingrad can no longer be held. Long live Germany! Long live the Führer!'

Some weeks later we saw photographs in British newspapers purporting to have been taken at Stalingrad. One of them represented Paulus negotiating the surrender with the Russians. The reproduction was very poor, and we could not recognise Paulus or anyone else with certainty. Hitler pored over those reproductions with a magnifying glass for a long time, trying to make up his mind whether they were authentic or false. Finally he shook his head and declared they must be fakes: that couldn't be Paulus. General Jodl agreed with him. According to Jodl, Paulus had told him on his last visit to Stalingrad that he had poison 'and in any case my pistol'. And Paulus had added: 'A German Field-Marshal just doesn't let himself be taken prisoner.'

But after a while we learned the truth. Those reproductions had certainly been poor, but they had not been faked; in fact, Paulus had gone even farther than negotiating the surrender of his men, and his behaviour led ultimately to the formation of the notorious Free German Committee, to which he lent his name, his rank and his benevolent support, even though he may not have gone so far as Seydlitz and some of the others did.

After the loss of Stalingrad and the collapse of the Caucasian front, violent disputes arose between Hitler and the generals of the Supreme Command, the OKW. General Haider was Chief of Staff at the time, and as no agreement could be reached, he resigned. His successor, General Zeitzler, occupied the post until 20 July 1944. Hitler now ordered that an exact stenographic record of all important discussions should be kept, so that at least in future there should be no more disputes about what had actually been said. A special staff of expert shorthand writers was now added to headquarters staff.

Hitler's bitterness over these terrible defeats and his disagreements with his generals now made him morose, withdrawn and mistrustful, and one result of this was that he no longer came to our common table, for now he feared that anything he said might be used against him, particularly as he was impulsive and accustomed to speak very frankly. He now took his meals alone in his own bunker, and only when he had highly placed and important guests did he sit down to table with them. In the mornings he was usually to be seen for half an hour or so exercising his favourite dog in the grounds. 'Die Blonde' it was called, and I don't think I ever saw a more beautiful dog.

It was very intelligent, too, and it seemed to understand every word Hitler said to it.

The tragedy of Stalingrad was the beginning of the end for Germany. Not only did Hitler lose a great army, but, in addition, the confidence which up to then had reigned supreme at home was suddenly destroyed. Naturally, a tremendous amount of discussion took place on the causes. Some of the questions went even deeper. For instance, many people were anxious to know just when Hitler decided to attack Russia, but only on one occasion did I hear him give a straight answer to that question. A visiting Gauleiter from somewhere or other dared to ask him, and Hitler replied: 'Four weeks before the war (with Russia) actually began.'

Whilst I was in Russia those prisoners who had 'the bird' tattooed under their arms were singled out for particularly bad treatment, and some of them were even executed. They were supposed to be particularly fanatical Nazis and SS men. Actually what they had under their arms was merely the record of their blood group, and nothing whatever to do with their particular state of mind or political outlook – whatever it may have been.

I was present at Hitler's table, together with Himmler, Keitel, Jodl and Professor Morell, when the idea was first mooted. Professor Morell expressed the opinion that in wartime – and even in peacetime, on account of the increasing number of road accidents – it would be a very good idea if every man, woman and child had his blood group indelibly tattooed on his body so that in an emergency a blood transfusion could be given at once, instead of, as at present, only after the doctors had discovered a patient's blood group. In this way, Morell declared, many lives would be saved which were at present lost because of the delay caused by ignorance of the patient's blood group. Morell then suggested that every child should be tattooed with its blood group at the time of its inoculation against smallpox, which took place in its first year.

Hitler thought the suggestion a good one, and Himmler immediately declared that he would introduce the tattooing into the SS at once. He did so, and within a few weeks SS men were being tattooed. Field-Marshall Keitel also accepted the idea for the Wehrmacht, but as far as the army was concerned the scheme was only in its preliminary stages when the war ended. But in fact a good many people did have this tattoo marking who had nothing to do with the SS – for example, the displaced persons. But somehow the Russians – and others, I believe – got hold of the wrong idea; I can well remember German prisoners being lined up for inspection with upraised arm to discover whether they were marked with the terrible brand of Cain – i.e. with details of their blood group. If they were, they could hope for no consideration, and I have known very sick and seriously wounded men to be struck off the exchange lists because they had this marking.

Professor Porsche, then a tank expert, but better known today as the designer of the famous Volkswagen, and of a car that actually bears his name, was often flown to Hitler's headquarters to discuss various problems of tank design. On one of these occasions the professor declared that the very best thing would be to fly him to all the tank commanders on the various sections of the front to discuss their difficulties with them at first hand. Hitler agreed, and placed his own famous D-2600 at the disposal of Porsche. I, of course, flew him.

In a week's tour we came from before Leningrad right along the front into the deep south, and with us there were several of Porsche's experts and a number of tank officers. Every time we landed, Porsche went off by car to visit the nearest tank division. Outwardly he was a small and not particularly distinguished-looking man, but he made a tremendous impression on everyone by his great ability, and during these discussions he collected a vast amount of valuable material which greatly facilitated the designing and construction of Germany's best tank types.

A few weeks after this I happened to be in Berlin. I went to visit him in his offices, as he had suggested, and there he presented me with a painting by Klaus Bergen of Smolensk on the Dnieper with my Condor in the air above it.

With the fall of Stalingrad the position on the southern front became very critical, and for a while it even looked as though the whole line might be rolled up. One night Hitler decided that an immediate conference with von Manstein was necessary, so we took off at 02.00 and touched down in Zaporozhye at 06.00 hours. There were two airfields there, one in the south-west and another, larger one, to the east. I had landed on the latter. The discussions lasted some time, and we were there for three days, during which I lived in one of the huts near the airfield. The third morning when I appeared at breakfast I was told that Russian tanks had broken through from Dniepropetrovsk, and were advancing towards the town along the very road which passed close to the airfield.

Fighter planes had been sent out to deal with them, but owing to mist and poor visibility they had returned without accomplishing anything – the weather was bad and the cloud ceiling was down to less than a couple of hundred feet. Storch planes sent out to reconnoitre came back with the report that a score or so of Russian tanks were only two hours away, and that there was nothing between them and the airfield. I took a car and drove into town to report the situation to Hitler, and ask for permission to take our planes to the airfield to the south-west of the town, where they would be safer. Hitler replied that this was unnecessary, as he would soon be there.

When I drove back I found the airfield commander doing his best to put the place into a state of defence; but the situation was not really one to inspire confidence, because there were no anti-tank weapons or even artillery available. Sure enough, the Russian tanks appeared after a while: twenty-two of them. But then fortunately Hitler came too, and as he was on board, our three Condors, whose engines had already been running, took off. As we flew off, two 'Gigant' planes flew in, huge six-engined jobs, rather belatedly bringing up anti-tank guns to defend the airfield.

Later on we heard that to everyone's surprise the Russian tanks had made no attack on the airfield, but had taken up their positions in a neighbouring *kolkhoz,* or collective farm, because they had run out of petrol. They would have found enough of it on the airfield! After a while the crews even abandoned their tanks altogether. When they saw an airfield with scores of planes on it, no doubt they expected strong resistance, and felt themselves helpless without petrol. This was the last Russian break-through – for a while. German troops were brought up, and the Dnieper line was restored.

'A bit of luck for us,' was Hitler's comment when I told him the story. But supposing those Russians had known . . .

General Hube was called to our headquarters to be decorated again; the 'diamonds' were added to his Knight's Cross, and Hitler wanted to present them in person. After the ceremony the celebrations went on until after midnight, but Hube insisted on leaving at 4 a.m. to fly to Breslau. His machine was ready for him at that time, and he arrived on the airfield with a number of others, including Ambassador Hewel. The pilot, an officer of the Luftwaffe, taxied his machine to the start, and the runway ahead of him was marked with lamps.

General Hube and his fellow passengers now entered the plane, which took off perfectly and flew away in a westerly direction, but hardly had it left the airfield than it veered left towards the hills, which were only a few miles away. The machine turned right again – no doubt the pilot had seen the lighted huts on the hills and had tried to turn away – but too late; one wing touched the ground and the plane crashed. All on board were killed outright, except Ambassador Hewel, who was seriously injured, and was in hospital for weeks before he finally recovered.

*   *   *

There was an Egyptian plague of mosquitoes in the marshy east, and we were not spared in Rastenburg. It was so bad that our sentries wore mosquito nets covering their faces. In addition to the mosquitoes, there were large numbers of frogs, too, and every night they would give tremendous concerts. But then one evening they were silent. It was a day or two before Hitler noticed it, but then he inquired the reason.

It appeared that some department or other had started a campaign against the mosquitoes by pouring hundreds of gallons of petrol into their pools. No doubt that destroyed many larva, which would afterwards have become mosquitoes, but there were more than enough left; in fact so many still that you hardly noticed any difference. But the effect on the frogs had been devastating: they had been wiped out altogether – hence the dead silence at nights, broken only by the whine of mosquitoes. Hitler was furious.

'Did you ever know such idiots!' he exclaimed. 'They set out to kill mosquitoes, but instead they kill all the frogs, which feed on thousands of mosquitoes daily.'

After that the ponds and pools had to be cleaned out, and the frogs reintroduced.

Von Neurath went off to Rome on a special mission, and I was instructed to send a machine to the Italian capital to fly him back to Rastenburg to report to Hitler. This machine made an intermediate halt in Munich to tank up; the pilot was informed that von Neurath was staying an extra day in Rome, and that he should therefore remain in Munich with his machine. The pilot made everything ready for a take-off the next day – and then went off to the cinema, leaving his wireless-operator and his mechanic with the machine.

But von Neurath did arrive after all, so they tried to find the pilot, but no doubt he was enjoying himself somewhere, and he couldn't be found. Von Neurath wanted to fly on to Rastenburg that evening, so the Luftwaffe provided a pilot, and the machine took off at 20.00. The weather was bad, particularly along the Vistula, and von Neurath's plane ran into a heavy storm moving from west to east. At first the pilot tried to fly through it, but then, because he had von Neurath on board, he got cold feet and began to fly along it. From Rastenburg we were in touch with the machine for a while, but then the weather made wireless contact impossible. By midnight we were aware that the machine must have run out of petrol, and Hitler grew very worried.

However, about an hour later a call came from a small Polish frontier station: von Neurath's plane had made a forced landing in the neighbourhood, but although the plane was wrecked, von Neurath and the other passengers were uninjured. Cars were sent off at once, and von Neurath arrived at Hitler's headquarters in Rastenburg at four o'clock in the morning.

Later that day I visited the spot in one of our Fieseler Storch planes. The pilot of von Neurath's plane told me that he had flown along the edge of the storm until his petrol was exhausted. As it was dark it was not easy to see the ground, but he found a small lake glimmering in the gloom, and beside it a stretch he thought might be suitable for a landing. Unfortunately there was not sufficient room, and the machine ran off the firmer ground into a bog, taking one or two birches with it on the way. When they got out of the plane von Neurath and his companions immediately sank up to their knees in the bog, but they managed to reach firm land and get to a telephone.

After that all that remained to be done was to teach that pilot what to do the next time he ran into a storm. Generally speaking, a storm area is not more than ten or twelve miles deep. In his case, as he could see the direction in which it was moving, he should have found the best spot he could and then flown at right angles into the storm. He would soon have covered that ten or twelve miles, and then he would have had calmer weather behind the storm front, and would have been able to reach Rastenburg easily.

*　*　*

Jodl was to make a visit of inspection to Dietl in Finland, and I flew him there. Our first stop was in Reval, where we received permission to fly into Finland and were instructed what course to set. We flew over Helsinki, but did not land there, and went on over a typical Finnish landscape of woods and lakes to Micheli near Viborg. The front was not far away from there, and one of the tasks I had been given was to report whether the airfield at Micheli was suitable for landing Condors – it was. Then I flew on to Rovaniemi, where we were amiably received by General Dietl, who lived in a small Finnish house which had been presented to him. It was very agreeably furnished, and in the large living-room there were several bearskins on the floor from animals which Dietl had himself shot, whilst on the walls were antlers from other animals he had bagged, together with sporting rifles and fishing-rods, for Dietl was not only a good soldier but also an enthusiastic sportsman.

Whilst I was in Rovaniemi I had an opportunity to ring up my observer from the First World War, Lieutenant von Hengel – now General von Hengel – whose sector was along the Polar Highway. He was astonished to hear my voice again, and warmly invited me to come and visit him. I would have loved to do so, but unfortunately I had to fly back again to Rastenburg with Jodl.

A little later I again flew to Sofia to fetch King Boris for a further conference with Hitler, to whom he invariably referred not as 'the' Führer, as Germans did, but as 'our' Führer. The next day I flew him back to Bucharest, and stayed the night as usual in the German Embassy. I had intended to fly back the following morning at 11.00, but before I went a messenger came from the King inviting me to come to the palace. As I was under no obligation to be back in Rastenburg at any particular time, I went there, and was received at once by the King, who said that he wished to show me round his capital – which he then did, sitting at the wheel of the 200-horsepower Mercedes Hitler had given him, whilst I sat beside him.

He showed me round very amiably, and everywhere he was saluted with respectful friendliness; he seemed to be a popular king. Then he drove me back to the palace, which was quite a small building but set in an enormous park. When we arrived the Queen and the two royal children, a girl of eleven and a boy of nine, were waiting for us in the palace garden. The tall, slim Queen was the daughter of King Victor Emmanuel of Italy, and she too spoke German. The King showed me over the palace, and then we went out into the grounds again to see his 'plaything', as he called it. It was a model railway with about half a mile or so of electrically equipped track. From what I could see of it, the King got at least as much fun out of it as his nine-year-old son.

After that we made a tour of inspection of the palace gardens and orchards with the Queen, and the King remarked that he would love to make a tour in my Condor over his capital with his family. I agreed at once, of course, but the Queen equally promptly refused, declaring that she would not allow the life of the successor to the throne to be risked for pleasure. 'I should be frightened to death,' she insisted.

The children begged hard, for they were very anxious to go, and King Boris added all his powers of persuasion, but the utmost the Queen would agree to do was to go and inspect my plane. Before we left in his car he took me to one side: 'I think we shall be able to manage it, Baur,' he said, 'but you must add your voice to help persuade the Queen.'

At the airfield we went over my Condor. I explained everything to them, and I was truly able to say that in my view there would be no risk at all for the heir to the throne in such a trip over Bucharest. And I added that I was really a very experienced pilot, having flown about 700,000 miles in all weathers. The Queen did not doubt this, but she refused to be persuaded, and the King had to give up resignedly.

In September 1943 I flew Hitler to Insterburg, where the latest models produced by the German aircraft industry were demonstrated to him. Practically all the high-ups were present, including Göring, Milch, Körner, Professor Messerschmitt and Professor Tank of the Fokke-Wulf concern. First of all we were shown rocket-firing planes, and then two types of jet, a bomber and a fighter; the formal part of the affair was concluded with a demonstration of the so-called Rotterdam radar apparatus.

When I was on my own I turned my attention to the models Junkers had on show. The Ju.290 struck me as specially suited for my purposes. It was a four-engined job, and each engine was of 1,800 horsepower. I was inside this machine and examining it very closely when Hitler put his head through the entrance. I invited him to come in and examine the machine with me, and he did. He was not long in recognising the advantages of a powerful, long-range, heavily armed plane that could carry fifty passengers.

In the meantime Hitler had been missed, and Göring was looking for him. He too looked through the entrance, and Hitler invited him in, telling him that I would very much like a Ju.290 for our flight. Göring immediately agreed to let me have one, but then changed the subject at once. Messerschmitt, it appeared, had undertaken to manufacture a thousand jet fighters by the spring of 1944, by which time it was supposed that the Allies would launch their invasion. Göring then went on to say that all the necessary material was available, except the nickel for the turbines.

Only recently, as Hitler knew, all available stocks of raw materials, including nickel, had been apportioned, so that unless other arrangements were made there would not be enough nickel for the jet fighters.

When Hitler, Göring and I got out of the Ju.290, Messerschmitt and Milch were waiting on the ground. Hitler confirmed from Messerschmitt what Göring had said, and then declared:

'Very well, I'll see to it that you receive the nickel; you see to it that you produce them. The jet fighter is enormously important.'

I WAS HITLER'S PILOT

But February 1944 arrived, and then March – but the jets did not. In the meantime the German fighter arm was running into more and more trouble. The bomber hosts invading Germany were growing larger and larger – on some days between three and four thousand planes flew in – but there were no jets to meet them. No one knew why, though there were many rumours. Something was wrong in the Air Ministry, it was said. In any case, a little later Milch was deprived of his post.

The invasion began in June, but there were still very few jets in the air, and our pilots in their old piston-engined planes were hopelessly outnumbered.

Hitler wanted to congratulate the Finnish marshal, Mannerheim, in person on his seventieth birthday, so it was arranged that I should fly him to Micheli to meet the marshal. At the test start the machine showed a tendency to veer to the left; a check indicated that there was something wrong with the brakes on that side, so they were adjusted. But even when I took off with Hitler on board there was the same tendency. However, we flew on towards Reval. It had been arranged with Helsinki that we were to have a Finnish fighter escort, and we picked up their squadron over the Baltic. The weather deteriorated rapidly, and it began to rain. Before long I was flying at about a hundred and fifty feet, and beyond Helsinki the weather grew worse, so I had to go down still lower.

By this time only one of the fighters was left – the others had lost us in the mist – and on account of the heavy rain the woods below us were steaming and there was less visibility than ever. Not wishing to lose us, the last Finnish fighter was flying very close, and because of the danger of a collision, I warned him off. Before long we lost him too. However, we reached Micheli safely, and as I touched down the tendency to veer to port showed itself again. I had to taxi between seven and eight hundred yards to where President Ryti, Marshal Mannerheim and a guard of honour were waiting to welcome Hitler.

As we rolled towards them I saw men running and pointing, and then I saw and smelt smoke. Something was burning under our Condor. We came to a halt, and Hitler got out of the plane without noticing anything. Whilst the ceremony proceeded, we got to work with chemical extinguishers: one of our wheels had caught fire. We discovered that once again our brakes on the port side had been out of order, causing friction and then fire.

We had been lucky. Had we had the same long distance to taxi at Rastenburg, the wheel would have caught fire there at the take-off, and I would have drawn up my undercarriage folding the burning wheel up beneath our rump, dangerously near to over two hundred gallons of petrol – and there would have been enough draught to encourage the fire! Later on we saw the newsreel of our landing at Micheli; Hitler noticed the smoke and asked me what it was. Just a burnt-out brake block, I told him.

There were more meteorological stations during the war than ever before, but their forecasts were not always as reliable as they might have been, because many of the new men had been hastily trained and some of them were inclined to give oracular forecasts which were open to almost any interpretation. Accurate weather forecasting was particularly important for me, all the more so as arrangements were sometimes changed right at the last moment, so I asked that an experienced and reliable man should be seconded to us to fly with me.

A Luftwaffe pilot who had flown General Dietl to Obersalzberg to see Hitler, and was now to fly him from there to Graz, consulted my new weather-merchant – because, as he said, he was not an experienced mountain flyer and was rather doubtful about taking the direct route. The weather that day was mixed: heavy showers to be met with all along the route, but with bright periods during which there would be ground visibility. My weather expert advised Dietl's pilot not to fly the direct route, but to fly along the Alps to Vienna and then turn south.

The pilot took this advice, and General Dietl arrived safely in Graz. The next day the same pilot was to fly him back to Finland. This time the reported cloud cover was at about two thousand feet and the upper ceiling at six to eight thousand feet, so although the Graz meteorological office advised the pilot not to fly over the Alps but to fly first eastwards and approach Vienna over the plains, Dietl objected, pointing out that the clouds were high and that he knew the Alps well, and would be glad to get back into them as a change from the eternal flatness of Finland. He therefore instructed the pilot to fly from Graz over the valley to Judenberg, and then along the Semmering railway line over Mürzzuschlag to Vienna.

The pilot flew as Dietl had instructed him. They got as far as Mürzzuschlag, but there the ground rises very sharply. The cloud cover was pressing down now and they had to fly much lower. Ahead of them the mountain peaks were already lost in mist and cloud. The Ju.52 flew over one ridge safely, but then found itself surrounded by cloud. The pilot turned right to get out of the clouds, but one wing hit a tree; the plane crashed, and everyone on board was killed.

In March 1944 I had flown King Boris of Bulgaria back to Sofia, and was on my way home to Munich. Not far from Belgrade we received a message advising us to land because strong US bomber forces with fighter escort were entering the area; such fighter planes had already shot down several of our regular planes to Belgrade. However, we had no passengers on board, so I decided to risk it, merely warning our machine-gunners to keep their eyes peeled, and asking both Belgrade and Graz to keep us informed of the enemy's whereabouts.

About ten minutes before Graz we received a W/T signal indicating that strong forces of American planes had just passed Udine flying towards Graz. Around Graz itself the weather was very clear, but as we approached the Alps we found cloud cover between about thirteen thousand and eighteen thousand feet.

I was flying at about twelve thousand five hundred feet. The Americans now appeared about five thousand feet above us: several hundred bombers escorted by fighters, and the Graz anti-aircraft guns opened up. At the same time the bombs began to fall on Graz. I changed course to the north-west.

So far none of the fighters had spotted me, but they might do so at any minute. I remained close above the lowest cloud level, and did my best to make an unseen getaway. Beyond Eisenberg I flew over the Leoben ironworks, and heavy flak began to come up. The firing was very accurate, too: at the right height, and all of it within a radius of fifty yards or so, with us in the centre. My propellers were constantly cutting through disagreeable little white clouds. I instructed Zintl to fire recognition signals, but he found it very difficult to get the cartridges into the rocket pistol, and quite impossible to fire them. As we discovered later, the cartridges were covered with an extra thick layer of colourless lacquer and wouldn't slide into the chamber properly.

In the meantime the firing went on, burst after burst of it. Our windows were holed, our wings were hit by splinters, and one of our tanks was leaking. As we were unable to give recognition signals, my wireless-operator put a PAN, or air SOS call, through to Munich, telling them that we were being heavily fired on by our own flak, a message which caused consternation. After about five minutes we were out of range, and we got back to Munich, where a couple of days' intensive repair work put us in order again.

Two weeks before Mussolini was arrested, I flew Hitler to Treviso with Field-Marshal Keitel and General Jodl. By 16.00 hours we were back on the airfield again. It was easy to see that things had changed in Italy. The population kept well in the background, and there were no enthusiastic crowds this time; in fact the whole atmosphere was cold and hostile. Hitler pretended to have noticed nothing, and when he took leave of Mussolini it was with stressed warmth.

At the take-off my outer starboard engine began misbehaving, but we got away all right. The weather was bad over the Brenner, so I flew via Udine to Wiener-Neustadt and on to Vienna, and from there to Obersalzberg. We hadn't been flying long when the engine which had been giving trouble cut out altogether, and I had to make do with three engines, but we arrived safely.

It appeared that in the special train which had taken Hitler to the conference Italian officers had tried again and again to separate Hitler from his companions, and this mysterious affair took on a sinister air a couple of weeks later, when we heard of Mussolini's arrest. Jodl in particular was furious, because during the conference the Italian General Staff officers had made promises and accepted undertakings which they could obviously have had no intention of keeping.

Hitler was very upset by the fate which had befallen his friend Mussolini, and he immediately made plans to release him. The coup was very daring, and it succeeded. But when Mussolini arrived at our headquarters he was obviously a broken man. He had lost so much weight and he looked so ill that it was not easy to recognise him at all. Hitler handed him over to Professor Morell for treatment. After Mussolini returned to Italy and took up his headquarters near Milan, Morell kept in touch by telephone, until one day the Italian doctors informed him that his treatment was no longer necessary – the patient was completely well again.

Things began to break up in Bulgaria, too, and a couple of weeks before his death I flew King Boris from Sofia to Rastenburg. On the return flight the weather was wonderful, but although the King, who had in the meantime become an enthusiastic flyer, greatly enjoyed the flight, he was unable to conceal his depression. He had staked everything on 'our Führer', and now he was compelled to realise that his card had been trumped.

Two days after his arrival in Sofia the German Embassy informed Hitler that King Boris was seriously ill. Hitler called me and told me to get ready to fly Professor Morell to Sofia, but the King thanked Hitler for his kindness, saying that he had good doctors in Sofia who could look after him. A matter of days after that we heard that he was dead. Our intelligence service reported that, in fact, he had not died of angina pectoris at all, as we had been told – he had been poisoned.

I flew Hitler to Rheims, and from there he went by car to a base on the coast to watch the discharge of the first V-2 on England. The next morning when we flew back, Hitler was full of it, and he seemed deeply impressed. What he longed to hear now was how the British had taken it. But the British didn't let on. Unarmed two-seater jet planes equipped with cameras were sent over to see what they could find out. Of course, they could easily outfly any British fighter plane, but they flew at between twenty thousand and twenty-five thousand feet, and the photographs they brought back told us very little.

Then the invasion took place, and scotched the idea that we could cripple Britain before it could be launched.* The first operations on the French coast definitely buried Germany's last hopes, and before long the bases from which the V-2s were fired were lost too. If the V-2 had become operational in strength twelve months earlier, things might have been different . . .

I often heard it said from informed quarters that Hitler had waited with the V-2 until a sufficient number could be accumulated, and I can remember the tremendous impression the first demonstration of this new weapon made on us. It was shortly after the successful culmination of the military campaign in the west, i.e. in 1940, and I flew Hitler to Peenemünde. On the testing grounds we took up our position behind a thirteen-foot-thick concrete barrier. A little distance away was the snail-like housing in which, we were told, the proper mixture of liquid oxygen and peroxide was obtained to fuel the rocket. Behind the firing platform was a great pit about sixty-five feet deep. I can't remember which impressed me most at the time, the ear-

---

* Baur gets his timings wrong here, as the first V-2 launch was in September 1944, after D-Day.

splitting noise as the rocket was discharged, or the tremendous white cloud which stabbed downwards into the enormous pit and blew out the great tree-trunks which lined it, tossing them into the air as though they were matchsticks. We were told that approximately 500,000 horsepower had been generated by the explosion – a simply gigantic concentration of power for the general technological level of those days.

Those responsible for the production and testing of the rocket believed that it could be made operational within a year, but in fact various difficulties were encountered, and there were long delays. The test rockets did not keep to the prescribed course, and for a long time it proved impossible to find out why. Finally it was discovered that the emptying of the tanks during the flight upset the flight stability and caused deviations. Special bulkheads were then incorporated, and finally the V-2 was ready to become operational.

The scientists responsible for the V-2 were well aware that they had opened up a new phase in the development of war, and that the V-2 was the pioneer of ballistic missiles which would one day soar over whole continents.

In July I once again flew to Romania, and brought Marshal Antonescu back to Hitler's headquarters in Rastenburg. It proved to be his last visit. I had orders to land at a certain time in Rastenburg, and in order not to get there too soon I made an intermediate landing in Cracow – which was just as well, because one of my engines had been giving me trouble on the flight from Bucharest, and in Cracow I was able to have it put right.

The marshal was to fly back to Romania the same afternoon, and when he arrived on the airfield he seemed very depressed. Hitler had obviously been able to offer him only very cold comfort. We hadn't been in the air more than a minute or two when an engine defect made itself apparent, and I put back and landed. Antonescu was very disturbed, and unwilling to believe that it was merely an accident; he feared sabotage. I ordered another machine to be made ready, but before this could be done our own machine was put in order, and we used that after all.

When we landed in Bucharest four hours later there were far more people on the airfield to greet the marshal than was customary. As soon as he descended he was surrounded by generals and other high officers and bombarded with questions. It was not difficult to see that the answers he gave satisfied no one – the general air of disappointment was too obvious. Clearly nothing he could do or say could now alter the conviction of them all that they were facing defeat. The commandant of the airfield told me that cases of sabotage were rapidly on the increase, and that there was a good deal of feeling in the country against Germany.

Within a couple of weeks the Russians occupied the whole of Romania. Another chapter had ended.

Weeks before 20 July I received special instructions from General Müller, the head of the Reich Security Service, to intensify all precautions and to take special care to ensure that all security arrangements were strictly adhered to. From time to time dummy attempts were made on Hitler's plane to test whether, in fact, these instructions were being carried out with sufficient care. And on one occasion something actually was overlooked. There were insistent rumours that an attempt was being planned on Hitler's life.

On 20 July I was with Flight-Captain Doldi at the dental clinic attached to Himmler's headquarters when I was called to the telephone, and told: 'Return at once and bring Doldi with you.' Doldi had just had an injection prior to having a tooth extracted, but he had to go off with me without the extraction. He was wanted to fly Himmler to Berlin. Within twenty minutes we were at Hitler's headquarters. There we learned what had happened, and saw the hut which had been devastated by the explosion. Colonel Stauffenberg, an officer who had lost an eye and an arm in action, was suspected, and there was a hue and cry after him.

The concrete bunker in which the situation discussions usually took place was not being used at the time. Work was going on to strengthen it by a further ten feet of concrete, because Intelligence had discovered that the Americans had perfected ten-ton bombs which were in all probability heavy enough to penetrate the thirteen-foot-thick concrete bunkers previously used. For the moment, therefore, meetings took place in an ordinary wooden hut above ground.

Gradually the investigation pieced together what had happened. A Heinkel landed on Rastenburg airfield with Colonel Stauffenberg and his adjutant, who drove together by car to Hitler's headquarters, where Stauffenberg informed the duty officer at the first control post that he had urgent instructions from the commander of the Reserve Army, General Fromm, and that he must speak to Field-Marshal Keitel at once. The duty officer immediately telephoned the field-marshal, who ordered that Stauffenberg should be allowed to pass. In this way Stauffenberg passed two controls, and presented himself to Field-Marshal Keitel. On hearing what Stauffenberg had to say, Keitel got in touch with Hitler, who ordered that Stauffenberg should take part in the situation discussion which was then just about to begin, as he, Stauffenberg, could then see the existing situation for himself and be able to report back according to the instructions General Fromm had given him.

The situation discussions usually started at midday, and this one was no exception. A large and heavy table had been brought into the hut for the discussion, and it was the solidity of this table which probably saved Hitler's life. When Colonel Stauffenberg entered the hut Hitler was already there, looking at a map which was spread out on the table-top. He was leaning forward with one arm resting on the table, and with the other hand he was holding his forehead. Stauffenberg put down the brief-case he was carrying – which contained the time-bomb – below the table opposite Hitler, so that Hitler's feet were not more than a few feet away.

Stauffenberg then walked out of the hut, saying to someone who asked him where he was going that he had to telephone and would be right back. He did telephone – to the airfield, ordering that the engines of his Heinkel should be warmed up for an immediate take-off as he had to fly back to Berlin at once. He then went to his car, which was waiting for him less than a hundred yards from the hut, and there he waited for the explosion. When it duly took place he assumed that his attempt had been successful, and the next task was to get to Berlin as quickly as possible to let it be known there that Hitler was dead. He got into his car, and instructed his chauffeur to drive back to the airfield. The first control post was less than two hundred yards away, and this he passed without difficulty. But the outer control post had already received the alarm, and Stauffenberg's way to freedom was barred by an anti-tank gun and portable barbed-wire entanglements. The duty officer informed him that the alarm had been given, and that he was not allowed to let anyone pass. Stauffenberg declared that he had come straight from the Führer with urgent instructions to fly back to Berlin at once, and that anyone who attempted to hinder him would undertake a heavy responsibility. This warning may have disturbed the duty officer, but it didn't make him give way. Stauffenberg then demanded to see the officer commanding the post, who happened to be at lunch. He was called from the mess at once, and because he knew that Field-Marshal Keitel had personally instructed Stauffenberg to be let in, he now gave the order to let him out again. The barbed-wire entanglements were removed, the pole rose, and Stauffenberg's car drove through and off to the airfield.

It was a ten-minute drive with no further control points, and when Stauffenberg arrived the Heinkel was waiting with running engines. There was, of course, no reason for anyone at the airfield to suspect that anything was wrong, and nothing was done to prevent the take-off. When Stauffenberg arrived in Berlin, fully convinced that Hitler was dead, his chief, General Fromm, was already aware that, in fact, Hitler was alive. He then took a step which subsequently gave rise to considerable differences of opinion – he ordered Stauffenberg's immediate execution.

In the meantime the most painstaking investigation into the whole affair was proceeding in Rastenburg. Stauffenberg's chauffeur was interrogated, and the only thing of any use he could say was that he thought Stauffenberg had thrown something out of the car on the way back to the airfield. A company of men was then set to search the sides of the road, and in a patch of stinging nettles a package of explosive was found – the same type which had been used in the attempt. It was of British origin, and it had a ten-minute mercury fuse. I had a look at it myself: it was a brown lump of plastic, looking something like wax, six inches square by two and a half inches thick. According to experts the explosive force should have been sufficient to kill everyone in the immediate neighbourhood – and in all probability would have been, had the conference and the explosion taken place in the confined space of the underground bunker. But in the lightly built hut above ground the walls were just blown outwards, so that the very important resistance factor was absent. In consequence the force of the explosion was dissipated in all directions, instead of being concentrated. Heinrich Berger, the official stenographer, who was sitting at the table opposite Hitler, lost both legs and quickly bled to death, but Hitler was just thrown backwards, and the only injury he sustained was a slight one in the arm.

Security precautions at Hitler's headquarters were greatly increased after that. Colonel Strebe, with men of the Greater-Germany Division, had previously been completely responsible for all security measures at Rastenburg, but now half the guards were Waffen SS units, and the other half men of the Greater-Germany Division. Precautions were also taken against parachutists; trenches were dug and mines were laid; and altogether Hitler's headquarters began to look very warlike. In addition, certain measures, such as the personal searching of visitors, etc., were introduced, and this gave rise to a good deal of resentment. The general atmosphere was much tenser, too, and as a result there were one or two incidents caused by sheer nervousness. On one occasion, for example, an anti-tank gun went off during an exercise. The shell tore through a hut and exploded against a tree, but no one was hurt, though the excitement was tremendous.

The fighting in the east was now rolling up to Germany's frontiers, and Hitler gave instructions that trenches and other defensive works should be prepared to resist the invader. After a while he had the impression that his orders were not being carried out with sufficient zeal by the Wehrmacht commanders, so he sent for Koch, the Gauleiter of East Prussia, and instructed him to carry out the work with the Volkssturm, or Home Guard, and the local civilian population. The whole of eastern Germany was to be defended with line after line of trenches, earthworks and tank-traps. And, in fact, during flights we made over the border areas we could see that Koch was conscientiously carrying out Hitler's orders.

By the autumn the fighting was only about sixty miles or so from Rastenburg. For the time being Hitler continued to occupy his headquarters, partly I believe under the impression that his presence would strengthen the resistance. Russian planes were more and more frequent visitors now, and I began to wonder how long it would be before they attacked our airfield. I had already taken precautions: most of my machines had been dispersed to various airfields in the neighbourhood, and I had sent away the greater part of my equipment and material, including our spare engines, to safety. As a matter of fact, the expected attack never took place.

When we were back in the Reich Chancellory again, Speer asked me if I would fly a jet plane for him and let him have my impressions. I agreed at once, but I pointed out that I should have to get permission from Hitler.

'Listen, Baur,' said Hitler, when I raised the matter, 'there have been so many unexplained crashes lately that I don't want you to take the risk. I need you still.'

So there was no jet flying for me, but one day I went along with Speer on a visit of inspection to Rechlin, for a demonstration of the new Volks-jet. This was a simplified jet with one engine only, and Speer reckoned that he could provide the Luftwaffe with a thousand a month. By this time the jets had become operational, and they had already booked some striking successes; for example, on one occasion a squadron of six jets attacked a bomber formation of thirty machines, shooting down twenty-eight with the loss of only one jet. Up to that time, when you heard that fifty enemy bombers had been shot down you knew perfectly well that at least the same number of our own fighters had been lost. But the jets had a speed of almost six hundred miles an hour, which was fantastic for those days, and far greater than anything the enemy could put into the air, so the jet fighter was obviously the answer to their mass bomber attacks.

When we arrived in Rechlin the weather was so bad and visibility was so poor that any demonstration of the new Volks-jet was out of the question, but at least we were given all the technical details and informed of all the latest developments. The old order, first given in 1943, for a thousand jets a month, was now repeated – but, as it turned out, with no greater success.

In December 1944 Hitler ordered the abandonment of his Rastenburg headquarters, and the greater part of my equipment and material was sent by rail to the south. Fifty of my men went off with a heavily loaded goods train towards Pocking in Lower Bavaria. On its way through Poland this train came into collision with another goods train. Seventeen of my men were killed on the spot, and many others were more or less seriously injured. It was the first time our flight had suffered such heavy casualties.

On 22 December the last members of the staff left Rastenburg, and I flew Hitler to Berlin. I was then given leave of absence for a few days, and flew to Munich to spend the Christmas holidays with my family. Soon afterwards the Russians captured Rastenburg.

Those of us from Bavaria had not gone willingly to Rastenburg, but we stayed there three years, and in that time we learned to appreciate the very different countryside of East Prussia and the sterling qualities of its inhabitants, so that in the end it was a real wrench to leave it, for we knew very well that we should not be going back there again. But at first there were other things to think of. In Berlin the last act was about to begin for Hitler – and for me the penultimate . . .

I spent New Year's Day 1945 in a maternity clinic in Seefeld near Munich, where my wife had just given birth to our third daughter. To celebrate the New Year, as well as the birth of my daughter, I had taken along sufficient glasses and champagne to supply all the nurses too; and when midnight came, many toasts were drunk and the usual good wishes exchanged. The atmosphere was cheerful enough for the moment, but I was secretly wondering – and I have no doubt a good many other people were too – what 1945 would bring for us. All hope of victory had gone, and the outlook was unpromising.

On 15 January I flew back to Berlin. The Russians had burst out of the Vistula bulge and were now fighting on German territory; and in the west Hitler's last card had failed. After great preliminary successes, the Ardennes offensive, which was to have driven the British and Americans back into the sea, had been brought to a halt. Hitler returned to Berlin, and never left it again.

The Allies were now bombing Berlin heavily, and the Supreme Command of the Wehrmacht, the OKW, which had its headquarters in Zossen, tried to persuade Hitler to move out to them, but he refused. The regular situation discussions now took place in the Reich Chancellery, and they usually lasted until early the following morning. One followed quickly on the heels of the other, because the situation was constantly changing – and always for the worse. The atmosphere in the concrete bunkers under the Reich Chancellery was becoming more and more macabre as one depressing piece of news followed the other, with never a ray of hope. The best news in those days was of a defeat which was not actually a disaster.

When any event gave Hitler a particularly hard jolt he would clasp his hands behind his back, and march up and down for a while with raised head. Then he would gradually become calmer; his face would assume its normal expression and he would behave as usual, though perhaps a minute or two before he had seemed almost at the end of his tether.

His fits of anger were becoming more and more frequent now, and sometimes he shouted and raved, usually when he suspected that his orders were not being carried out, or that they were being carried out unwillingly and with resistance. I have read a good many newspaper reports purporting to describe these outbursts – the alleged carpet-biting, and so on – but I can only say that although Hitler was certainly temperamental, I never witnessed anything of that sort in all the years I knew him.

By the beginning of 1945, we who were closest to him had the impression that he had aged by at least ten years since 20 July. His right arm often trembled now, and his back grew more and more bent. It frequently happened, of course, that men came into his presence who had not seen him for some time; and then we could see from the expressions on their faces how shocked they were at his changed appearance. He was obviously going downhill fast, and nothing Professor Morell could do for him – pills, injections, hormones, vitamins and so on – did him any good or held up the process of decline. Towards the end he rarely slept more than three or four hours a night, which was not enough to counteract his increasing exhaustion.

When the air-raids on Berlin became heavy the bomb-proof bunkers under the Reich Chancellory were thrown open for children in Hitler's absence, and they had been brought in from all parts of the capital so that they should at least be safe at nights and get undisturbed sleep. Every evening after that the bunkers were like a great children's home. The little beds were there, the towels, the hair- and tooth-brushes, the glasses, the night things – everything the children needed. Round the walls were illustrated nursery rhymes. And as the raids grew heavier, and many hospitals were hit and damaged, part of the bunkers was turned into a maternity clinic where women could have their babies in safety. But when Hitler returned to Berlin for good in 1945 the maternity clinic became a hospital for seriously wounded men of Hitler's own Leibstandarte, and by April there were about a thousand men being attended to there.

The Reich Chancellory had been hit and damaged, and Kannenberg, who was still in charge of the domestic side, was very much worried about the fate of his precious wines, so he evacuated them to Dresden – a proceeding which annoyed Hitler, because, as he said, fuel was needed for more important purposes. By March the Russians were still advancing, and Kannenberg feared that his wines would no longer be safe even in Dresden, so he got hold of a couple of army lorries, drove to Dresden, loaded up his wines, and went off to Upper Bavaria. In the neighbourhood of Bayreuth he was stopped, and his lorries were requisitioned, but at least they let him unload his wines. He managed to find provisional shelter for them and then he went back to Berlin and tried to enlist Hitler's aid, but Hitler told him bluntly that the lorries had been very properly requisitioned. Kannenberg then appealed to Bormann, who showed more understanding for his wines, and provided him with two log-burning lorries. With these Kannenberg drove back to Bavaria, loaded up his wines again, and found a home for them somewhere in the south – and that was the last Berlin saw of him.

As the situation grew worse, Göring used to visit us in the Reich Chancellory about every other day. One day when Hitler had once again reproached him bitterly for the failure of the Luftwaffe – not so much for its fighting qualities, as for the way in which research and development had been allowed to lag – he came to me.

'Baur,' he said, 'you're one of the old guard. You've seen the development of flying from the beginning right down to the present day; and I don't mind telling you frankly that I don't know anything about modern flying. The thing has just passed over my head.'

'How right you are!' I thought. 'It would have been better for you if you'd kept up your flying instead of rolling around in special trains all the time.' And I remembered those days just after Hitler came to power in 1933. I flew Göring a lot then, and he was still an enthusiastic flyer. He would sit next to me in our old Ju.52, and even try to learn instrument flying, but later on he was given his own pilot, a very experienced colleague of mine, Flight-Captain Hucke of the Lufthansa. Now and again Göring was flown in very bad weather, and he didn't care much for the experience. Gradually his enthusiasm for flying declined, and he flew less and less.

I remember one day when we were in Vinnitsa. Göring arrived in a four-engined Condor from Cracow. Afterwards he was going back to Berlin. It was excellent flying weather and I pointed out that it would save a good deal of time if he flew straight on to Berlin, but he refused, saying that a special train was waiting for him in Cracow. By that time it had already become clear to us all that the head of the Luftwaffe didn't care for flying any more, and did as little of it as he could. For example, we knew that he had come by plane from Cracow to Vinnitsa only because, partisan activity having made any journey overland dangerous, Hitler had given instructions that VIPs should travel only by plane. It was already a joke amongst us that Göring ought really to have been Railway Minister, not Air Minister. And now, at a time when the Luftwaffe could get off the ground at all only with difficulty and at the cost of lives, the person responsible for it, the Reich Marshal and Reich Air Minister, was forced to confess that technical developments in the air had gone beyond him!

* * *

The work to convert the new Junkers 290 plane for our use began in the summer of 1944. It was a machine originally designed as a long-distance Atlantic reconnaissance plane; it had four engines, each of 1,800 horsepower, a total weight of forty tons, and a range of almost four thousand miles. Its normal cruising speed was well over two hundred miles an hour, and its top speed was well over three hundred miles an hour. Its crew consisted of a pilot, a mechanic, a wireless-operator and observer, and ten men to man its heavy machine-guns. In fact, it was a veritable fortress, and it represented tremendous progress. In all it could carry fifty passengers, and I am convinced that in ordinary circumstances it would have proved a worthy successor to the famous Ju.52 which conquered the world – peacefully – in 1932.

Three of these splendid machines were now converted at Pocking, between Braunau and Passau, for our use. The place where Hitler sat was protected with armour-plate, and the safety-glass was of a thickness calculated to withstand bullets. From Hitler's seat to the cabin entrance was over fifteen feet, which was much too far in an emergency, so a powerful hydraulic device was installed capable of opening a special trapdoor at his feet against the strongest air-pressure, whilst a parachute was built into the seat in such a way that it could not be seen. All Hitler had to do in an emergency was to pull a red-handled lever situated at a convenient spot beside his seat. This operated the hydraulic mechanism and opened the trapdoor. Hitler could then escape by parachute. We tried this mechanism out repeatedly with a dummy of the correct weight and size, and it always worked satisfactorily.

As soon as one of these machines was converted I went down to Pocking to try it out for its flying qualities, and it came up to my highest expectations. It was equipped with an advanced type of W/T apparatus which allowed more accurate beaming and position-finding, and it had fully automatic three-axis steering linked with the gyro-compass. All these things are a matter of course nowadays, but then they were quite new.

The day before I was to take over this machine and fly it to Berlin, there was a very heavy raid on Dessau, where the machine had been flown for its final check before handing over. I found a great part of the town devastated and a great deal of damage on the airfield itself – but our new Ju.290 was unscratched!

By this time the hopeless trek of hundreds of thousands from the outlying areas of Germany into the interior was reaching its height, and in Berlin there were large numbers of women and children from East Prussia who no longer knew what to do or where to go. Every time I flew down to Pocking in connection with the new Ju.290 I would load my plane with as many of these unfortunates as I could carry. When I returned from Russia after my long imprisonment I was delighted to find that a good many of these people whom I had flown had settled down satisfactorily and made themselves new homes.

Shortly before 09.00 on 17 March I touched down with my Ju.290 on Munich airfield. Almost every morning large formations of American bombers coming from Italy would pass over Munich on their way into Germany. I had already given orders for my plane to be rolled into a hangar, for were it left out its unusual size might attract unwelcome attention from the passing enemy. Then I drove into town. I had not been gone more than ten minutes when an air-raid warning sounded. We drove out of town again as quickly as possible, and stopped under trees in Laim to await developments. Before long bombs began to fall to the east of Munich. The attacking bombers then turned away to the south, and I drove home. Before long there was a telephone call for me. The airfield had been heavily attacked; the Ju.290 had been burnt out, and there were casualties.

This time the Americans had done a good job. They had often attacked the airfield before, but usually their bombs had fallen harmlessly in nearby fields, only occasionally damaging a building. Previously they had always flown from south to north, or from north to south on their way back, but this time they had flown from east to west, and it seemed to have improved their aiming, for the airfield and its installations were devastated. I rang up Berlin and ordered a machine to pick me up. When it arrived I flew to Berlin – and that was the last I saw of Munich until 1955. In Berlin I reported the fate of our Ju.290 to Hitler, but he took it very calmly, just nodding his head.

In March, Giesler, Inspector-General for the reconstruction of Munich, came to visit us in the damaged Reich Chancellory, and under the present circumstances we wondered what on earth there was to discuss about Munich's ultimate rebuilding. But Giesler saw nothing incongruous in his arrival, and informed us that his plans were now ready. For example, they provided for the rebuilding of the famous Frauenkirche with its double towers, which had always been Munich's distinctive architectural characteristic. Giesler was particularly delighted at the thought that this would please Cardinal Faulhaber.

When Hitler heard what Giesler had come for he positively beamed – we hadn't seen him look so cheerful for a long time and the two of them went off by themselves to discuss the rebuilding of Munich. In the meantime Berlin was being rapidly flattened. Hitler spent hours on the plans, and made many sketches to show what he wanted. He seemed very happy, but for the rest of us, who knew that the final disaster was at the gates, it was an extraordinary and unreal experience.

At the end of March I went out to Schönwalde to inspect my machine park and visit my men. Whilst I was there an air-raid warning sounded, and the machines were put away as rapidly as possible in the hangars in the woods. But before all the planes could be got out of sight a big formation of bombers flew over accompanied by the usual strong fighter escort. Two of the fighters spotted us and dived down. One of them shot up the four-engined Condor of Grand Admiral Dönitz, which had sixteen hundred gallons of petrol in its tanks and flared up tremendously, whilst the other attacked Ribbentrop's machine, a Ju.52.

As the fighting came nearer and nearer to our airfield I had to reckon that such losses would increase, so I had some of the machines, my spare engines and the greater part of my supplies and stores transferred to Pocking and Reichenhall. By April the front was even nearer to Berlin. By this time everyone knew that the situation was hopeless, and Berliners spent most of their time in cellars and air-raid shelters. There were even rumours that Hitler was no longer in Berlin, but, in fact, he was still in the Reich Chancellory. On 1 April the various ministries were instructed to leave the capital, and by 10 April only the Foreign Office, part of the Propaganda Ministry, and Hitler's Reich Chancellory staff were left.

Barriers were going up everywhere in the capital now, but they looked very sketchy and not as though they had been planned in any detail. My machines were distributed amongst various airfields in the immediate neighbourhood: Rangsdorf, Finsterwalde, Gatow, Schönwalde and Tempelhof. Before long Rangsdorf and Finsterwalde had to be evacuated. Colonel Böttger, the commandant of Tempelhof airfield, came to see me in Berlin.

'Herr Baur,' he began, 'I have done what I can to put Tempelhof in a state of defence, and we'll hold out as long as possible. But if the Russians take the place I don't propose to let them take me.' On 22 April the Russians took Tempelhof airfield, and Colonel Böttger shot himself.

Hitler had personally taken charge of the defence of the Reich Chancellory, and on 15 April – it was a beautiful sunny day – he appeared in the garden to give various instructions. Mortar positions were being built, walls were being knocked down in order to obtain a free line of fire, anti-tank gun positions were being set up, and concrete defences with loopholes were being built. A thousand men of his Leibstandarte under the command of General Mohnke were there to defend Hitler's last stronghold to the end.

Frau Goebbels arrived in the Reich Chancellory on that day, and when Hitler saw her he went up to her, exclaiming: 'For heaven's sake, Frau Goebbels, what are you doing here in Berlin? You should have gone away long ago. Baur here will fly you to the Berghof whilst there's still time. You will be safe there with your children.'

'If the Russians take Berlin my husband will be killed,' she replied calmly, 'and what point would there be then in our living on? I didn't bear my children for them to be put on show in the United States or Soviet Russia as the progeny of the Nazi propagandist Goebbels. No, I am going to stay here in Berlin with my husband.'

As she was obviously quite determined, Hitler arranged for her to live with her children in the bunkers, where Goebbels himself was now spending his nights. I was living in the Kanonier Strasse at the time, but when the house was bombed I was given quarters in what had been the Yugoslav Embassy. I was shaving one morning near the window when mortar shells fell. There had been no air-raid warning, and there was no sign of any air activity, but about a couple of hundred yards away was a flak bunker and the Russians were obviously getting the range. I happened to mention it to Hitler, and he was startled to find that I was still living outside the Reich Chancellory. He now ordered that I should be given quarters in it. Cubicles had been run up in the bunkers, and I was there now with Martin Bormann, Rattenhuber, Betz, and the detective Högl, who had been with Hitler at the time of the Röhm putsch – he was now a high police official.

The new Reich Chancellory looked pretty depressing. There was no longer any life above ground-level. All the windows were gone, and the curtains, torn and dirty, waved wildly backwards and forwards in the constant blast. The Wilhelm Platz and the Voss Strasse were already in the firing line, but underground for five hundred yards or so there was a network of cellars and bunkers linked up with each other. It was possible for lorries to drive down from the surface into the bowels of the Reich Chancellory. At one time they had brought coke; now they brought wounded – when they came at all. During the last few days about six hundred wounded were brought in; and almost a thousand civilians, mostly women and children, were allowed to take shelter after desperately running here and there on the streets trying to find a refuge.

Hitler had his own bunker with just a few rooms for himself, his doctor, his servant and the absolutely necessary personnel of his staff. This bunker was about forty feet underground, though the entrance which led down to it from above was only about three feet or so below ground level. During the last days of the fighting a shell penetrated the cover of this entrance corridor and burst inside. Light was supplied by a sixty-kilowatt diesel engine, which also provided power for the water-pump. Fire-brigade hoses were laid through the underground corridors to serve as water-pipes. In this way Hitler's bunker and the general underground city of the Reich Chancellory, including the sick-bay, had light and water right to the end, long after all outside sources had been cut off.

On 17 April Göring arrived in the Reich Chancellory accompanied by Major-General Christian, who had been our Luftwaffe adjutant for a while. I asked him what Göring had come for, and he said it was to persuade Hitler to come to Obersalzberg, where Göring himself was going that evening by the Autobahn, which was still open, but might not be much longer. Göring was with Hitler for about an hour and a half, and then the two of them appeared in the anteroom. They shook hands, and I heard Hitler say: 'Mind you send reconnoitring parties on ahead. Fighting is taking place between Nuremberg and Bayreuth, and American tanks might break through. Good luck, anyway.'

The next day Hitler told me that Göring had arrived safely. 'At least someone I can trust can influence the development of affairs from outside,' he said optimistically.

The fighting increased in violence on 18 and 19 April. After a breakthrough from the Seelow hills the Russians launched a pincer drive to encircle Berlin, and after that the battle for the centre of the town began to take shape. I was constantly on the airfield we were still using, and in the night planes were still taking off with documents, and so on, for Munich. Part of the Reich Chancellory personnel was also flown out.

Hitler's last birthday was a sad affair. Grand Admirals Raeder and Dönitz appeared with Himmler and Goebbels to congratulate the Führer. On 22 April, by which time the Russians were already in the suburbs and pressing forward to the centre of the town, Hitler declared that he was determined not to leave Berlin. At the same time he gave instructions that as many others as possible should be flown out. Every night after that my machines carried people out to the south. The only airfield we had now was Gatow, and it was from here on 25 April that people and material were flown out to Munich and Salzburg for the last time. They would take off at 2 a.m. in order to be at their destination before dawn. The last machine to leave was piloted by Major Gundelfinger. Unfortunately he could not get away on time, because some of his passengers didn't arrive punctually. When he finally took off we reckoned he would have nearly an hour's daylight flying before he reached his destination. All the other planes reported their safe arrival either during the night or in the early hours of the morning, but we heard nothing of Gundelfinger's plane.

Hitler was very upset at this, because one of his favourite personal servants was with this plane.

'And I entrusted him with extremely valuable documents which would show posterity the truth about my actions!' he exclaimed in dismay.

It was eight years before it was discovered that Gundelfinger's plane had been shot down near the Bavarian Forest – in daylight. The machine was burnt out. Peasants buried the bodies which were found in the wreckage.

That same night Professor Morell was also flown out, but in another plane. A couple of weeks before that he had himself suffered a slight stroke and needed treatment. I was astonished at the extraordinary expression given to his face by the paralysing of the muscles of the left side of the mouth and the eyelid. Powerful doses of his own medicine gave him temporary relief, but it was a warning signal. Morell wept when he left Hitler. He told me that Hitler had said that during the very short time that he, Hitler, still had to live, Dr Stumpfegger would look after him.

On 25 April Hitler received a telegram from Göring, who was in the Berghof. It said in gist: 'You have appointed me to be your successor. You are now cut off in Berlin, and can no longer exercise your authority except within a very limited area. I therefore call upon you to transfer full powers to me.' At first Hitler did not take this telegram very seriously and merely commented that Göring probably had no idea of the situation in Berlin. We were still able to broadcast on long and medium wavelengths, but a short-wave broadcasting station had been overlooked, which meant that we needed an outside aerial. This was a great nuisance, because the aerial was constantly being damaged by bombardment and we could not always repair it immediately. All incoming news was heard on ordinary receivers, and our signals section put together a daily bulletin for Hitler from the British and American broadcasts, which were already being issued in German.

That same evening a report came through that Göring had opened negotiations with the Americans. At this Hitler became really angry, and instructed Bormann to despatch a message to Göring at once. Bormann showed me the message before it went off. Its gist was: 'Your action represents high treason, which, in the ordinary way, would be punishable by death. Only your long and valuable services persuade me not to impose such a sentence. However, I order you to lay down all your offices and appointments within twenty-four hours.' An answer arrived from Göring the very next morning. He came to heel and relinquished all his authority. Hitler then appointed General

Ritter von Greim as Göring's successor, and instructed him to fly into Berlin at once and report.

As all our airfields were now lost, a runway for planes was established on the avenue from Brandenburger Tor to the Victory Column, and I was instructed to supervise the work. The Russians were bombarding this area very heavily, because they knew that it was used by us for transport and communication, and on the way there a shell exploded a few yards away from our car. The chauffeur was wounded in the hand and the car was damaged, but I didn't get a scratch. Colonel Ehlers was waiting for me at the Victory Column to discuss the undertaking. The first thing I pointed out was that the avenue, though wide as such, was much too narrow for our purpose. It was about seventy yards across, whereas even a Ju.52 had a wing span of ninety-five feet, which meant that even if it landed in the exact centre there would be less than sixty feet to spare on either side. I therefore gave orders that the trees should be cut down on each side of the avenue in order to extend the width to a hundred and thirty yards. Whilst I was standing there with Colonel Ehlers we heard the engine of a Fieseler Storch, and saw it touch down some distance away just before the Brandenburger Tor. I got into my car and drove to it at once to find out who had arrived, but when I got there whoever it was had already gone. Two soldiers told me that a wounded general and a woman had got out of the plane, taken a car and driven off at once.

When I got back to the Reich Chancellory I discovered that Hanna Reitsch was the woman pilot, and that she had flown in with General Ritter von Greim. I knew the general well from the days of the First World War, and I found him now lying on an operating table. He had received a bullet in his calf on the way in. Hitler appeared too, welcomed von Greim, congratulated him on his successful flight into the beleaguered city and wished him a speedy recovery.

Von Greim stayed a couple of days, and I talked to him on several occasions. He told me that Hitler had given him a detailed description of what had happened during the past few days, and particularly the incident with Göring. Von Greim, it appeared, had also been appointed chief of the Luftwaffe, and promoted to the rank of field-marshal. In the night of 28 April Hanna Reitsch flew him out of Berlin to take up his new command.

On 29 April Hitler married Eva Braun. It was all done very quietly, and even I knew nothing about it until Hitler told me when he said good-bye to me. On the same day several other marriages took place in the Reich Chancellory. Dr Naumann performed the ceremonies, which took place above ground. There was a good deal of firing going on at the time, and the various couples were married to the accompaniment of breaking glass, falling masonry and heavy explosions. They were then given separate rooms in the bunkers for a honeymoon perhaps unique in its tragedy, for not one of those pairs could hope for any happiness, or, indeed, for any future at all.

That evening I spoke to Eva Braun, or Eva Hitler as she now was. She told me what, in fact, I already knew, that Himmler had also broken away. He was expelled from the National Socialist Party that evening. On 26 April he had tried to persuade Hitler to leave Berlin, sending a young officer with an armoured group, spearheaded by six Tiger tanks, into Berlin. On the way to the Reich Chancellory they had shot up nine Russian tanks. Beaming with delight at his success, the young officer saluted Hitler and delivered his message. Hitler received him very amiably, but repeated that it was his intention to stay in Berlin. The young officer was then seconded to General Weidling, the last commander of Berlin, and later on I met him again in Posen.

SS Group-Leader Fegelein, the liaison officer between Hitler and Himmler, was married to Eva Braun's sister, which now made him Hitler's brother-in-law. The day Hitler married Eva Braun he summoned Fegelein, who couldn't be found. Then someone got the idea that he might be still in his own flat on the Kurfürstendam. General Rattenhuber rang him up there –

incidentally, the Berlin telephone network worked right up to the last moment – and Fegelein answered the telephone. The general informed him that Hitler wanted to see him at once, and that everyone had been looking for him for hours. Fegelein replied that he was drunk and couldn't appear before Hitler in such a state. But Rattenhuber declared that orders were orders, and he would send along a car to fetch him. A car with several SS men set off, but they discovered that the area in which Fegelein's flat was situated was already in Russian hands. However, they fought their way through – one man was wounded – and reached Fegelein's flat, where they found him tipsy, as he had said, and in civilian clothes. He was still unwilling to come, but promised that as soon as he sobered up he would come.

But he didn't, and after several more telephone calls – Fegelein was still in his flat – another car was sent round at about nine o'clock in the evening. This time an officer of the Wehrmacht and a number of soldiers went. Once again one of their number was wounded. This time Fegelein gave his word of honour that he would come later, and at about midnight he actually did come. When Hitler was informed that Fegelein had arrived at last, he said that he no longer wanted to see the man, and he ordered an investigation on a charge of desertion.

At Hitler's instructions General Mohnke, the commander of the Leibslandarle, deprived Fegelein of his rank insignia and his medals, and he was then lodged in the GPU bunker, which was below a church opposite the Hotel Kaiserhof. Eva Hitler now came to me in horror, declaring that Hitler would show no mercy: he would shoot his own brother in similar circumstances. It was her sister she was thinking of primarily, she declared, above all because she was about to have a baby.

Early that morning the results of the investigation were laid before Hitler: Fegelein had been found guilty of desertion. Hitler then ordered his immediate execution. An execution squad was sent off to carry out the sentence. Every attempt to move in the open was very dangerous by this time, but the men managed to reach their objective, and Fegelein was executed in the garden of the Foreign Office.

On 28 April I had a talk with Frau Goebbels. We sat together calmly chatting, but I was very conscious all the time that I was talking to a woman who knew that she had only a very short time to live, and that as a mother she must first kill her children.

'You know, Herr Baur, life hasn't really given me very much,' she said. 'I bore children to my husband; I went to all the big meetings because he wanted me to; and I did my best to devote my life to him and my children. It wasn't always easy. My friends, who envied me, made me see a good deal. They would tell me about this or that woman I ought to keep my eye on. I knew quite well, of course, that my husband – who was surrounded with attractive women – didn't take his obligation of marital fidelity very seriously. Perhaps it was the fault of the women; they certainly flung themselves at his head. He often hurt me, but I have forgiven him. I know that we shall never get out of this bunker alive . . . In any case, I have nothing more to hope for – and it isn't only just recently that I have felt that. Every evening I put the injections for my children ready, and when the time comes the doctor will make them for me. The Russians are not more than a couple of hundred yards away now, and every night when I tuck my children in and say goodnight to them I never know whether it's for the last time.'

As she spoke, her children were playing around us, or talking to the wounded, to whom they sometimes sang little songs. When the bombardment occasionally reached new heights and the whole place shook, they would dance and clap their hands and wish 'the wobbling' would go on – it was such fun.

The last hope of the men fighting in Berlin was the almost legendary relief army of Generals Steiner and Wenck. On 29 April Hitler called me and told me that he was sending Colonel von Below, who had been liaison officer between him and Göring, and was now his personal adjutant, with various instructions to General Wenck. Then he went on:

'The way westwards is still open, and I want you to leave Berlin with Colonel von Below. I don't need you here any more.'

I replied firmly that I had already made my decision clear to him, and that my opinion had not changed in the meantime: 'I am staying here,' I said, 'and I've no doubt I'll find various things to do. For example, I can take Colonel von Below's place when he's gone.' There wasn't very much left for an adjutant to do, but Hitler agreed, so once again I had a job.

Looking back on it now it seems astonishing that there were people even then who still wanted to see Hitler. For example, the nurses, who had been working night and day for weeks in our underground hospital, asked that he should visit them. Professor Haase and Frau Goebbels went to Hitler and told him, and he agreed to do so.

You had to go through a canteen before going down to the hospital below, and the nurses were gathered there with Frau Goebbels and her four children and about twenty other children. When Hitler came into the room the children began to sing. With his hands in his jacket pockets he walked past the nurses nodding to them; then he halted and stood there for about half a minute without saying anything. There was silence, and most of the nurses were in tears. Still without saying anything, Hitler turned and left the room, and the nurses went back to their patients.

On 29 April 29th the battle for the Reich Chancellory itself opened up. The following day I was repeatedly called into Hitler's bunker, for, after all, I was now his adjutant. The last time I was called in I was told to bring my own adjutant, Colonel Betz, with me. Hitler's room was quite small, and the furniture consisted of a couch, a small sideboard, a table and a few chairs. The concrete walls had been covered with wood panelling.

As soon as I entered, Hitler came up to me and took both my hands in his.

'Baur, I want to say good-bye to you.'

'You don't mean . . .' I began in dismay.

'Yes,' he answered. 'The time has come. My generals have betrayed me; my soldiers don't want to go on; and I *can't* go on.'

I tried to persuade him that there were still planes available, and that I could get him away to Japan or the Argentine, or to one of the Sheiks, who were all very friendly to him on account of his attitude to the Jews. Hitler made himself many enemies over the Jewish question, but he also won a number of friends. After the war – which, of course, he had expected to win – he proposed to take Madagascar away from the French and turn it into a national home for the Jews. It was to be a sovereign and independent state; and all Jews, including those living in Egypt, would be sent there. This plan naturally won him the sympathy of the Mufti, who was living in Egypt, and had visited Hitler on a number of occasions in the Reich Chancellory. I had seen him there once or twice myself, and Hitler told me when he was gone that he was a very cunning fox indeed.

Hitler declared once again that he would under no circumstances leave Germany. He could go into the mountains, of course, or he could go to Grand Admiral Dönitz in Flensburg. But what would be the good of that? In a couple of weeks at the outside he would be in the same situation as he was now.

'The war will end with the fall of Berlin,' he declared. 'And I stand or fall with Berlin. A man must summon up courage enough to face the consequences – and therefore I'm ending it now. I know that tomorrow millions of people will curse me – that's fate. The Russians know perfectly well that I am here in this bunker, and I'm afraid they'll use gas shells. During the war we produced a gas which could put a man to sleep for twenty-four hours. Our Intelligence tells me that the Russians now have this gas too. The consequences would be unimaginable if they captured me alive. There are gas-locks here, I know, but can you rely on them? In any case, I'm not – and I'm ending it today.'

Hitler then thanked me for the many years' loyal service I had given him, and he looked round the room.

'I want to give you something,' he said. 'What about this picture on the wall here? – It's a Lenbach of Frederick the Great. I've owned many pictures in my life, some of them much more valuable than this one, which cost me thirty-four thousand marks in 1934. I want it preserved for posterity; it has considerable historical value.'

I replied that I would gladly accept it, and that in more peaceful times I would present it to some art gallery.

'No,' he said, 'that's not what I want at all. It's for you. It's enough if it's in your hands. I know you've often grumbled about my pictures, including this one – but that was another matter.'

I must have looked at him in astonishment, for he explained: 'You remember that whenever I changed my headquarters for more than a day or so this picture had to go along. They told me long ago about the way you used to grumble.'

And then I remembered that awkward item of baggage that was never allowed to be sent on with the baggage plane but always had to go in our machine, leaning in the gangway in everybody's way. I knew, of course, that Hitler was very fond of his pictures, and liked to have them around him – so that when we went away from one place for long, his pictures had to go along too.

I tried to excuse myself and explain that other people used to complain when they had to pass that large package in the gangway . . . but Hitler smiled and interrupted:

'All right, Baur. All right.'

And then he went on more seriously: 'Now I've still two jobs for you, Baur. I am making you responsible for burning the bodies of my wife and me. And then, I have appointed Dönitz my successor, and Bormann has important instructions from me to be communicated to Dönitz, and I want you to get him out of here. It is very important that Bormann should get to Dönitz.'

Hitler then shook hands firmly with me and turned to Colonel Betz, thanked him for his services and shook hands with him too. I had already turned to leave the room when Hitler walked

185

after me and caught hold of me impulsively with both hands. 'Baur,' he exclaimed, 'on my tombstone they ought to put the words: "He was the victim of his Generals!"' When I made some comment, he went on: 'Baur, there's a good deal you don't know, and you'll find out some things that will astonish you.'

Later on in prisoner-of-war camps I was with generals who had been urging our men to throw down their arms and go over to the enemy since 1944, when they were taken prisoner, and I knew then what Hitler had meant.

When we left Hitler I said to Betz that we should have to try the break-out that very night, and that we needed different clothes, for we should have to make our way to the planes on foot. It was 19.00 when we left Hitler, and not 16.00 as I have since seen it said. I went down to Professor Haase, who was operating day and night on the wounded and hardly ever got away from the operating-table except to snatch a little sleep, and I asked him for a couple of camouflage capes and packs from the kit brought in with the wounded men.

He found me the camouflage capes, but said that he hadn't any packs, because the men were being brought in from positions close at hand and therefore had no packs with them. I then handed over all my spare personal clothing, shirts, socks and so on, for the wounded. I managed to get a pack from a Luftwaffe man, but it had no straps, so Bormann gave me some and I sewed them on myself. Then I burnt all my papers.

About an hour and half had passed, and to find out what had happened in the meantime I went with Betz through the ruined corridor which led under the garden of the Reich Chancellory to the Führer's bunker. Even before I had gone down the twenty steps which led to it I smelt cigarette smoke, which was unusual here because Hitler was a non-smoker and smoking was forbidden anywhere near his quarters. I went quickly down the steps, and there I found Goebbels, Rattenhuber, Müller and Bormann, with perhaps a dozen SS men, all very obviously on edge. I asked Goebbels if it were all over, and he nodded. I then asked if Hitler's body were still in his bunker, whereupon Goebbels replied that it was already being burnt. When I told him in surprise that Hitler had made me responsible for burning his body, he replied that Hitler had given everybody those instructions when he said good-bye.

'Hitler committed suicide shortly after I left him,' he added.

I asked whether he had shot himself.

'Yes, in the temple. He was lying on the floor. Eva Braun took poison, and she was sitting on the sofa as though she were asleep.'

It appeared that Hitler's body had been wrapped in blankets and carried upstairs into the open. Hitler's chauffeur, Kempka, had brought along tins of petrol. Goebbels, Bormann, Rattenhuber and Müller had been present at the burning of the body. Rattenhuber told me that during the burning Eva Braun's body had twitched violently, and it is, in fact, well known that this phenomenon is common. Hitler's body had shrunk in on itself.

With this I regarded the matter as ended, and I didn't even go up and look – an omission I was to have cause to regret later on in Russia, because investigations showed that the cremation of the bodies had not been complete, and that certain parts, though charred, had not been destroyed.

When I was ready to go I reported to Martin Bormann, who told me that it depended on General Rauch, who was now in command of the defence of Charlottenburg, whether we made the attempt today or tomorrow. Rauch would be arriving at the Reich Chancellory at 22.00. Bormann also said that there was a suggestion that surrender negotiations might be opened up, because it was now well established that the Russians were raping every woman they got hold of, irrespective of age; for example, all the nurses and even bedridden patients at the Weissensee Hospital had been raped.

When our nurses heard this – and some of them were very pretty and attractive girls – they all began to clamour for poison to do away with themselves rather than fall into Russian hands.

There were also quite a large number of women in the bunkers, and they were all obviously threatened with the same fate.

Goebbels had been asked to hand over the Reich Chancellory officially to the Russians, in order, if possible, to prevent the sort of thing that had happened at Weissensee. General Krebs, who spoke Russian, was to go to Marshal Zhukov to open up negotiations and see if reasonable conditions could be obtained.

After that I went to Linge, who was Hitler's valet, to get my Lenbach portrait of Frederick the Great. We took it out of its frame, and rolled it up – the actual size of the canvas was about twenty-four by sixteen inches – and tied it on top of my pack.

It was 22.00 hours now and General Rauch arrived. Through Bormann I learned what Rauch had to tell us: the Russians were already in Grunewald and Spandau, but the Heeres Strasse was still open, and the bridge over the Havel was being successfully defended by Hitler Youth detachments under Axmann. There was therefore no urgent reason why our departure should take place at once.

Frau Goebbels, Rattenhuber and I were together that evening, and our conversation was not very cheerful. At 03.00 hours a policeman arrived and reported to Rattenhuber that the bodies of Hitler and Eva Braun had been consumed, apart from negligible remains, and buried in shell-holes – the garden and forecourt of the Reich Chancellory was pitted with shell-holes. I learned only later in Moscow that this report was inaccurate.

Ambassador Hewel, who had been liaison officer between Hitler and Ribbentrop, sat at a little distance from us, looking at a photograph of his young wife – they had been married only a few months. I asked him whether he was going with us. There were tears in his eyes when he replied:

'I don't know, Baur. I really can't give myself up to the Russians.'

I pointed out that none of us intended to give ourselves up to the Russians. 'It doesn't look very hopeful,' I admitted, 'but we might manage it; you never know.'

'Right,' he said with determination, 'I'll come along. And if it looks as though they're going to take me I can always shoot myself. I don't want to become a traitor to Hitler, though I often disagreed with his policy.'

When we started out the next day, Hewel could see that the situation was hopeless, and he blew his brains out before the Russians got him.

A little later that evening General Burgdorf asked me to shoot him, but I refused, and then he shot himself. General Krebs shot himself, and so did Schädle, who was wounded in the leg and therefore couldn't come with us. General Müller, the chief of the Gestapo, also decided not to come with us.

'I know Russian methods too well to take the risk of falling into their hands, Baur,' he said. 'They'd shoot me in any case, but at least I can save myself the preliminary beatings and the torture.'

A wave of suicides now swept through the bunkers, for many highly placed people preferred a quick death at their own hands to imprisonment by the Russians. I often thought about them later on when I was in Russian hands and subjected to endless ill-treatment, and I once told a Russian commissar that I envied my comrades who had decided to end it with a quick shot – they were better off than I was.

At dawn the following day General Rauch set off to return to his men, but at midday he was back in the Reich Chancellory in a very downcast mood. He had been unable to get farther than the Zoo bunker, for during the night the Russians had driven a wedge through the Tiergarten, and we were now completely surrounded.

The reports on the situation reaching the Reich Chancellory were very confused, and it was difficult to get a clear picture, but General Weidling decided that as the westward escape route seemed closed, we should try to make our way out northwards over the Weidendamm Bridge, where the first Russian lines were situated. The second line was in Oranienburg, but to the north of that was an SS division under Steiner. If we could get through to them we should be safe – for the moment at least. Orders were now given that the break-out should start at 21.30 hours that evening.

Shortly before we left I went down to Dr Goebbels to say good-bye. He was in his bunker room with his wife. I didn't see the children, and I didn't ask about them, so I don't know whether they were already dead then or not. When I went in they both got up, and there were tears in their eyes.

'Berlin is completely surrounded now, Baur,' Goebbels said, 'and it won't be easy for you to get out, but I wish you luck. Do your best; Bormann has important instructions for Dönitz. If you manage to get through tell Dönitz what the situation's been like here this past three weeks. And tell him that we knew how to live and fight, and then how to die.'

I shook hands silently with them both, and then I left.

Just before 21.30 hours we were ordered to go forward in small groups. I kept with Bormann, as I had been instructed to do. There were about fifteen of us in our group, and we went out of the Voss Strasse entrance – where the SA sentries had always stood, and from there we ran towards the Kaiserhof underground station. It had been badly damaged, and there were no steps left, so we went down into the station on our behinds. Apart from where bombs and shells had broken open the tunnel it was quite dark. We had no torches, and we went forward in the dark over the Friendrichstrasse crossing and on to Gendarmenmarkt, where we came out again and found everything in flames. We now went back to the Friedrich Strasse, and from there towards Weidendamm Bridge. A little way before this there was an anti-tank barrier, and about a hundred yards further on burning lorries in front of the Russian lines.

The Russians knew that anyone attempting to get out of Berlin to the north would have to pass over this bridge, and so they put up a concentrated barrage, with the result that casualties in this area were very heavy. Martin Bormann crouched on the stone steps of a house doorway on the corner of Schiffbauerdam. A young Russian lay dead just in front of him. I was still trying to find a way forward. From the Friedrich Strasse we were to make our way into the Ziegel Strasse, and from there into a big brewery, which was our meeting-point. But every time I tried to go forward I had to turn back.

'Stay where you are, Baur,' Bormann called out. 'I don't want you shot. You can see for yourself how many wounded are streaming back. I need you. Stay with me.'

I told him that it was impossible to stay put. We must try to get forward. The night was short enough as it was, and we had a long way to go.

Then I went forward again to a ruined house. It had once been a hotel, and beyond it we could almost reach the corner of the Ziegel Strasse. It was about two o'clock when Bormann and I ran forward. The Russians were firing persistently from the direction of the Chausee Strasse, as we sprang and clambered over heaps of rubble to get to the ruined hotel. We took refuge in a doorway and discovered that the hall behind it, and the cellar below, was full of people, most of them wounded. Their position seemed pretty hopeless, but there was nothing we could do about it, and I went out onto the street to see if there were a possibility of going on. German and Russian tanks were fighting it out in the streets. Several giant Russian tanks were destroyed by anti-tank weapons, and I was standing quite close to a German tank when it suddenly opened fire, and I was thrown to the ground by the blast. Afterwards I discovered that my face had been so seared by the explosion that it took me months to get the little black powder spots out of my skin. I scrambled to my feet and ran back to the doorway. Then I heard the sound of shooting from the courtyard at the back, and I ran up the stairs to look down.

In the flicker of burning cars I saw about a score of Russians down below. As quickly as I could I ran back to Bormann and told him that all the Russians had to do to finish us off was to open the back door, and it was therefore time we moved. It was time anyway, for there was only about an hour's darkness left.

There were only four of us left now: Bormann, Naumann, Dr Stumpfegger and myself, and we all knew that once it was light there would be no chance at all of getting out of the trap. There was, we had heard, a possibility of getting out of inner Berlin underground. Youths and girls, who knew their way around through the cellars and the passageways that had been knocked between them for air-raid purposes, had taken out many soldiers under the Russian lines. In fact you could go for hundreds of yards under great blocks of buildings, though, of course, during the bombardment and the fighting it often happened that the way was blocked by fallen debris.

But we came across no one who could have guided us through the underground labyrinth, and we had no torches with which we might have found our own way, so, for better or for worse, we had to chance our luck above ground. We had very little time left now, and after a short discussion we decided to make a final desperate attempt.

Dr Naumann of the Propaganda Ministry went first, followed by Martin Bormann; then came Dr Stumpfegger, and I brought up the rear. But we had hardly put our noses outside the house doorway in which we had been sheltering than the shooting started up again. We got to the Ziegel Strasse and ran along it in Indian file. The shooting seemed to be coming from everywhere, windows, doors and corners. Cars were burning, and the wounded were groaning. Shortly before the University Clinic I threw myself to the ground. When the shooting died down I looked up again, and there was no one to be seen. They were not troubling to pursue anyone; they merely fired on anything that moved.

To this day I have never heard any more of Bormann and Dr Stumpfegger, but I feel sure that they were both killed. Bormann was wearing a simple brown uniform with no special distinguishing marks, and in all probability his dead body was picked up together with the thousands of others that lay around in the streets at the time and buried as the body of an unknown man in one of the mass graves. No doubt the Russians carefully examined all the dead bodies they picked up in the neighbourhood of the Reich Chancellory, but Bormann was killed some distance away, and in any case his features were not so well known as those of many of the others. Naumann did survive, as I discovered later.

It was daylight when I ran back in the other direction. Others were running now, and I ran with them. We went along the Spree Canal as far as the bridge leading down to the Wilhelm Strasse, and there well-aimed fire made us turn back. Then we went along the Stadtbahn towards Lehrter Station, but again we were turned back by heavy fire, this time from the direction of the Reichstag. Then we tried again in the protection of the railway embankment, aiming to get past Charité Hospital, but the Russians were already in occupation, and there were many casualties. Quite close to Lehrter Station we raced through a courtyard right into the line of fire of Russian tommy-gunners. I felt a violent blow in the legs and I fell down.

The first searing pain probably made me cry out, and men grabbed me and dragged me into a house that was already burning and had lost the greater part of its facade. Good Samaritans splinted one leg with pieces of wood and cardboard, and bandaged the other leg, which had got a bullet clean through it without touching the bone. In the first excitement I didn't even notice that I had also been hit in the hand and chest.

The fire was spreading now, and I could feel the ground under me getting hotter and hotter. By my side lay a pistol with which I intended to blow my brains out rather than be burnt alive. The house was still under fire, and bullets were ricocheting wildly off the walls. Somewhere quite close wounded were crying out. After about four hours of this a Russian arrived with three German prisoners to collect the wounded. It was from this Russian that I first heard the words that were to become so familiar to everyone at the time: '*Ury, ury*,' from the German word *Uhr* – watch, wrist-watch in this case. My watch, an airman's job with every possible device, pleased my captor tremendously. He seemed to have been doing well, for he already had about a dozen wrist-watches, but mine was the best of them all and he was delighted, for he kept repeating '*Khorosho*! *Khorosho*!' – 'Good! Good!'

In the cellar in which I was lying there was a bedstead, and this was taken to pieces to form a stretcher for me. I was laid on this and carried out into the Invaliden Strasse.

PART FIVE

In Russian Hands

I WAS A Russian prisoner now, and there were fifty or sixty of
us at the collecting centre to which I was taken. There was
a German policeman who spoke Russian there, and he was
helping to take down our particulars. When he asked me my
rank and I told him lieutenant-general, he looked up in surprise.
No one had taken any particular interest in me so far, but after
that it was different. The policeman rushed off to the Russians
with the news, and after a while a Russian colonel arrived with
a piece of paper on which he asked me to write my name. This I
refused to do, saying that I didn't propose to give anyone a blank
cheque.

The colonel then condescendingly explained that he needed
the signatures of all field officers under an appeal to those
German soldiers who were still holding out, calling on them to
lay down their arms. I told him that I was a pilot and that I had
nothing whatever to do with military affairs. As far as I knew,
the defence of Berlin was in the hands of General Weidling: that
was the man he should apply to. He looked at me suspiciously
and then began to threaten me, but when this had no effect he
ordered my removal to an empty room, where I was laid out on
a table and left.

I was very weak from loss of blood, and now I had an attack of ague. I remained on that table for about two hours, and then I was carried off to my first interrogation by the GPU – or MVD, as it called itself by this time. Having found out who I was, they now wanted to know what had happened to Hitler, whether he was really dead, and, if so, whether his body had really been burnt. This was the first time I was questioned on the matter. It was not the last, and at the time I had no idea how much trouble the whole business was going to give me.

At my insistent request I was finally given a glass of water. I was seriously wounded, of course, but I wasn't to be spared 'the march through Berlin'. It appeared that there was a general order that all prisoners should be carted through Berlin to see how many white and red flags there were hanging out everywhere; so I was hoisted into a car, and off we went – a light Russian tank following in the rear. We drove out of Berlin to Schönwald, Bernau and back. The roads were, of course, in a very bad state, having been shot to pieces. As the car drove along at speed I was sometimes thrown right into the air by the bumping, and at such moments the pain in my leg was so excruciating that I screamed. There was a Mongol soldier sitting next to me, and he just nodded his head. Beyond that it didn't seem to bother him. I was driven round Berlin for a couple of hours – orders were orders.

If by chance I had supposed that after this form of torture I should be taken somewhere for treatment, I would have been mistaken – though I had been promised it. I was now questioned by another GPU interrogator, and at the end of it came the renewed promise: 'Hospital will be!' That night I was taken by car to a farm near Straussberg, where there were a dozen other generals, including General Weidling. I still received no medical treatment, and there were further interrogations – for a week! And always on the one theme: Hitler's death.

At the end of a week I told the interrogating commissar bluntly: 'From now on I'm not answering any of your questions until you provide me with medical treatment. In any case, you keep asking me the same thing over and over again. Hitler is dead as far as I know, and I believe his body was burnt.'

Once again I was asked to sign something; once again I refused; and once again I was threatened.

'Shoot me or give me medical attention; one or the other,' I said with determination.

When the fellow saw that there was really nothing more to be got out of me he must have given orders to take me to another farm, where operations were going on. There were four couches covered with American cloth there, and on three of them lay wounded Russians still under a general anaesthetic. I was put under an anaesthetic too, but it hadn't worked before someone started to cut. I let out a wild yell of pain, as a result of which they gave me another whiff, whereupon I really went off. When I recovered consciousness both my legs were in plaster, but I noticed that the plaster on the right leg was soaked with blood. However, for a while I was free of pain.

The unwounded generals were taken away a couple of days later and sent off to Moscow by plane. The sick and wounded went to Posen, where there was a vast hospital camp with about thirty-five thousand inmates; there was a desperate shortage of medicine and no surgical instruments at all. Professor Schneider informed me that it would be necessary to open up the plaster, as there was no X-ray apparatus because in their initial enthusiasm the Comrades had destroyed them all. I was put under an anaesthetic, and what he had to tell me when I came to wasn't encouraging:

'They've just slit your whole calf open from top to bottom. Why, I can't tell you, for they didn't even extract the bullet. It was still embedded in the bone. Some of the bone is missing, by the way; but later on when things settle down you can have a bone-grafting operation.'

But even that wasn't too encouraging, because now my leg began to suppurate and I fell very ill. I had weighed a hundred and ninety pounds; now I weighed a hundred and ten. At last, and with a heavy heart, I had to give permission for my leg to be amputated. There was no scalpel available, so the German surgeon amputated with a pocket-knife. On my return I received a letter from a pastor who said he still had the pocket-knife with which the job was done.

After the operation I was put in a tent. It was heated by a stove whose chimney pipe went through the canvas roof – with the result that the canvas often caught fire. And one stormy night the whole thing fell in on us and the pipe dropped down on my bed. After that at least I was put into a proper building, and that would have been a great advantage but for the bed-bugs. There were two things which stayed with me throughout my imprisonment: one of them was *kasha*, the coarse millet porridge which was the chief source of our nourishment, and the other was bed-bugs. There were myriads of them in Posen; in one night I took the trouble to count my bag – six hundred and forty. Not that there was any sense in killing them even in such numbers; there were far too many of them, but at least it gave you something to do.

A woman doctor with the rank of captain was in charge of our hospital, and one day she came to me and informed me that I was now well enough to be sent to a sanatorium in Moscow with the other German generals, where I should be well looked after and get plenty to eat and a daily ration of schnapps – a point which the Russians seemed to regard as of great importance. It sounded all right. I had succeeded in getting a former telephonist in the Reich Chancellory, a corporal named Misch, allowed as my batman, and now, with some difficulty, I got permission for him to accompany me to Moscow, though I'm not sure that it turned out to his advantage. Incidentally, whilst I was still in Posen I sent twelve letters to my wife through fellows who were going back, but, as I learned afterwards, she received only two of them.

On 24 November, four hundred and fifty of us were loaded into cattle-trucks to make the journey to Moscow. The train had eighty trucks, but they were not all at our disposal because some of the booty of war was being taken back to Moscow with us: furniture, factory equipment, pianos, horses, cattle, old stoves, stove pipes, baths, old water-pipes and so on.

We actually went to a prison camp at Moshaisk, about seventy miles this side of Moscow, and because I was to be sent on to this 'generals' sanatorium' I was quartered outside the camp. After a while I set off with a group of other officers, and my batman Misch. In Moscow we had to wait for a long time in a waiting-room, and then a small Opel car picked us up. The 'sanatorium' turned out to be a prison – one look at the forbidding gates was enough. It was, in fact, the notorious Butirka.

Misch and I were put together in a cell, which was just about big enough to take two, and there we waited – waiting was another thing we were to get very used to. At about four o'clock in the morning we were woken up to have our particulars taken, and an officer informed me that henceforth the wearing of rank badges, medals and so on was forbidden. When he had taken away everything there was to take away I was given the usual assurance that some day I should get it all back again. It didn't take us long to learn that the phrase we were constantly fobbed off with, 'Will get everything', needed the words 'taken away' added to bring it into line with reality. We were not alone: Generals Weidling and Rattenhuber, for example, were both in prison with us.

By comparison with what we had so far been given in Russian hands the food wasn't too bad, though I couldn't get enthusiastic about the fish soup. You could spot a fish's head, or fish bones in it occasionally, but never a piece of fish. And we had that soup every day of the year. From time to time my stump was given light treatment, and I was assured that before long it would be all right – *budit*, 'will be', was another expression we got very used to. It was the future tense, and therefore it never needed to be true, though it was always 'going to be': jam tomorrow and tomorrow, but never jam today.

The interrogations went on, and on and on, and I made the acquaintance of a man who was to stick to me like a leech for years. He was the GPU agent who had my case 'in hand', and his name was Dr Saveli. At first everything was more or less right and proper, though my examiner preferred night-work – as being more inconvenient to me. The first night he just got me to tell him about the final hours in the Reich Chancellory, whilst he scribbled away like mad.

Neither Misch nor I told them that we had known each other in the Reich Chancellory, and Misch, having seen what being in the Reich Chancellory had done for me, was very anxious to avoid any mention of the fact that he had been there too. But they got to know about it somehow, and one evening during an interrogation, this Dr Saveli suddenly threw a book at Misch and said:

'Well, Misch, how was it in the Reich Chancellory? Tell me all about it.'

Poor Misch was so flabbergasted that he couldn't conceal his astonishment. After that we were separated. When I met him again later he told me that he had been badly knocked about. The Russians had beaten him unconscious five times, thrashed him on the soles of the feet, and then thrown a bucket of water over him, brought him to, kicked him in the backside and sent him back to his cell. They knew he had been a telephonist in the Reich Chancellory, and therefore they assumed that he must have heard everything. They weren't prepared to believe that there was an ingenious device which prevented the telephonists from hearing a thing once they had put the call through.

I was interrogated almost daily for two months, and then I was transferred to the Lubianka, the no less notorious GPU prison, where, as I learned at once, Grand Admiral Raeder and his wife, and Field-Marshal Schörner were also being held. In the Lubianka they weren't satisfied with hearing what we had to say: we had to write it all down. Sometimes I was scribbling away for six hours a day – all about . . . Well, all about what?

Three guesses! The last hours in the Reich Chancellory. I wrote a hundred and thirty pages of it, but when my interrogating commissar read it he just tore up the last thirty pages in front of my eyes and asked me whether I was silly enough to think they were going to be deceived by such rubbish. They just weren't prepared to believe that I had told them all I knew, and my commissar told me menacingly that there were ways and means . . . The machinery of intimidation started up in earnest now.

First of all they cut down my food until I was so weak that I couldn't stand properly, and had to be half-carried along to interrogation. I also began to suffer from fits of giddiness, for which the doctor prescribed some very bitter medicine which did no good at all. And why should it have done? All I needed was a bit more to eat.

One night I was taken out of my cell and brought before General Kapulov – he was afterwards shot with his chief, Beria.

'Now look, Baur,' he said. 'You were in everything, we know; and now you want to tell us you don't know anything.'

I pointed out that I had already written a hundred and thirty pages setting out all I knew, and that there was nothing more I could say. At which he laughed, and said I would have to change my mind one day, so why not now? In the meantime he was leaving me in good hands. The two officers with him had instructions to persuade me to talk freely.

'They won't hesitate to treat you very rough, Baur. We, naturally, don't like beating up generals. But your attitude forces our hand.'

After that I was taken from the Lubianka and sent back to the Butirka – and the whole thing started again from scratch as though nothing at all had happened in the meantime. There were endless series of interrogations in the old fashion. Myself, Rattenhuber, Hitler's valet Linge, Admiral Voss, two German detectives named Hofbeck and Hentschel, Sturmbann Leader Günsche and my unfortunate batman, Misch, were all taken together to the examination room one night, and there everything we had was taken away from us: – even any bandages were ripped off; I happened to have a nasty boil at the time. Then some old rags were given to us. My share was a pair of trousers about right in size for a boy of fifteen. I was also given a bast shoe for the one foot I had left.

In this get-up, and objects of great amusement, we suffered twenty-one successive nights of interrogation from midnight until five o'clock in the morning – and when we got back to our cells we were not allowed to make up for the sleep we had lost. A favourite trick was to play one of us off against the other; but when you asked to be confronted with the fellow who had allegedly said that or this about you, your examiner always changed the subject.

My particular examiner was always running round in excited circles, and when he paused for a moment it was usually to swallow all sorts of pills, apparently to set him up again. What he wanted me to tell him was that Hitler wasn't really dead at all, and that I had flown him away to some place of safety. According to him this was also what the Americans believed. Now where had I flown him? You might wonder why – if I had flown Hitler to safety – I had returned to the Reich Chancellory and let myself be taken prisoner. But that was just the devilish ingenuity of it all – it was to put them off the scent! Nor was this all. My adjutant, Colonel Betz, had been in the know, and as such knowledge was dangerous, I had murdered him to make sure he could never talk. This was the first I had heard that he was dead. However, if I only told them where Hitler was now, everything would be all right. In fact, I would be liberally rewarded and given a good job in Chile – or if I felt I wouldn't be safe abroad after that, I could stay in Russia . . .

The whole thing was ludicrous, but grimly so; and sometimes I used to wonder whether I was still in my right mind, for they insistently asked me exactly the same questions over and over again, using exactly the same threats – and then exactly the same promises. Throughout all this I wasn't allowed to sleep properly, and I was given less and less food.

One day, after swallowing a handful of pills, my examiner sprang a special surprise on me: Hitler hadn't committed suicide at all, and the body which had been burnt in the forecourt of the Reich's Chancellory had been that of a double, who had been shot and then burnt. Now it was a fact that on one occasion there had been some talk about using a double to represent Hitler, and as early as 1934, Rattenhuber, who was then head of the Reich Security Service, had approached me and asked me to let Hitler know in the course of conversation that he, Rattenhuber, had a man who greatly resembled him, and that with a little titivation the man could easily pass for him if necessary.

I passed on the information as requested, but Hitler only laughed, saying he wasn't Stalin and didn't need a double. I told my examiner to ask Rattenhuber about it; he might still know where the man was. If by chance he happened to be still alive they could convince themselves that nothing of the sort had taken place. Four weeks later my examiner was beaming.

'Baur!' he exclaimed. 'We've got hold of that man.'

You could never tell when they were telling the truth or not; in any case, as far as I was concerned that was the last I heard of Hitler's double. But it wasn't the end of my interrogations. The Russians were ingenious at concocting new methods. For example, at one period we were all busily engaged in drawing sketches of the Reich Chancellory, showing all the actual entrances, and all the possible ones.

One night I was given a terrible shock. I went along to my interrogation as usual, and the examiner glared at me and shouted triumphantly:

'Baur, you're going to tell us what you know now – or else. In a day or so your wife will be here, and if you don't talk then we'll rip her knickers off in front of you. And if that's not enough we'll turn her over and thrash her. And if even that doesn't loosen you up we'll make her into a whore.'

That was a bad night for me. Such threats may sound fantastic, but from one or two things that had already come to · my knowledge they were to be taken seriously. In fact, when I returned home in 1955 I learned that at the time an attempt had actually been made to kidnap my wife. A man got into touch with her, telling her that I was in Czechoslovakia, and claiming to be able to get me released. He would need two thousand marks, however, and as an earnest of his authenticity my wife would have to go with him. In their desperation, my wife (who has now been dead two years) and her mother fell for this swindler, and my wife went with him by train as far as Marktredwitz, from where they went on foot through the woods to the Czech frontier. But shortly before the frontier my wife's strength gave out, and she could go no farther. The man went off, allegedly to get help, but he never came back, and in the meantime a frontier patrol came along and found my wife.

One day I and others were given our things and put on a train. From the position of the sun we could tell that we were travelling westward. We travelled for nine days, and during that time our daily rations consisted of some brownish water from the locomotive, half a salt herring and about a pound of bread. We arrived – in Berlin! – half starved. We thought that we knew a thing or two about bad prison conditions, but Berlin-Lichtenberg prison under the Russians beat the lot. The warders were sadists who took pleasure in beating up their prisoners. One day my cell door was wrenched open and I was beaten up and left half-unconscious on the floor – vaguely I heard through a mist of pain that it was because I had been sitting on the edge of my bed.

However, we hadn't been brought to Berlin just for those brutes to kick us around – or to make the acquaintance of cells in which there was often nothing but one pail for all purposes: washing, fetching soup, urinating, and so on. So after four weeks of this I was brought before a GPU commissar, a man whose face I knew from Moscow. He told me that the bodies of Hitler and his wife had not been burnt at all, but preserved, and that I had been brought to Berlin to identify them. Linge, Hitler's valet, was also with us, and he was taken to the ruins of the Reich Chancellory and made to explain all the ins and outs of the place.

A man who had been a member of the anti-Hitler movement in Germany, and was now a trusty in Lichtenberg prison, told me that he had been present when the Russians dug up all the corpses buried in the forecourt of the Reich Chancellory. They had found two charred bodies, and these had probably been preserved, as had the bodies of Goebbels and his family.

Actually I was never called upon to inspect any body. One day I was interrogated by a Russian colonel in connection with a statement allegedly made by Detective Hofbeck, that I had actually been present at the burning of Hitler's body. And then I was asked whether I was quite certain that the man who had said good-bye to me as Hitler actually was Hitler. Now I had been with Hitler for hours on end on many hundreds of occasions throughout the years, and I had known him as well as a man can know anyone; in particular I knew that odd mixture of Austrian and Bavarian accent which was typical of him. It was therefore really out of the question that anyone – no matter how alike – could have been palmed off on me as Hitler. I made this statement to the colonel, and signed it. After that I was sent back to Moscow.

On the way we stopped in Brest-Litovsk, and there I was taken to the local prison and forced to crawl up the prison steps because I couldn't manage it alone with my crutches. The pail in my cell leaked, with the result that the floor was damp with urine and excrement and stank abominably. The warder then ordered me to wipe up the floor with the one handkerchief I had, and this I steadfastly refused to do. After four days of this – with a plague of bed-bugs to enliven the nights – I was taken out of this cell and put into another. An hour later I was taken back to the old cell, which, in the meantime, had been wiped up. But in one corner the damp floor-cloth had been used to write the name 'Misch' – so my unfortunate batman was here too!

It may sound astonishing, but all things are relative, and we were glad to get back to the Butirka. A few days later I was told that in all probability we should soon be sent to 'a camp'. For anyone in prison such a prospect is the promise of 'the little freedom'. You're still a prisoner, but at least you're amongst other people, and life isn't quite so monotonous and circumscribed. But it turned out to be a false hope, and it was almost a year before they thought of me again. Then I was brought before General Kapulov once more – the sands were running out fast for him, though he didn't know it.

'Well, Baur,' he demanded, 'have you changed your mind? Are you prepared to tell us what you know now?'

There it was again! All I could say was that I had already told them all I knew, to which he replied:

'Please yourself, Baur, but you'll stay here two years, five years, ten years – to the end of your days. Unless you do decide to tell us what we want to know.'

And with a cynical grin he had me sent back to my cell.

What he said sounded only too true. And it *was* all true – except the words 'to the end of your days' . . .

By the time I had suffered this sort of thing for three and a half years, I felt that I had had enough. I had not been allowed to receive any letters from my family or to write any. In my desperation I now decided that I would end it – one way or the other, so I presented an ultimatum: unless you release me and send me home within three months I shall go on hunger-strike – to the end.

Nothing at all happened, so when the three months were up I went on hunger-strike. On the third day a doctor, a woman, came into my cell and informed me that hunger-striking was forbidden in Russia; it was regarded as an anti-government demonstration, and as such it was severely punished. When I refused to be moved she tried to persuade me: it was very silly; what good could it do? And, in any case, I certainly shouldn't be allowed to starve myself; she would see to that. I remained firm. I wanted to get out; I wanted to see grass and green leaves again; I wanted to hear from my family.

The next day I was taken down to a punishment cell, which happened to be in the women's wing, and there the forced feeding began. There were quite a lot of them for the job; several officers, several men, and a nurse, carrying a long flexible piece of rubber tubing with a glass nozzle at one end and the other immersed in a container with some frothy liquid in it. I was asked whether I would consent to eat, and when I refused, four men seized me by the arms and legs, whilst the sister resolutely bored the glass nozzle into my nostrils. She couldn't manage it because it was much too large, but she ripped my nostrils and the blood poured down over my chin and on to my chest. Then I lost consciousness. When I came to, the nozzle was down my throat. I immediately vomited everything up, nozzle, liquid and all. Then a thinner nozzle was produced, and the game started up again. The men who were holding me seemed to enjoy it, and my howls of pain only made them laugh. When they had pumped all the liquid into me they left me half-unconscious on the floor of the cell and went off, promising me another performance the next day.

The next day the sister came in alone, no doubt hoping that the previous day's performance had been sufficient to intimidate me, but I still refused to eat, so then the warders trooped in, and the thing was repeated. This time I shrieked so wildly that the women in the neighbouring cells began to panic. Once again the party went off, again with the promise that they would return the following day, which they did. I asked the sister to get a thinner nozzle, but she refused. I then appealed to the doctor, who was usually quite conscientious, but she said that it was entirely up to me: I held the solution in my own hand – I should eat, until I did she could do nothing for me. She could not order a thinner nozzle, and she could not order the forced feeding to take place through the gullet just because my nostrils were torn and the mucous membrane injured.

On the fourth day the doctor herself stood in the doorway and watched the proceedings, and before long the tears were streaming down her checks, but she couldn't interfere – she had her orders too.

When I was alone again I started to get out a small thin piece of steel which was hidden in the collar of my coat, keeping my eyes on the Judas-hole whilst I worked. I had whetted that piece of steel to razor sharpness on the stones of my cell, and I was determined that if I couldn't end it one way I would end it the other. But suddenly the door was wrenched open and a warder came in who from time to time had shown me a little human sympathy. He looked at me and then went out again. Hastily I rolled my coat up and put it away. But GPU men now came in and took away the coat. At first they found nothing, but they were thorough, and patient, and experienced; and finally the small piece of steel came to light.

After that they searched everything. The pail was taken away, and even the bench on which I sat. I also had to strip stark-naked, and they took every stitch of clothing away from me; after which I was given new 'old clothes'. I was pretty whacked now. Apparently I couldn't end even my sufferings, and going on with that forced-feeding torture was useless, as the doctor had said in the first place. I could have starved myself slowly to death, but I wasn't to be allowed to. For about an hour I sat there on the cell floor, and my thoughts were despairing. I was helpless: there was nothing I could do. So I decided to start eating again.

The doctor came in, beaming. The warder came in, beaming. You would have thought I had done something kind and wonderful for them all. They even wanted to send me to hospital, but I told the doctor I would prefer to go back to my own cell – there was just one more job I had to do: warn a Hungarian fellow-prisoner against following my example.

In my cell I was provided with special food at the doctor's orders, and I was given pencil and paper, on which to compose a request to be brought before the prison governor. I wasn't, but three days later I was sent off to a camp. There were other Germans there with whom I could talk, and I no longer had to sit for hours and hours in a cell on my own. At least my sufferings seemed to have done some good.

About a hundred miles or so due south of Moscow lies Stalinogorsk, the centre of a large coal-mining area. There are a good many forced-labour camps in the area, whose inmates are largely Russian. But from 1945 to 1950 there were sixteen of these camps from which many thousands of German prisoners of war trudged out every day to work in the mines. The seams are not very deep, the workings are very damp, the equipment is primitive, and the safety measures very inadequate by German standards.

After a night in a prison train I arrived at Stalinogorsk the following morning and got out of the train with thousands of Russian prisoners, to be met by large numbers of guards with tommy-guns and dogs. I was new to the game, and so I was surprised when on reaching the ground everyone knelt down. I spent the night in the Stalinogorsk *Upravlenie*, and the next morning I was taken by lorry to Camp No. 3. The first thing I saw was a wretched column of men in ragged clothing wearing miners' hats. At first I thought they were Russians, but when one or two people recognised me and called out my name, I realised that they were German prisoners of war going off to work in the mines.

In this camp one pleasant experience did at least await me: I was allowed to have a bath and shave – in prison all we ever had was scissors with which to trim our beards. A medical examination showed that I was undernourished, and I was told that I should stay in the sick-bay for two weeks. I asked for newspapers, and I was given them, and for the first time for nearly four years I got news of the outside world – even though it did come through the East Zone filter.

Before long the first faces began to appear at the window, and it turned out that I had quite a lot of acquaintances in the place. Everyone grumbled bitterly about life in the camp, and they found it a bit difficult to understand that – by comparison – I found it wonderful. I could speak my mother-tongue with fellow-countrymen (although for the moment it was forbidden), there was a window I could open, a bed I could sleep in, and there were trees and grass to be seen. It was paradise! For the first time since 1945 I was almost happy!

My comrades immediately declared that I must have a wooden leg and get off those crutches, so in the carpenter's workshop they made me the sort of wooden leg I used to see, when I was a little boy, on our men who had lost their legs in the Franco-Prussian War. That wooden leg served me well; at last I could throw away my crutches.

I hadn't been there long when I had a birthday. At about six o'clock in the morning I heard slight sounds outside the door. Then soft music struck up and the door was opened to reveal three fellow-prisoners playing a violin, a guitar and an accordion in my honour. Then many comrades appeared to congratulate me, bringing small presents with them. I say small presents, but your idea of what's small and what's large change according to circumstances – in my present situation what they brought me was valuable in the extreme. But it wasn't that so much which affected me – it was the way it was all done, and the solidarity with which all these men bore their common fate. The warmth and comradeship just bowled me over, and I wept unashamedly.

During this so-called quarantine period I was frequently visited by the Russian camp commandant, together with officers from the political department. They expressed great astonishment at what they called my political ignorance, but I told them that I never had been a politician. I had, it was true, like so many others, believed in Adolf Hitler, but now, I told them, I had come to the conclusion that any form of extremism in politics, whether right or left wing, would only lead to disaster.

As things stood, of course, it was impossible for me to form any very reliable opinions about what was happening in Germany, because all I had to go on was the reporting of the East German Communist newspapers; and my comrades, who had been away as long as I had, couldn't help me much either, because all they had to go on in the meantime was from the same unreliable source. Twice a week there were meetings of the so-called Antifa, a camp anti-Fascist organisation, and we were regaled with political speeches, but there was never any proper discussion – how could there have been in that atmosphere of political terror? The camp commandant tried many times to make me 'take up a position', as he called it, but I always evaded the issue, insisting once again that I knew nothing about politics. He used to grin incredulously at that, but in the end he left me in peace.

'The little freedom' brought another great pleasure for me: I was allowed to write home. But, as I learned afterwards, my first two cards did not arrive. The third one did. But I didn't get any answers from my wife! Then one day the leader of the Antifa came to me and said: 'Herr Baur, if you give me your word of honour to say nothing about it I'll let you see a postcard from your wife.' Naturally, I gave him my word of honour at once, and then he showed me my first card from home. I copied it and handed it back to him. The same thing happened with her second and third cards, and I couldn't complain because I had given my word of honour to know nothing about it. But then one day chance came to my aid: a fellow-prisoner who worked in the postal department happened to mention that a postcard had arrived for me with the current mail, so when I didn't get that one I complained at once. The day after that I got it. I still don't know how many cards I lost in this way, but what I do know is that to some extent we all suffered like this.

There was an official order of the Russian Government that unconvicted generals were not to work, so I systematically appealed to this ruling whenever the camp commandant tried to get me to do anything which looked to me as though it were just an attempt to exploit my position and reputation amongst my fellows. The retaliation for such refusals usually consisted of visitations during which I was bodily searched and my effects ransacked.

The year 1949 was, so the Russians said, to be the year in which we were all to be sent home, and the prospect created a good deal of tension and irritability amongst us. The suspense was relieved for me by the very welcome announcement that I was to go into a hospital, be fitted for a proper artificial leg, and then be sent home.

I was to be operated on in Moscow, but I didn't care for the idea, so I was told that I would be given a temporary fitting, and when I got back to Germany I could be operated on there. Everything seemed to be going smoothly, and it looked to us as though the Russians were doing what they very often did – making sure that everything went right in the end. I was given my temporary leg, which, as it turned out, had to last me another five years, for after a short stay in Lublino they sent me back to Stalinogorsk.

From there I was sent to Moscow, after having been told that as a general I was not to travel in cattle-trucks like the others. Personally I wouldn't have given a damn how I travelled, so long as I got back to Germany, but I didn't. In Moscow I found myself in the Butirka again, and there I was put in the tower, the place where as a rule specially watched prisoners came. After a while I learned that there were sixty-five other generals in the Butirka. The food was very poor, ordinary Russian prison food, though as unconvicted prisoners we were entitled to hospital food. I was there with the others for two months, during which nothing at all happened, and we seemed to have been forgotten again.

But then for some reason or other our dossiers were taken out of their pigeon-holes, and the machinery began to grind once more. I was brought out for interrogation, and a new record was put on the old gramophone. A GPU examiner asked me two questions. One, had I ever been with Hitler to Mussolini? – and two, what did I think about Katyn? The juxtaposition of these two questions seemed odd, but I answered the first one: Yes, four times. That was enough, and I was sent back to my cell. Three weeks later I was allowed to know the nature of the indictment which was now being prepared against me: as I had been with Hitler to see Mussolini on several occasions the charge would be one of having taken part in war preparations, because during those discussions Hitler and Mussolini had hatched their criminal plot to attack the Soviet Union.

The GPU men seemed to find their indictment very impressive. I immediately pointed out that my only share in the whole business had been that I had flown Hitler to the meetings and back again, and that I had had no part or hand in the actual discussions. They just shrugged their shoulders. On 31 May 1950, I came before a tribunal to answer this ludicrous charge. The solemnity of the day was marked by the special issue of a salt herring in addition to my normal bread ration, and after breakfast I was taken from the Butirka to the court. The President was a general, and to the left and right of him respectively sat a colonel and a lieutenant-colonel. In addition there was a woman interpreter and a clerk. Behind me stood two guards armed with tommy-guns. And, no doubt, in a drawer was the signed and sealed verdict only awaiting delivery. But, of course, a certain amount of palaver had to precede that.

'Were you with Hitler in Russia?'

'Yes, often. For example, for several months in Vinnitsa at his headquarters there.'

'And where else were you with Hitler in Russia?'

'Pretty well everywhere where there was trouble: Leningrad, Smolensk, Zaporozhye, the Ukraine, the Crimea, and so on.'

The President then wanted certain details, and I explained that usually I flew generals to Hitler, but if the circumstances made it seem advisable I flew Hitler to their headquarters, where he would stay perhaps a few hours, after which I would fly him back. This seemed to satisfy the President's curiosity, who then announced that the court would retire to consider the verdict.

About an hour and a half later I was brought back into court and the verdict was read out to me: 'As the prisoner was in various towns with Hitler, and there planned crimes against Soviet citizens and against prisoners of war, he is to be regarded as co-responsible with Hitler, and he is therefore sentenced to twenty-five years in a reformatory labour camp.'

I declared once again that I bore no more responsibility than a train-driver, and that I had never taken any part in any military discussions, but the general declared shortly that such matters were no longer open to discussion and that I was now validly convicted and sentenced. However, if I felt that I had been wrongfully convicted I could lodge an appeal within seventy-two hours. Two others got their twenty-five-years' labour camp that day, and then we were taken back to the Butirka; not to our old cells, but to common cells for convicted persons, containing between twenty and twenty-five prisoners.

The same day a number of other generals who already had their twenty-five-year sentences were put into the same cell. The whole thing would have been ridiculous but for the fact that we knew that the idiocy was deadly serious. I lodged my appeal promptly, of course, but just as promptly – within twenty-four hours – it was rejected.

On 15 July 1950, we were taken out of the Butirka and sent to Krasnogorsk, together with several hundred others collected from various Moscow prisons, all with twenty-five-year sentences. Some of the stories the convicted men had to tell would have been very funny, except that the result was far from amusing. Some had been convicted on indictments which had obviously been drawn up for other people. There were cases where Cuba had been mixed up with Baku, and Athens with Aden, and so on. But just to wipe the grins off our faces there were some very disagreeable gaps in the ranks – some of our comrades had been unable to stand the strain, the merciless chicanery, the constant interrogations and the senseless accusations. And at night when each man was alone there was the thought of that twenty-five years stretching away into the future. Which, if any, of us would survive that long?

For the moment, however, we weren't left a great deal of time in which to think about anything. We were first reshuffled according to Russian practice, and then pushed around first here and then there. Some of us were sent from Krasnogorsk to Stalingrad, and others went to the Urals. Some of us stayed for a while in Krasnagorsk, and then went after the others to the Urals – and none of us could tell why one went here and the other went there.

Special difficulties arose in my case: in the night of 31 July I was taken from Krasnogorsk to Borovitchi, a place between Moscow and Leningrad. But when we got there the local prison governor declared that as I had been convicted he couldn't accept me: his was a remand prison. Whereupon the leader of my escort insisted that he had specific instructions to deliver me to Borovitchi Prison. It looked like a deadlock, but after hours spent on the telephone in an effort to resolve the impasse, the governor of Borovitchi Prison won, and my escort had to cart me away again.

There were two prison camps in Borovitchi in addition to the prison itself. One was a camp for prisoners who worked in the mines. I was taken to the other one. I was glad, at least, to find that I was still with Germans. Now that I was a convict I was no longer entitled to 'generals' food', but at least the camp food was better than prison food.

From the beginning of the conviction phase all contact with home had ceased. We had received nothing, but we had been allowed to write – now and again we had even been generously allowed to write an extra letter, as a special privilege. Later on we learned that all these letters, after having been solemnly collected, were destroyed. Out of thousands of letters and postcards not one was forwarded. When we realised the situation we began to fight for the right to send and receive letters from our families, and there was more than one dramatic scene in which the Russians played a deplorable role. More than once, after a discussion about the simplest rights of man, the local Russians would shrug their shoulders shamefacedly and hide behind their government in Moscow, assuring us that one day, 'for certain', it would allow us to write and receive letters. In this situation, without news, and without being able to give news, we suffered grievously; but at last, after many months, contact was re-established and letters began to go backwards and forwards again to encourage us and give us renewed strength.

In our camp at Borovitchi there were about three hundred Spaniards. Some eighty of them had fought for the Spanish Republican Government during the civil war, and after Franco's victory they had sought political asylum in Soviet Russia; the rest had fought with Franco's 'Blue Division' on our side and had been taken prisoner. During our stay in Russia we often came across these unfortunate 'Red' Spaniards. Some of them had been little more than children when they first came to Russia. Now they were rotting in some labour camp or other, or, if they were 'lucky', they were 'semi-free' labourers on remote building sites.

In Borovitchi the Spaniards, whether 'Red' or 'White' originally, were solidly in opposition to the Bolshevist system. The former 'Reds' had seen Communism at first hand, and they were thoroughly fed up, but none of them was allowed to write home or receive letters from home. Somehow these men from sunny Spain seemed almost more out of place in Russia's great barren plains than we were. The Russians declared that as there were no diplomatic relations between Spain and the Soviet Union it was impossible to arrange for post. The 'Red' Spaniards knew what this meant – they were to be pushed around in Russia until one day Franco was replaced by a 'people's government'. At one time, no doubt, that had been their hope, but by 1950 they knew that it was very unlikely. And all the Spaniards, of course, knew perfectly well that this business of the missing diplomatic relations was just an excuse – all that was really missing was goodwill on the Russian side. The Spaniards pointed out that if the International Red Cross could organise an exchange of letters in wartime between belligerent countries, it could certainly do so now between two countries which were at peace even if they weren't friendly. And when the Russians just trotted out the old excuse, the Spaniards acted.

Fifty men went on hunger-strike. The following day it was a hundred, the third day it was one hundred and fifty, and so on. Many of these Spaniards could speak Russian, and this gave them a big advantage in making life awkward for the Russians. Thirty of the hunger-strikers were now seized at random and put in the punishment cells. Then something quite fantastic for Russian conditions took place – rebellion! The imprisoned Spaniards broke down the doors and knocked out the windows, and rejoined their fellow-countrymen in the huts. The Russians in the camp then withdrew, and machine-gun posts were set up covering the huts of the Spaniards.

But then, as the Russians didn't want a blood-bath, the usual soft-soap commission arrived. This was another Russian manoeuvre to channel discontent into harmless byways. Such commissions never had any authority, but they were often very successful in persuading prisoners to content themselves for the time being with formal protests – which never led anywhere.

This time they didn't succeed, however: the Spaniards stood firm. We did our best to help them by smuggling in food, but this they refused, and all they would take was sweets to suck with their tea. Most of the Spaniards – two hundred of them – stayed on hunger-strike for nine days, and finally the Russians promised to allow them to write home. On this promise the Spaniards discontinued their hunger-strike, and quite a number of them were removed to hospital.

And the epilogue? The promise was a lie, like most other Russian promises. The Spaniards were not allowed to write, and in order to prevent concerted action in future, the Spanish contingent was broken up and distributed over a variety of other camps.

One day certain building work began in our camp. A small area was cut off from the rest, and one hut was surrounded with treble lines of barbed wire. Naturally we wondered what was going on, and, having been made wise by experience, the first thing we thought of was stricter punishment isolation, and so on. But we were wrong. Women were brought into the camp and put into this hut – German women. We knew some of them; they were the wives of German diplomats or diplomatic employees, or they had themselves been employed in German diplomatic and other institutions in the Far East. They had been taken prisoner when Russia hurried to take part in the war against Japan before it was all over.

There was, for example, Frau Bischoff, the wife of the German consul-general in Manchuria. She had been sentenced to fifteen years. Her daughter, as a fifteen-year-old, had played the accordion at a meeting of the League of German Girls. For this she had been sentenced to ten years. The wife of Ambassador Wagner was serving ten years because at official receptions she had naturally functioned as the lady of the house. And so on, and so on. All the men had – of course! – been sentenced to twenty-five years. Ambassador Wagner had died of a heart attack in the Butirka. His wife had learned of his death only very much later.

Imprisonment is bad enough for men; it must be very much worse for women, and to see these women in a hard labour camp when we had naturally thought them all safely at home again was sad and bitter.

In July 1951 hope flickered up again for a while – preparations were obviously being made for a 'transport'. Perhaps we were going home at last? No, we were merely being carted a little farther eastwards for some reason or other. Even in the ordinary way the transport of prisoners in Soviet Russia is bad enough, but the transport of 'twenty-five-year men' like ourselves is something truly terrible. 'Mallet' transports they are called, and for a very good reason. To check as quickly as possible from time to time whether any board has been loosened on the way, through which prisoners might escape into the open, parties armed with mallets go right along the train, hammering away at every board in the sides, bottoms and roofs of the carriages. The effect on those cooped up inside is shattering. Horses or cattle would never stand such treatment; they would just die. And then the constant countings to make sure no one is missing! The transport guards seem to be chosen for their brutality and their delight in knocking their charges about, and to the accompaniment of curses and shouts and a stream of obscenity they drive their prisoners from one side of the train to the other with shoves, blows and rifle-butts, so that anyone who can't move quickly is badly off.

At normal temperatures such a 'transport' is bad enough, but in hot weather it is hell itself. All the doors are closed, and the prisoners are lucky if the small slits guarded with barbed wire are open. To lie on there is nothing but hard benches or the floor, and before long you ache in every limb. Only too often the water-tubs are empty, and at halts the guards can't be bothered to let the prisoners whose job it is go out and fill them. At certain doors down the prison train there are grooves to allow the urine to pour away on to the track; the neighbourhood of such doors always stinks, but in hot weather . . .

And in the wagons the atmosphere is stifling. You pant for breath, and find your body trembling despite the heat, and you know that your lungs aren't getting enough oxygen. You sweat, and the water trickles down your body. And then it seems to happen only too often that your food consists of boiling-hot soup. Of course, the prisoners are hungry – they are always hungry – and so they swallow the hot soup; there isn't time to let it cool down. And after that they are hotter and thirstier than ever.

Far into the night, when the searchlights are on everywhere and the guards on the platforms are already huddling up into their greatcoats against the cold night air, it is still oppressively hot in the wagons, and the sweat-dripping prisoners roll restlessly from side to side seeking sleep. And when perhaps they have dropped off at last an infernal noise will start up and creep slowly throughout the length of the train as men crawl along the sides and the roofs hammering away with their mallets at one board after the other.

Towards dawn things are a little better; at last the oppressive heat inside the closed wagons has been dissipated. But it does not stay like that for long, because the sun rises, and soon its pitiless rays are beating down on to the prison train again. In such circumstances time seems endless. With a tremendous effort of will I pulled myself together and began to give lectures to my fellow-unfortunates on my experiences as a flyer, and others followed my example.

The last blow during our transport fell in the neighbourhood of Molotov, when the shutters were closed over the ventilation slits, so that we then had no fresh air at all.

Our train, which, to any innocent outsider, would have seemed to contain the worst criminals in the world, stopped at Pervo-Uralsk. The Soviet Government had decided to concentrate German prisoners in this neighbourhood, and in order to accommodate them many hutments recently built for the civilian population were requisitioned. When we were put into them we could see from pencilled observations and sketches here and there on the wooden walls, in the lavatories, and so on, that they had been built by our fellow-countrymen. But the tremendous thing about this new camp was that the hutments had never been occupied by Russians, and so they were free of bed-bugs. Our own fellows now adapted them for camp purposes, making store-rooms for potatoes and so on, big kitchens, and other requirements.

But the lack of bed-bugs was about the only bit of luck we had in that camp; for example, the commandant was a brute of the worst type, and he seemed to take a particular pleasure in persecuting the sick prisoners and the older men who were no longer strong enough to do any outside work.

Because I had only one leg I counted as an invalid, and I was allotted to the tailoring workshop, where I made hundreds of pairs of gloves. I never saw any money for my work, and then one day I was told to report to the *natschalnik*, or overseer. As you never knew whether you were coming back from such summonses, I put on my padded jacket, etc., so as to be prepared for the punishment cell. How right I was! The *natschalnik* bellowed at me, declaring that I was lazy and just wasted my time. I replied calmly that my foreman obviously didn't think so, and the *natschalnik* must be wrongly informed – would he please call the foreman? This request was ignored, and the *natschalnik* went on to ask me what hours I did, although he knew perfectly well that at doctor's orders I did only four hours a day. He then said that I was perfectly well enough to do an eight-hour day. After all, tailoring wasn't really work at all. I refused, and he then ordered me five days in the cells.

It was the usual sort of place, but executed in ferro-concrete this time. As I had only one leg, they gave me a stool to sit on. The other prisoners had to sit on the concrete floor. At nights we were given benches to sleep on. In the next cell there were seven men. The *natschalnik* never allowed the cells to become empty. At night it was very cold, for, although there were heating arrangements, there was never enough fuel. The first morning the guard arrived with a piece of paper and a pencil and ordered me to write down what I was in the punishment cell for. I refused, saying that if the *natschalnik* didn't already know, I certainly didn't. On the third day he arrived with the punishment-cell register, and in it the *natschalnik* had written that I was punished for laziness and bad work. I told him to take it away and tell the *natschalnik* it was a lie.

The food in this camp was like the food in all the others – just enough to keep you alive, though sometimes we doubted it. Fortunately we hadn't to find out, for now we began to receive parcels from home. Quite apart from what was in them, it is difficult to describe just what those parcels meant to us. They were comforting proof that we had not been forgotten; they strengthened us morally and physically, and gave us renewed hope.

In all prison camps in all countries there is – and must be – some sort of control on the part of the authorities over the contents of such gift parcels, but what the Russians did – sometimes before our eyes – to our parcels, which had been made up with love and care by our fellow-countrymen and women at home, used often to fill us with impotent rage. At first we thought it was just the clumsy pawings of people who had never seen such things before – the way in which the gifts were packed, the tinfoil, the bright paper, the fastenings, and so on, often made a greater impression on them than the gifts themselves. But before long it became clear that there was system in the way in which our parcels were wrenched open, things torn and often destroyed, or perhaps senselessly jumbled up.

Of course, the very fact that starving Germany – every country in Europe outside the Communist orbit, is *ipso facto* half-starving – could send such wonderful parcels was a mystery. But it was soon explained: the parcels were really being sent by the Americans, who hoped to be able to use us as war criminals again one day. Most of the guards could readily be fobbed off with such rubbish, but there were those who had had too much to do with us not to know the truth. And, be it said, there were Russians who did not allow themselves to be incited against us. It would sometimes happen that a Russian would secretly hand us things – a flower, a decorated twig, a beautiful bow – which had been in our parcels but had been deliberately thrown away by those responsible for searching them.

A Soviet Russian has to know everything, even things he doesn't know; and he must never confess to surprise at anything he sees, for Soviet Russia has everything and can do everything – and better. One day a coconut arrived in a parcel. Three Soviet officers were present, and it was obvious from their behaviour that not one of them had ever seen a coconut before. They handed it round, put it to their ears, rattled it, listened to the milk being shaken up inside, and so on. Finally they called a man with a brace and bit from the carpentry workshop, and he bored a hole in it. The milk was then poured out into a cup. At which the faces of the three officers lit up. The mystery was solved. It was obviously a new way of preserving liquid, using wood instead of sheet metal.

'We have a factory in Leningrad manufacturing such things,' declared one of them blandly.

It was a bit too much, and all the Germans present burst into uncontrollable laughter. It was only when a German doctor who spoke Russian produced a Russian encyclopaedia and showed them the entry relating to the coconut, complete with illustration, that the affair was finally laid to rest – one theory had been that it was an ingenious way of smuggling schnapps in to the prisoners.

The war, and the consequent willy-nilly touch with the Western world, undoubtedly did a great deal to broaden the horizon of the Russians, but many things which we take for granted are far from being accepted by them. For example, the question of going abroad – in fact, not merely going abroad, but even writing to people abroad. By this time life in Germany was beginning to grow normal; people were going abroad, for business and pleasure, and writing to friends in foreign countries, particularly to Britain and America in the hope of finding long-lost relatives and so on.

But for a Russian it is an axiom that anyone who goes abroad must do so at someone's instructions and on someone's behalf – in all probability he's a spy. These specifically Russian views on foreign travel and foreign contacts were, of course, held by the people who censored our letters, and when there was any mention of foreign contacts in them the recipient was hauled before the GPU and called upon to explain on whose behalf this or that person had been abroad, and what he had been doing there. It was all very disconcerting.

My stay in this particular camp ended as suddenly as it had begun. One day I was told to get my things together, and two hours later I went off. My new camp was only about twelve miles away, and it was known generally as the 'Austrian camp', because most of its inmates (four hundred of them) were Austrians, though there were two hundred Germans as well, and thirty of our wretched Spaniards had ended there. I found a lot of friends and acquaintances in this camp, and there were joyful meetings.

Here too I worked inside the camp, for I was still regarded as an invalid, and it was here that for the first time I received money for my work – forty roubles a month. Thanks to the regular arrival of parcels from home it was now possible for us to celebrate special occasions, such as birthdays; then there would be tea or coffee, sandwiches, chocolate and so on to mark the day. And stories were told. During the long hours in camp the art of telling a good story blossomed again. I, for example, had a good deal to tell. There were my experiences as a flyer, including a visit to Africa; my experiences during the war; and my experiences during the last days in the Reich Chancellory.

But the Russians always had spies and tale-bearers even amongst us, and before long I was hauled before the camp commandant, who strictly forbade me to say anything more about the last days in the Reich Chancellory, because this was, allegedly, pro-Fascist propaganda – though, in fact, I always did my best to be strictly objective. Perhaps it was these stories which were responsible for sending me from camp to camp; but, on the other hand, the Russians don't like sustained personal relations anyway, and they are always anxious to end them, so these sendings here and there broke up groups, and, so to speak, re-shuffled the pack.

In 1953 we thought we spotted a ray of hope. Negotiations were taking place in Moscow between the East German Communist Grotewohl and the Soviet Government, and according to the East German newspapers we were allowed to see, all German prisoners of war, 'except serious war criminals', were now to be released. Naturally this gave rise to excited discussions amongst us, and some of our 'experts' even thought they knew who would be released and who not. But none of their fine theories worked out. Some prisoners were returned – and amongst them were men who would have said they hadn't a chance; whilst left behind were men who would have said equally confidently that it was their turn next. You could, of course, subsequently work out some theory to fit the known facts – but you could never formulate a theory beforehand which would afterwards stand up to the facts. The ways of the Soviet Government were mysterious, and, as far as we were concerned, unintelligible.

In the autumn and winter of 1953 thousands of prisoners did go home. For us who were left behind there was at least the consolation that they would take back news and that the efforts to get us all home would now continue with renewed hope and energy. By December the last man of the batch had gone. There were fewer of us now, but we were still hoping that one day . . .

On 15 February 1954, all the generals who were being held anywhere in the neighbourhood were brought together in our camp. A few days later all thirty of us were taken to Volkovo, where there had always been a generals' camp. Some generals had been there all the time, whilst others – usually those the Russians particularly disliked – were hauled around from camp to camp. With our arrival there were a hundred and eighty-six generals of various grades in Volkovo. After a while ten Hungarian generals were added to the bag, and a little later forty Japanese generals.

By this time the camp was over-full, and all the work was done by the inmates. I used to peel potatoes and prepare vegetables.

A special feature of this camp was its park and its flower-beds. The seeds came from Germany, and some of our generals were really expert gardeners. The odd thing was that the Russians were very proud of our lovely display, and were always showing it to visitors as though in some way it was their doing. We also bred rabbits, and this greatly improved the food. All the work at this camp – with the exception of harvest-time – was done in the camp itself.

In our spare time we had Russian and satellite newspapers, and there was wireless; it was centrally controlled, so we never heard anything the Russians didn't want us to hear, but during the long years of imprisonment we had learned to read between the lines. The Russian camp commandant, a colonel, kept himself well in the background, and on the whole life at Volkovo was quite pleasant.

In the spring of 1954 our hopes rose again – probably merely because hopes just do rise in the spring; there was no sound reason for them. Summer came, and then autumn – and finally winter closed in. And we were still there. The New Year in 1955 opened like all the others before it, and there was absolutely no reason to suppose that it would be any different. We hoped; our hopes were cast down; we hoped again; and again our hopes were cast down. It was the old physically and mentally exhausting round once more until really we only pretended to believe that there was still hope.

After the death of Stalin we had, of course, seen certain changes, but we had learned that apparent changes were merely temporary deviations from the general line of Russian policy 'for tactical reasons'. Sooner or later everything would be as before. With anxiety we now saw Russians smiling at the West and trying to create the impression that the leopard had changed its spots. We saw some things which were said to have been black, and were now said to be white. We saw Malenkov's star rise, and we were told by Russians that he was particularly popular because he had helped to open the doors of many forced-labour camps – to Russians, of course. But after a while Malenkov was pushed into the background, and other names came to the fore.

But then the much-abused Adenauer came to Moscow, and our camp was wild with rumours. Our hopes rocketed from zero to fever-point – and then fell back again. This latter was when Bulganin publicly declared that we were the scum of the earth, and that our crimes had robbed us of all human semblance. We cautiously but closely followed the course of Adenauer's hard-fought negotiations, and we could sense that even the Russians respected the determination and integrity of that old man. But long years of bitter experience had taught us not to count too certainly on any advantage coming out of it for us.

Then three Russian generals turned up in our camp and informed our camp leader, General Meinert, that they proposed to organise a so-called *Heimkehrer* meeting, i.e. a meeting of those who were to go home. At the instructions of the Soviet Government, and following on the negotiations with Adenauer, they had come to inform us that we were now all free citizens, and this information must, of course, be conveyed in a suitably impressive fashion. They wanted the formation of a presidium consisting of themselves and three German generals to organise the meeting.

General Meinert replied that he thought it very unlikely that any German generals could be persuaded to have anything to do with such a meeting, because they deeply resented being slandered as common criminals, when in reality they had only done their duty as soldiers. This embarrassed the Russians, and they made evasive replies, saying that 'of course' we knew that we had been kept back for political reasons only, and so on. But now Russia and Germany had decided to pursue a policy of friendship and to exchange ambassadors, so that there was no longer any reason to keep us. The Russian generals even appealed personally to General Meinert to help them, or at least not make their job difficult. They had been instructed to organise the farewell meeting in such a way that the Germans should go home as friends and no longer as foes. Meinert promised to speak to his colleagues, and then get into touch with the Russians again.

Such a lot depended on it for us that in the end we agreed to hold the candle to the devil, and the *Heimkehrer* meeting took place. Chairs and benches were set up in the garden before a table covered with a red cloth. Film newsmen and press photographers were mobilised, and everything was ready for the last act of the long-drawn-out drama.

The meeting was opened, and one of the Russian generals made a long speech in which he described recent developments, and then concluded by telling us that we were now all free men.

Then various details were announced. We were to be divided into groups of thirty-two, and all of us were to be out of the camp within a week; but before that we would all be provided with new clothes – underwear, socks, shirts, suits, overcoats, hats. We subsequently reckoned that this must have cost the Russians about three thousand roubles per man, or a total expenditure of half a million German marks. The route was to be from Ivanovo to Moscow, where special sleeping-cars would be attached to the normal Moscow–Berlin express for us.

When the Russians had finished, General Meinert said a few words as our camp leader, and as soon as he sat down the meeting broke up, leaving the Russians still sitting at their red-clothed table. They seemed very astonished, and told General Meinert that they hadn't said good-bye to us properly, and that they wanted to give us a farewell banquet. General Meinert agreed to raise the matter with his colleagues, and finally we agreed that the farewell banquet should be held provided that we Germans invited the Russians, and not they us. The Russians were so relieved that the banquet was to take place at all that they agreed, stipulating only that they should provide the food and the service.

Then lorries rolled into the camp with everything necessary for the huge banquet: crockery, cutlery, food, cooks and waiters.

We subsequently learned that the Russians had just closed down
the Hotel Moscow in Ivanovo, and brought everything along,
including the staff. The banquet took place in two parts: in the
restaurant and in the recreation room or 'Hall of Culture'. The
three Russian generals were in the restaurant with some of our
men, and the rest of us were in the recreation room on our own.
There was wine, including champagne; and beer and vodka.
Then there was a soup, schnitzel, pudding, pastries and coffee –
an excellent meal, but somehow the right spirit to enjoy it wasn't
there. The leading Russian general came in to us after he had
delivered a speech in the restaurant, and exhorted us to forget
the past now and be happy. I must say we didn't find it as easy
as all that.

The whole affair lasted about two hours, and then the Russian
generals went off, and everything was packed up again and
returned to Ivanovo.

That same afternoon fourteen comrades were delivered into
the camp from Vladimir prison, where they had been held for
ten years and six months; for nine years they had not been able
to get into touch with their families in Germany. Some of them
had been kept in solitary confinement, and they all looked very
ill. They had obviously had far more to put up with than any of
us had. The meeting with them was moving and sobering. If any
spirit had been generated by the banquet, this grim aftermath
effectively doused it.

We received our new clothes as promised, and I left with the
third batch for Ivanovo. From there we travelled to Moscow,
where the Russians had another surprise for us – a sightseeing
tour! We drove round the town and saw the sights, including the
Kremlin, and were taken out to the vast Lomonossov University,
which greatly impressed us. By 14.00 hours we were back again
at the station to catch the regular Moscow–Berlin express.

Our meals in the restaurant car were provided, and all we
had to pay for was the drinks. In Brest-Litovsk we halted for
a few hours whilst the change from broad to narrow gauge

was made; and then we went on to Frankfort-on-Oder. We were on German territory again at last, though it was occupied. There were ordinary Germans to be seen, but they were kept well away from us. Here we changed trains and went on past Berlin to Luckenwalde, where nurses brought hot coffee into the train for us. There were civilians here, too, but no chance of getting into conversation with them. Then we went on to Erfurt, where nurses again brought us hot coffee. Wherever we stopped it quickly became known that German prisoners of war were returning home on the train, and people would come running up and stand there looking at us silently and, it seemed to me, sadly.

It isn't easy to return home after ten years. You are overjoyed, but everything is so new that things spring at you like a clumsy dog, almost bowling you over. However, when the Russian officers who accompanied us handed us over to the representatives of the Federal Government at Herleshausen over the border, and our names were read out and ticked off one by one, a tremendous burden fell from our hearts. We really and truly were free at last! We were in our own country again after long and painful absence. German soil was under our feet. Our fellow-countrymen, whom we could still see as yet only as through a mist, were real. It was no dream from which we could wake up into the bitter reality which lay behind us. There were GPU men still there, but they had no power over us here in our country. They could no longer haul us back to prison and drag us from camp to camp. They belonged on the other side of the frontier. This side was our land.

But the first few minutes in our homeland, which had been the focus of all our longings for so many bitter years, left us little time to think. People called out. Names were shouted. Flash-bulbs went off, camera shutters clicked and film cameras hummed. I heard my name shouted too, and I shouted back and waved, without knowing who I was waving to. Nurses were there to look after the sick and the halt, and I was led to a small tent outside the railway station where we were to have a snack. I badly wanted my first glass of good German beer, but I didn't get it – I was immediately surrounded by reporters; more photographs were taken, and the German news cameras were turning busily. Coaches were waiting for us and we piled into them and were driven off to Friedland, the big reception centre.

The memory of that journey is like a film that keeps breaking off; the impressions were too overwhelming. Every village and hamlet we passed through gave us a tremendous reception. There were tears in our eyes, and we were so moved by our welcome and by the many presents showered on us that we could hardly speak for emotion. Again and again hands were stretched out to us, and we shook them warmly. We saw faces so clearly marked by deep sympathy that we felt the urge to say something, but our tongues cleaved to the roofs of our mouths. And then there were new scenes and new faces. We saw children carrying lighted candles to welcome us; whole villages were decorated with lighted lampions in our honour; and everywhere we heard the church bells ringing out in thanksgiving. And at last we came to Friedland, the scene of much gladness and much sorrow in German history.

I shall never forget those tremendous scenes as we were welcomed, and I shall never forget the sad eyes of those who had come and waited once again in vain. After an evening meal in Friedland there was an official gathering. Vice-Chancellor Blücher welcomed us home in the name of the Federal Government; and one of our own representatives replied to him on behalf of us all.

But there was one man there in particular I wanted to see and thank, and that was Bishop Heckel, the leader of the Evangelical Relief Work, a man better known to us prisoners of war than anyone else. I introduced myself and shook hands with him warmly, thanking him sincerely for myself and all my comrades, telling him how tremendously important his work and that of his colleagues had been for us. It was not too much to say that it had saved the lives of thousands, and given us all new hope and courage. The Bishop was obviously deeply affected by what I said to him and he held my hand for a good moment.

But I was soon surrounded by reporters again, and many of them asked me questions about Hitler. I deliberately said very little. It wasn't the time; and I am convinced that I acted rightly. In the first excitement at Friedland a good many things were said which were made up into sensations, but they were not really very helpful.

After a good night's sleep the reporters and the photographers and the cameramen were buzzing around us again, before we had even shaved. But we got through the day somehow, and that evening I took the night train – for the first time as an ordinary civilian, with my own ticket in my pocket, and at ten o'clock in the morning I saw Munich, my old beloved Munich, again. But was it the old Munich?

I was astonished at the number of cars on the streets, and at the many buildings I had never seen before. Much was new and strange to me, and yet behind it all I could feel that it was the same old Munich after all, the great city I had known for forty years and not seen for ten. How many times in those years had I longed desperately to be back in its streets?

And greatest joy of all – here was my family, here were my children. I was not only back in my own country again; I was home at last.

Index